# QUEEN KATHERINE AND THE HOWARDS

# QUEEN KATHERINE AND THE HOWARDS

## A Tudor Family on the Brink of Disaster

### MARILYN ROBERTS

PEN & SWORD HISTORY

AN IMPRINT OF PEN & SWORD BOOKS LTD.
YORKSHIRE – PHILADELPHIA

First published in Great Britain in 2025 by
PEN AND SWORD HISTORY
An imprint of
Pen & Sword Books Ltd
Yorkshire – Philadelphia

Copyright © Marilyn Roberts, 2025

ISBN 978 1 03611 252 3

The right of Marilyn Roberts to be identified as Author of this work has been asserted by her in accordance with the Copyright, Designs and Patents Act 1988.

A CIP catalogue record for this book is available from the British Library.

All rights reserved. No part of this book may be reproduced or transmitted in any form or by any means, electronic or mechanical including photocopying, recording or by any information storage and retrieval system, without permission from the Publisher in writing.

Typeset in Times New Roman 10/12 by
SJmagic DESIGN SERVICES, India.
Printed and bound in the United States of America by
Integrated Books International.

The Publisher's authorised representative in the EU for product safety is Authorised Rep Compliance Ltd., Ground Floor, 71 Lower Baggot Street, Dublin D02 P593, Ireland.
www.arccompliance.com

For a complete list of Pen & Sword titles please contact
PEN & SWORD BOOKS LIMITED
George House, Units 12 & 13, Beevor Street, Off Pontefract Road,
Barnsley, South Yorkshire, S71 1HN, England
E-mail: enquiries@pen-and-sword.co.uk
Website: www.pen-and-sword.co.uk
or
PEN AND SWORD BOOKS
1950 Lawrence Rd, Havertown, PA 19083, USA
E-mail: uspen-and-sword@casematepublishers.com
Website: www.penandswordbooks.com

# Contents

List of Illustrations ........................................................................................... vii

Acknowledgements ........................................................................................ ix

Family Trees .................................................................................................... x

Introduction .................................................................................................... xii

Prologue ......................................................................................................... xvi

Chapter 1    The Howards of East Anglia ........................................................ 1

Chapter 2    The Mowbray Inheritance ........................................................... 6

Chapter 3    The Duke of Norfolk ................................................................. 10

Chapter 4    Rehabilitation ............................................................................. 16

Chapter 5    Saviours of the Realm: Flodden ................................................ 20

Chapter 6    A Great Matter .......................................................................... 28

Chapter 7    Times of Change ....................................................................... 34

Chapter 8    Choler and Agony ..................................................................... 39

Chapter 9    The Northern Rebellions ........................................................... 44

Chapter 10   A Birth, a Death and a Betrothal ............................................... 51

Chapter 11   Lord Edmund Howard ............................................................... 56

Chapter 12   Our Wife Agnes ......................................................................... 62

Chapter 13   Chesworth and Lambeth ............................................................ 67

Chapter 14   The Maidens' Chamber ............................................................. 74

Chapter 15   Mistress Katherine Leaves Home ............................................. 80

Chapter 16   1540: Two More Wives ............................................................. 85

Chapter 17   No Other Wish but His ............................................................. 90

Chapter 18   Faces from the Past .................................................................... 97

Chapter 19   The Northern Progress ............................................................ 101

| | | |
|---|---|---|
| Chapter 20 | A Time of Reckoning | 107 |
| Chapter 21 | Master Thomas Culpeper | 115 |
| Chapter 22 | As Long as Life Endures | 122 |
| Chapter 23 | The Fate of Dereham and Culpeper | 129 |
| Chapter 24 | The Sorrow of the Women | 135 |
| Chapter 25 | That Vicious Life Before | 141 |
| Chapter 26 | All Has Changed | 148 |
| Chapter 27 | Those Katherine Left Behind | 151 |
| Chapter 28 | Scotland and France | 153 |
| Chapter 29 | Lieutenant General of the King on Sea and Land | 155 |
| Chapter 30 | The 'poure prisoner' | 159 |
| Chapter 31 | A Question of Heraldry | 163 |
| Chapter 32 | 1547: A New Regime | 168 |
| Epilogue | | 171 |
| Appendix: What Became of Norfolk House? | | 172 |
| Notes | | 175 |
| Bibliography | | 202 |
| Index | | 209 |

# List of Illustrations

1. Elizabeth (Talbot) Mowbray, the last Mowbray Duchess of Norfolk, with Elizabeth (Tilney) Howard, Countess of Surrey, grandmother of both Anne Boleyn and Katherine Howard. (Courtesy of Long Melford Church, Suffolk. © Marilyn Roberts)
2. Memorial commemorating lives lost on both sides at Flodden, looking south towards Branxton Hill. (© The Remembering Flodden Project)
3. Old photograph of what survives of Framlingham Castle, Suffolk. (Author's collection, courtesy of Margaret Bell)
4. Thomas Howard, third Duke of Norfolk by Hans Holbein the Younger, 1539. (Royal Collection Trust / © His Majesty King Charles III 2024)
5. The Humber Bridge lies approximately where Robert Aske made his fateful ferry crossing in October 1536. (© Marilyn Roberts)
6. Romsey Abbey, Hampshire, was dissolved in 1539. Henry VIII sold its church to the town for £100 in 1544. (© Marilyn Roberts)
7. Lambeth House [Palace] 1647, by Wenceslaus Holler, detail showing its gatehouse, beside St Mary's Church, with Norfolk House to the right between the trees. (Courtesy of the Metropolitan Museum of Art, Harris Brisbane Dick Fund, 1917. Public Domain)
8. View from Lambeth Bridge, 2023; buildings on the right are where Norfolk House stood. (© Marilyn Roberts)
9. Gainsborough Old Hall, south façade. (© Marilyn Roberts)
10. Foundations of the north façade of Norfolk House now lie beneath the Novotel on Lambeth Road, SE1 7LS. (© Marilyn Roberts)
11. Artist's reconstruction of the detail on Duchess Agnes's tomb. (© Shaun Clark, Whisker Hills Pottery)
12. *Portrait of a Young Woman*, workshop of Holbein the Younger, c.1540, possibly Katherine Howard. (Courtesy of the Metropolitan Museum of Art, New York, Julius Bache Collection, 1949. Public Domain)
13. Henry VIII in his mid-forties, after Holbein. (Author's Collection, Public Domain)
14. Suit of armour of Henry VIII, designed by Holbein the Younger, made at the Royal Workshops in Greenwich in 1527. (Courtesy of the Metropolitan Museum of Art, William H. Riley Gift and Rogers Fund 1919. Public Domain)
15. Field Armour of Henry VIII worn at the siege of Boulogne, 1544. (Courtesy of the Metropolitan Museum of Art Harris Brisbane Dick Fund, 1932. Public Domain)

16. Mannequin of Katherine Howard wearing a recreation by Pauline Loven of Crow's Eye Productions of the cloth of silver dress. (http://www.periodcostume.co.uk/a-gown-for-queen-catherine-howard/)
17. Lincoln Cathedral Great West Door. (© Marilyn Roberts)
18. Lincoln Cathedral Great West Door, detail. (© Marilyn Roberts)
19. Ruins of the Bishops' Palace Lincoln, with the cathedral behind. (© Marilyn Roberts)
20. The Alnwick Tower, Bishops' Palace, Lincoln. (© Marilyn Roberts)
21. Pontefract Castle in the seventeenth century, J. Dicks, London, 1850. (Public Domain)
22. The retrospective arms of Edward the Confessor with the arms of Thomas of Brotherton as granted to Thomas Mowbray, Duke of Norfolk by Richard II. (*A Complete Guide to Heraldry,* Fox-Davies, Arthur George, Jack T.C. and E.C., London, 1909; Public Domain)
23. Henry Howard, Earl of Surrey, engraving after Holbein; Lodge, 1835. (Public Domain)
24. Sir Thomas Wriothesley, aged 30, Holbein the Younger, 1535. (Courtesy of the Metropolitan Museum of Art, New York, Rogers Fund 1925. Public Domain)

*Back cover*: Arms of Edward Fitzalan-Howard, eighteenth Duke of Norfolk. (Sodacan. File licence Creative Commons Attribution-Share Alike 4.0 International Licence)

# Acknowledgements

My journey with Katherine Howard and her extended family has, for various reasons, been a very long one and, as always, along the way I have been amazed by people's good wishes and willingness to help a complete stranger. To them, many of whose names I do not know, I give my heartfelt thanks.

Very special thanks are also due to Clive Hallam-Baker of the Remembering Flodden Project; Philip Norman of the Garden Museum, Lambeth; Sara Rodger, Arundel Castle Archives; Kevin Booth and Jeremy Ashbee, English Heritage; the British Library; the National Archives; Lincolnshire Archives; Society for Lincolnshire History and Archaeology (SLHA); staff at Lincoln Cathedral; the Royal Collection Trust; Berkeley Castle Muniments; the Surrey History Centre; Warwickshire Record Office, Stratford-upon-Avon; the Metropolitan Museum of Art, New York; the National Portrait Gallery, London; Epworth Mechanics Institute Library; Shaun Clark of Whisker Hills Pottery; Susan Scott, former curator of Gainsborough Old Hall; Lauren Brie and Niamh Tame of the Medieval Bishops' Palace, Lincoln; the late Joy Woods; Sharon Bennett Connolly; Alison Weir; Nathen Amin; the late Christopher Warwick; Pauline Loven, Crow's Eye Productions; Lynne and Colin Guthrie; Margaret Bell; Rio Rawlings. Many thanks also to Christine and Peter Hopwood of York, who for decades have kindly offered the most excellent hospitality and taken me on so many fascinating excursions throughout Yorkshire, and to the editors and staff at Pen & Sword Books including Sarah-Beth Watkins, Lucy May, Sarah Hodder, Laura Hirst and Jon Wilkinson for his excellent cover design.

Last, but not least, endless thanks to friends and family, who have for far too long suffered my moaning and whingeing about some of the more outrageous behaviour of the larger-than-life character known to the world as King Henry VIII.

# Family Trees

## THE MOWBRAY AND HOWARD DUKES OF NORFOLK

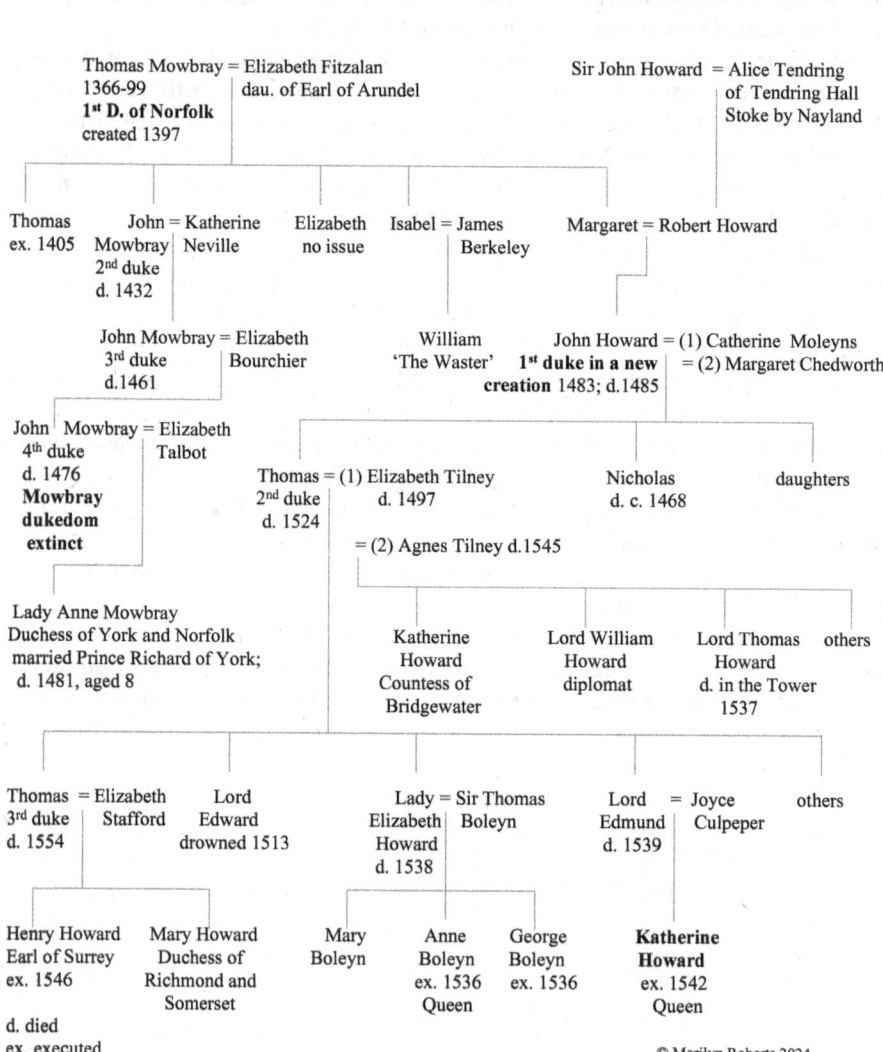

© Marilyn Roberts 2024

# THE DESCENT OF HENRY VIII AND HIS WIVES FROM EDWARD I

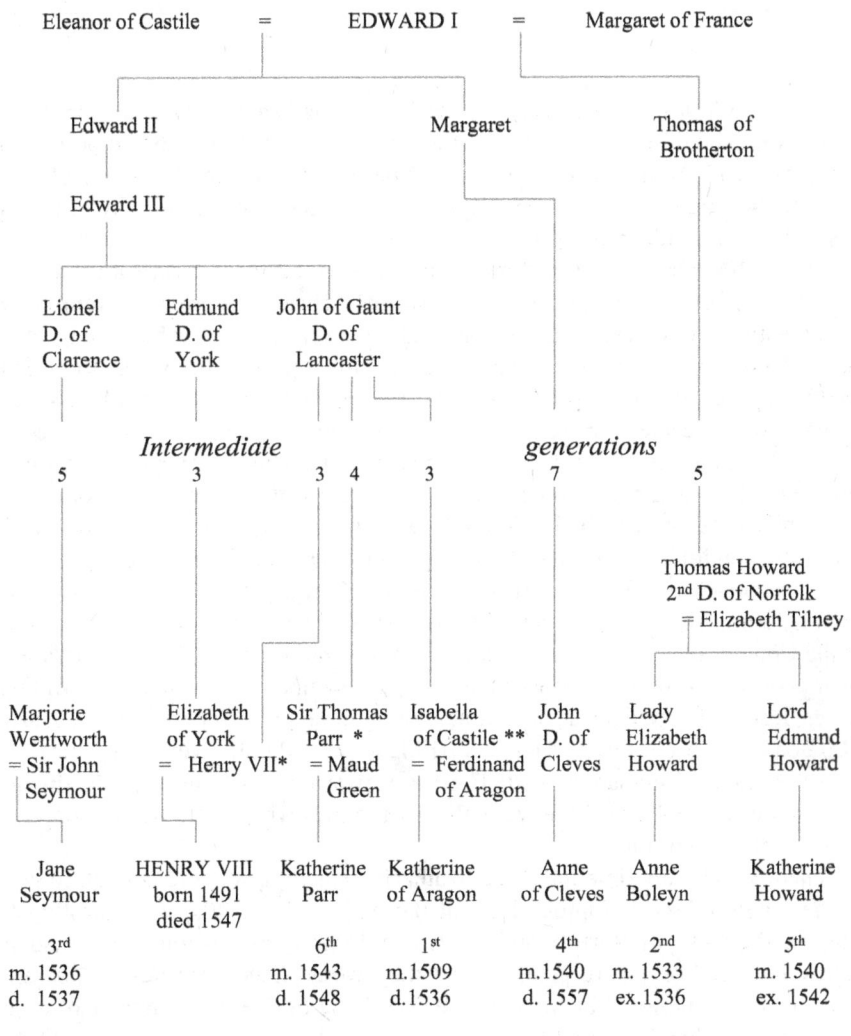

D. duke
d. died
m. married
ex. executed

\* descended from John of Gaunt and Katherine Swynford
\*\* descended from John of Gaunt and Blanche of Lancaster

©Marilyn Roberts 2024

# Introduction

There can be little doubt that certain members of the extended Howard family had laboured on and off for seven years in the late 1520s and early 1530s to oust Henry VIII's first wife in favour of Katherine Howard's cousin Anne Boleyn. But could the same be said to have happened again in 1539 into 1540, especially in light of their current difficult circumstances?

The 1530s had been something of a horror story for the Howard patriarch, Thomas, third Duke of Norfolk, whose position had been dangerously compromised by the actions of some of his nearest relatives. Apart from the beheading of his niece, Anne Boleyn, and her brother George, his wife had been sent from court for her support of Anne's predecessor, Katherine of Aragon, and his half-sister's husband was executed for treason. Norfolk himself, a man never much cared for by Henry VIII at the best of times, was accused of giving a disrespectful burial to the king's illegitimate son and expected to be sent to the Tower, where one of his young half-brothers, who had fallen in love with the wrong woman, would soon die in terrible conditions accused of planning to interfere in the succession.

Even though in 1536–37 Norfolk had played a large part in saving his sovereign from uprisings that were the greatest threat in his reign, the plum job of President of the Council of the North eventually went to someone else.[1] The Howards were even accused by their enemies of harbouring sympathies towards the northern rebels, leading to the duke's son and heir being imprisoned for punching a courtier who goaded him over it. As Henry VIII blew hot and cold over the political and religious situation he had created, Thomas Howard was as vulnerable as the next man; more so in fact, as there were always enemies who would be very happy to facilitate the end of him.

Therefore, by the time his niece, Katherine Howard, was old enough to come to the notice of the libidinous king at the end of the 1530s, it is questionable whether the Duke of Norfolk and the Howard family as a whole were in such a highly favoured or secure position that they would have been able deliberately to engineer the removal of his then fiancée, Anne of Cleves, in favour of a new Howard protégée whom, up to that point, the king had probably never met. Or that they could have insinuated Katherine into his life as a mistress. So, has the part played by the Howard clan in guiding Katherine into King Henry's rapidly ageing arms been overstated? Was the young woman pushed, or did she unexpectedly fall into the clutches of an already very dangerous man?

Like, I suspect, many readers of the life story of Katherine Howard, one of Henry VIII's least-known wives, I gave little thought to the plight of those family

*Introduction*

members and retainers incarcerated with her in November 1541 after her liaisons with other men were brought to her husband's attention. It was only through research into the history of Norfolk House, her home in Lambeth, as a follow up to years of specialising in the Howards' Mowbray ancestors that I began to look more closely at some of the sources that have been used to put across their very disturbing story.

Popular culture has not been kind either to Katherine Howard or her step-grandmother Agnes, Dowager Duchess of Norfolk, who is criticised for giving her a questionable upbringing, yet little has been written about what the girl's disgrace would actually have meant for the old lady herself, or for the others detained in the Tower for not having disclosed what they knew of Katherine's colourful past. The reader of certain of the nineteenth- and early-to-mid-twentieth-century popular works, which did so much to create what is still the continuing wider public perception of these wretched human beings, is frequently presented with a narrative of events embellished with excessively liberal servings of fiction, speculation, or wishful thinking.

More often than not, the impression given is that once the best-known of the major players were so hideously disposed of, the rest of the accused were released from captivity and instantly able to pick up the wreckage of their traumatised lives as effortlessly as though nothing of any great consequence had befallen them. In reality, imprisonment in the Tower of London was terrifying, often terminal and most definitely not considered by *any* section of Tudor society as being merely a minor inconvenience. The demise of Katherine Howard was of potentially life-threatening consequence for all those who found themselves incarcerated there because of their association with her.

The reliable primary sources that have come down from Katherine's own times are, for various reasons, incomplete. On the basis of those that do exist, the idea that proliferated in the nineteenth century of the elderly dowager being an out-and-out failure as a mentor and even a deliberately evil influence who neglected Katherine and treated her like an unpaid drudge, can be challenged. The primary sources tracing the twenty-six months from the first known mention of Katherine Howard when selected as one of the maids of honour to Anne of Cleves, up to her execution in February 1542, are made up of official documents, including records of interrogations and confessions, reports and other correspondence sent to Henry VIII, together with his responses, witness statements and also the correspondence of those on the periphery of the court, in particular the French and Imperial ambassadors, as well as correspondence between members of the public.[2]

The majority of the very little detail that is known of Katherine's early life derives from what came out in the few weeks after her fall from grace in the autumn of 1541 and what can be gleaned from her father's difficult circumstances when she was a child. We do not even know when or where she was born.[3] Then there is also the less reliable 'evidence' coming from what at first appear to be learned sources of the time, or from soon after the queen's death. One such is *The Spanish Chronicle*, still frequently quoted today although its unknown author, writing some years later, had not even managed to place Henry VIII's wives in the correct order and has Katherine being chastised over her behaviour by Thomas Cromwell, who by then had been dead over eighteen months.[4]

It is, however, largely the popular Victorian and Edwardian accounts which shaped the way in which Queen Katherine and Duchess Agnes are frequently still viewed today. In the 1840s, 300 years after Katherine's death, the author Agnes Strickland was one of the earliest writers to present history in an accessible way that would appeal to the masses, for which she should be applauded. But she also improvised, and some authors and historians writing well into the twentieth century were still relying on her as a valid source.[5] 'Facts not opinions' was Miss Strickland's motto, but the popularity of her books was in some measure due to speculation, the insertion of trivial gossip and of doubtful details, which can also be said of the contributions of some of her emulators and successors.[6]

Today we accept a certain amount of artistic licence in historical dramas although, in the main, the subject's real story is far more thrilling than the invented version. Nevertheless, we might wonder whether the makers of a television drama series which began in 2007 and had an enormous following, especially in the United States, really needed to portray Katherine Howard as a stupid, giggling fool who spent much of her time stark naked, and whether it was necessary to make her trembling character suffer the indignity of wetting herself on the scaffold as she prepared for execution, when an actual witness to the event, who had no reason to lie, reported she made a most brave and dignified end.[7]

There can be little doubt that the teenage Katherine brought to court in the autumn of 1539 was physically attractive, elegant, charming, beautifully mannered and always at her most dignified in public, but was, it would seem, intellectually unremarkable. It was this erstwhile rather insignificant girl's sexual misdemeanours when in Duchess Agnes's care, and her stunning lack of judgement over a male courtier when she became queen consort, which brought about her downfall and death.

Modern historians have assessed her as being anything from a high-class good time girl with no thoughts of the consequences, to a victim of sexual abuse at a very early age, but poor Katherine, no matter what she had done, in her hour of need had nobody to turn to in her fear and despair. The great and powerful, the self-seeking and the just plain terrified all abandoned one isolated young woman in order to placate a dazzling and terrifying giant of a man, who today might be seen as being well on the way to becoming a homicidal maniac.

However, in the circumstances, the context of the times and the evidence available to us, it could be argued that by holding out as long as was possible under intensive and terrifying questioning and by not speaking ill of her, Katherine's step-grandmother Agnes and Agnes's daughter, the Countess of Bridgewater, yet another Katherine Howard, did as much as they could to save Queen Katherine, and, of course, themselves. Nevertheless, when Henry VIII walked out of her life on 6 November 1541 her days were numbered, with her murky past already being meticulously trawled over by his leading advisors, including her own uncle.

This book, tracing the rise of an obscure East Anglian family, its producing of two queens consort and its fate after both were executed, has evolved entirely out of my own curiosity. Most of all I hope it may present the players as human beings with aspirations, weaknesses, fears and failings just like the rest of us, and place the story of Katherine Howard in the context of her times and of Henry VIII's often strained relationships with her relatives. I hope it will also perhaps encourage interest in the Dowager Duchess of Norfolk, an important woman in her own times but today largely overlooked.

By presenting the final weeks of Katherine's life in what amounts almost to a day-to-day narrative, I hope to have shown how terrifyingly easily and rapidly, in the evil and twisted world of Henry VIII, her step-grandmother, a godmother to Henry's two daughters and widow of the premier nobleman of the land, could be brought to her knees by terror and lose her liberty, her possessions and her beloved home because of someone else's actions.

In our own times, every autumn droves of young women of 18 leave home for the first time as students about to make their way in the wider world. In the late autumn of 1539, the old Duchess Agnes was getting her step-granddaughter prepared to leave Norfolk House to become a student of the behaviours and etiquette of the court of Henry VIII. The resulting whirlwind of events and Katherine's shockingly short adventure that ended in disaster for both women, would cause the great House of Howard to quake in its luxurious boots. But, even when it was all over and young Katherine was dead and buried, Henry VIII was not yet done with them.

## A note about dates

Prior to 1752, when for the first time the New Year officially began on January 1 and ended on December 31, the new Civil and Legal year had begun on Lady Day, 25 March (the Feast of the Annunciation) and ended a year later on 24 March. Therefore January, February and up to 24 March, which had been the last months of the Old Style, became the first three months of the New Style. Whereas a date such as the birth of Elizabeth I would have been recorded as November 1533 in both styles, Duchess Agnes's will, which she dated 12 March 1542 would, according to New Style, date from 1543, and in some sources is recorded as 12 March 1542/3. Unless stated otherwise dates used in this book are New Style.

## Katherine Howard's age and the spelling of her name

Records of births were not kept until 1538; born some years earlier, Katherine Howard's date and place of birth were unrecorded. This account will follow the theory she was born around 1521 and was 20 or barely 21 when executed. There are various spellings in documents of the times but for the purposes of this account, with the exception of a signature *Katheryn* believed to have been written by her at the end of the 'Culpeper' letter, her name will be written as *Katherine* throughout.

# Prologue

Seven miles northeast of the city of Lincoln, sticking out of the seemingly endless flat Lincolnshire landscape like a sore thumb, lies a surviving section of a high and very substantial dressed-stone wall, once part of a large, important and no doubt beautiful building. Now this sad ruin, with its lonely wide-mouthed grotesque, is all that remains of the pillaged and long forgotten medieval Barlings Abbey.[1]

Its abbot, Matthew Mackerel, was the prominent clergyman who, at the funeral in 1524 of the second Duke of Norfolk, had preached the hour-long fire-and-brimstone sermon at Thetford Priory in Norfolk taken from the Book of Revelation, which, according to witnesses, he performed with such gusto that some in the congregation fled in terror. In the spring of 1537 Mackerel himself would face the ultimate terror when hanged, drawn and quartered for apparently having assisted rebels in the Lincolnshire Rising the previous autumn, which he denied having done willingly. His downfall aptly demonstrated what an unpredictable, perplexing and terrifying country England had become under the rule of Henry VIII.

Thomas Howard, second Duke of Norfolk, a survivor of the Battle of Bosworth and victor over the Scots at Flodden, had lived for an astonishing eighty years. Powerful, a brave soldier, cunning, politically and financially astute, he had led a life on a par with that of a late medieval prince and was one of the last of the great magnates to refer to himself in the plural, 'we Thomas, Duke of Norfolk' and 'our wife Agnes'. His funeral was the last of its kind for a commoner in the Tudor era in terms of sheer magnificence, expenditure and the volume of people who witnessed it, either as participants or onlookers.

Among the mourners were his sons Thomas Howard, who succeeded him as third duke, and Lord Edmund Howard, whose daughter Katherine was about 3 years old. When the late duke had planned the new Howard family vault at Thetford he could have had no inkling that not only would he be the first but also the last Howard to be laid to rest in it, and even that was not going to be for very long.

# Chapter 1

# The Howards of East Anglia

On 28 July 1540, Henry Howard, Earl of Surrey who, barring any unforeseen catastrophe would eventually become fourth Duke of Norfolk, was gloating over the demise and execution of Henry VIII's chief minister, Thomas Cromwell. Surrey, a first cousin of the late Anne Boleyn, was an intelligent and emotionally sensitive young man in his early twenties, one of the most colourful and complicated members in the whole history of the Howard dynasty before or since his times, and just about as well-connected as any non-royal person could possibly be.

On that day he might have been feeling even more pleased with himself than usual. For not only did he have the gruesome satisfaction of witnessing in the forenoon Cromwell's head being messily removed by an inept executioner on Tower Hill, but his teenaged first cousin Katherine, who woke in the morning as Mistress Katherine Howard, had by nightfall become the king's latest wife. The transformation in her young life that took place at Oatlands Palace near Weybridge that afternoon marked the 19-year-old bride's first venture into matrimony and her 49-year-old husband's fifth. Full of arrogance and youthful optimism, Surrey, unlike the older generation of Howards, perhaps, did not stop to consider whether this might prove to be yet another poisoned chalice, for they had been in this situation before and the outcome had not been good.

According to a statement given by his cousin, Sir Edmund Knyvett, six-and-a-half years later, Surrey had opined that the death of Cromwell, the son of a Putney blacksmith, was a good thing: 'Now is the false churl dead, so ambitious of others' blood. These new erected men would, by their wills, leave no noble man a life. Now he is stricken with his own staff!'[1] It was not just Cromwell, but most of the other 'newly-erected' men, including higher nobility, at the court of Henry VIII that Surrey and his father so resented, those still-rising stars the Seymour brothers being no exception.[2] And yet, in 1540 it was little more than half a century since the Howards themselves would have been regarded by the then 'old' higher nobility as being 'newly-erected men', for in reality the early Howard lineage was rather mundane. Their spectacular rise within one generation from untitled East Anglian gentry to what is still the premier non-royal dukedom of England today, they owed to a marriage made in the 1420s. Although at the time it was of no importance dynastically to the bride's family, some sixty years later it proved to be of enormous consequence for that of the groom.

The first Howard of any real importance had been William, a lawyer born in Wiggenhall near Lynn in north Norfolk, who rose to the position of Chief Justice of Common Pleas and was knighted by Edward I in 1297. From then on the family flourished; his great-great grandson, Sir John Howard, becoming a Member of Parliament and standard-bearer to King Richard II. Sir John's two sons by his second wife Alice Tendring, Robert and Henry Howard, could expect only whatever was willed to them by their mother, since the bulk of the inheritance, as was usual, would go to the son from his first marriage and thence to that son's only child, Elizabeth, who married the Earl of Oxford.

The great medieval Mowbray family was far above the Howards on the social scale. Descended from some of the most powerful and wealthy of the Norman feudal tenants-in-chief, they could also claim to have the royal blood of the Plantagenets and the French Royal House of Capet in their veins.[3] John, third Lord Mowbray (1310–1361) married Joan Plantagenet, a great-grandchild of Henry III. Their son, another John, born at Epworth in Lincolnshire in 1340, married Lady Elizabeth Segrave, a granddaughter of King Edward I's younger son, Thomas of Brotherton, Earl of Norfolk.

Elizabeth Segrave and John, fourth Lord Mowbray died young, but Thomas, their elder son born in 1366, also in Epworth, was elevated by his close kinsman King Richard II to the dukedom of Norfolk in 1397 in its first creation. Shortly afterwards, however, Richard took his revenge on Mowbray for the part he had played in the removal and execution of his favourites a few years earlier by banishing him for life. Banished at the same time and for the same reason was Henry Bolingbroke, son of John of Gaunt, Duke of Lancaster and therefore also a grandson of Edward III, who returned in 1399 and seized the throne as King Henry IV. Eight days earlier Thomas Mowbray had died in Venice at the age of 33.[4]

Thomas Mowbray had left behind in England his wife, Elizabeth Fitzalan, a daughter of the Earl of Arundel, sons Thomas and John and three daughters. Although the dukedom had been forfeit, his elder son lived in the hope it would soon be restored to him, but sadly was impatient and joined the rebellion against Henry IV, for which he paid with his life in 1405 at the age of 19; the dukedom was eventually restored to his brother John Mowbray in 1425. Of the first duke's daughters it was Lady Margaret Mowbray who made the marriage that even now defies explanation, as the bridegroom was none other than the rather lowly Robert Howard who would eventually inherit only a small legacy from his mother Alice Tendring. Unfortunately, relatively little is known about him.

Historians invariably call him *Sir* Robert Howard but documents reveal the possibility that he was only ever a straightforward *esquire*, that is, an arms-bearer for a knight.[5] Some specific Howard historians have claimed, without giving references, that Robert Howard was an important naval commander during Henry V's campaigns against the French, commanding a fleet of 3000 men that set sail from Lowestoft, and might also have seen service at Agincourt. Although documentation from these campaigns abounds, there does not appear to be any documentary record to back up claims Robert Howard played any significant part. Anne Crawford, Robert Howard's son's excellent biographer could find no reference to this either.[6]

Robert Howard and Lady Margaret Mowbray had been married perhaps ten or eleven years when he died in 1436 leaving two daughters and a son, John, the heir who shortly afterwards inherited from his grandmother Alice a small group of manors and Tendring Hall in Stoke by Nayland, Suffolk. This was a substantial residence, which remained the favourite Howard family home for the next two generations. Never in their wildest dreams could this John Howard's parents, an impecunious underling and a banished duke's insignificant younger daughter, have anticipated their son's greatest achievement: he was the progenitor of the dynasty that today, after more than five-and-a-half centuries, still holds the premier dukedom of England.

Two long-running conflicts overshadowed life in fifteenth-century England. The first, fought on foreign soil and known as The Hundred Years' War, had begun in 1337 when Edward III of England challenged the right of the House of Valois to rule France, which he saw as being his by right of his late mother.[7] The second, fought on and off on home ground for thirty years by his descendants from the royal houses of the dukes of Lancaster and York, is known nowadays as The Wars of the Roses. John Howard, who definitely fought in the latter, was possibly also involved very briefly in the final stages of the former. The fact that the then still insignificant Howards are barely mentioned until the last twenty-five years of this long and exceptionally well-documented period, makes their subsequent rise to the highest rank of the nobility all the more remarkable.

John Howard, born in East Anglia in the mid-1420s, was an intelligent and enterprising boy whose mother's brother happened to be a duke. For him it was the right time and place both geographically and politically and he grew up to become a local politician, Member of Parliament, soldier, entrepreneur, one of the greatest shipping magnates in the country, courtier, Treasurer of the Royal Household, ambassador, one of England's foremost envoys to France, Deputy Lieutenant in Calais and eventually one of his country's leading noblemen.[8]

After his father's death, John, who was about 11, was taken under the Mowbray family's wing. At their great castle at Framlingham in Suffolk he was gradually introduced into public life which included learning military, administrative and chivalric skills, and, if his later life is anything to go by, how to keep comprehensive household accounts such as those now known as the Howard Household Books.[9] Like his Mowbray relatives, he later supported Richard, Duke of York, a great-grandson *and* great-great-great-grandson of Edward III, who was calling for reform and the curbing of the power of the favourites of his kinsman King Henry VI of the House of Lancaster, a great-great-grandson of Edward III, Although John was a Member of Parliament, this put a stop to his wider public advancement in the 1450s.

However, Howard accounts of the 1460s show a thriving and expanding shipping business involving the provisioning and leasing of ships as well as construction, and it is apparent that during the chaotic 1450s, between the ages of 25 and 35, John had fully appreciated that an island nation would always be in need of ships, irrespective of who was in charge.[10] After the late Duke of York's son was declared King Edward IV in 1461, meaning England thus had two kings living, Howard was knighted at the notorious Battle of Towton in March. He and his Mowbray cousins remained loyal to the Yorkist cause throughout the continuing Wars of the Roses.

In the autumn of 1467 he was awarded his first major diplomatic appointment as a member of an embassy to Louis XI of France, and was also made a member of Edward IV's advisory council; thus the one-time small-town East Anglian boy was at last becoming a recognised player on the national stage. His diplomatic career continued against the background of the York-Lancaster war, with Howard and his elder son, Thomas, both active on the battlefields on several occasions.

A cursory glance into the life of John Howard appears to show he was raised to the peerage in October 1470, but although that date was indeed his first summons to the House of Lords by writ, it was actually in late February or early March of that year that he is referred to in documents as Lord Howard.[11] However, Edward IV's situation was deteriorating rapidly and in October he fled the country. His Lancastrian predecessor, Henry VI, was released and restored after six years in the Tower and Howard was finally called to the House of Lords on 15 October, for the Parliament which would meet in November, but it is not thought he attended.[12]

On 19 February 1471 Edward IV returned from the Continent and, although Henry VI was re-arrested, the struggles for the crown continued. In April John Howard could have been at the Battle of Barnet, or perhaps was still some distance away bringing up reinforcements; the Earl of Oxford, his cousin Elizabeth's son, had already scoured East Anglia for suitable recruits for the Lancastrians, so Howard's task had taken longer than expected. What is in no doubt is that Thomas Howard, his heir and only surviving son from his marriage to Catherine Moleyns, was 'sore hurt' during the engagement. Had Thomas died this might have been the end of the Howard family, as it is thought his younger brother Nicholas died in 1468, the last mention of whom is found in their father's accounts for five pairs of new shoes for him in November of that year.[13]

With her only son killed on 4 May after the Battle of Tewkesbury, Henry VI's wife, Margaret of Anjou, who had come to England twenty-seven years earlier as a 15-year-old bride, was finally a spent force and, with no options left to her surrendered to Edward IV. On the night of 21 May, when her pitiful wreck of a husband died in the Tower 'of pure displeasure and melancholy', possibly with a little assistance, the Wars of the Roses appeared to be over, at least for the foreseeable future. Lord John Howard, his son Thomas and their kinsman John Mowbray, the fourth Duke of Norfolk, had survived to the end.

With the return to power of Edward IV in 1471, Lord Howard was restored to his former post as Treasurer of the Royal Household. The King's Lieutenant in Calais would frequently be absent on business in England and on 25 July Howard was appointed his deputy. Except for the occasional visit on leave, it would keep him and his second wife Lady Margaret away from their English home for long periods throughout the 1470s. Calais was the last English foothold on the Continent, and apart from its importance as a military stronghold and trading hub it was also a vital enclave enabling diplomats and other important travellers to arrive from England and depart from the Continent on 'English' soil.

'Calais' was not just the town and castle of that name: the Pale itself covered a strip of coastline approximately eighteen miles long and stretching eight to ten miles inland. John Howard, therefore, was a major player in what was also a very important and sophisticated English outpost with a constant stream of English and foreign diplomats, sometimes accompanied by their families, passing through his domain, necessitating that he keep a welcoming and lavish household. Calais definitely was not a posting for a man of limited means.

The family made a trip home in April 1472, when Howard and his Mowbray lord and kinsman were invested with the Order of the Garter on St George's Day. A week later his son Thomas, then 29 and recovered from his battle wounds, married the wealthy widow Elizabeth, Lady Bourchier, née Tilney, who must have delighted her father-in-law by presenting him with a brood of healthy grandchildren – Thomas, Edward, Elizabeth and Edmund – before the end of the decade, thus ensuring the continuity of the Howard family name. John Howard could never have anticipated that his great granddaughter, Elizabeth's daughter Anne Boleyn, and his grandson Edmund's daughter Katherine Howard, would become queens of England.

## Chapter 2

# The Mowbray Inheritance

The untimely death at Framlingham Castle of the fourth Mowbray Duke of Norfolk in January 1476 at the age of only 31 was a disaster for that ancient family. Lady Anne, his only child, born on 10 December 1472, as a female could not hold a dukedom in her own right, so the title became extinct; she was created Countess of Norfolk instead.[1] There were no Mowbray cousins to marry Anne and save the dynasty's name in the hope the dukedom would be revived for the family in a second creation. Indeed, the banished original first duke who had left behind five children when he went into exile, was the last Mowbray to produce more than one surviving child, all of which offered a golden opportunity to the grasping Edward IV to snap up the heiress for his own younger son, Prince Richard, Duke of York.[2]

At the end of 1477 and the beginning of 1478 Lord Howard was on diplomatic business at the French court, meaning he was absent for a royal wedding and a royal decision that robbed him of the potential of a massive inheritance. Prince Richard had been granted a Mowbray subsidiary title of Earl of Nottingham in June 1476, followed by Earl of Warenne and Duke of Norfolk in a new creation in February 1477; he married Anne Mowbray on 15 January 1478, almost two years to the day since her father's death, making her Duchess of York and Norfolk. The spectacular wedding at St Stephen's Chapel in the Palace of Westminster is described in some detail by an observer, possibly a herald. It is difficult for us today to comprehend that the bewildered bride and groom were still only 5 and 4 years old respectively and for part of the ceremony the exhausted little boy needed to be carried.[3]

Edward IV had been so determined to secure Anne's fortune that instead of a pre-contract, which would have been a solemn promise of marriage at a later date, this ceremony was the real thing, complete with a papal dispensation for 'nearness of blood', both parties being descended from two of the Neville sisters: the Prince from Cecily, Duchess of York, his grandmother, whereas Lady Anne's great-grandmother was Katherine, Dowager Duchess of Norfolk, widow of the second Mowbray duke. Had Anne died before an actual wedding took place her betrothed would have had no claim on the Mowbray fortune. Of massive concern, therefore, to the noble and wealthy of the land in the wake of Anne Mowbray's wedding was the alarming news that King Edward had brazenly set aside the laws of inheritance for his own gain, arranging that if she died childless her fortune, instead of reverting to her nearest relatives, would remain with his son.[4]

If every man had been awarded his legal dues, then Anne Mowbray's true heirs at law if she died childless were her now elderly kinsmen – cousins Lord John Howard and Lord William Berkeley, sons of her great-grandfather's sisters

Lady Margaret (Mowbray) Howard and Lady Isabel (Mowbray) Berkeley. By the time the wedding took place John Howard had faithfully and competently served Edward IV in various capacities continuously for seventeen years, making his shabby treatment over his lawful inheritance even more appalling. He offered no resistance, as far as is known, but although by then a very wealthy, self-made and ennobled man in his own right, he must nevertheless have felt aggrieved.[5]

At Greenwich Palace on 19 November 1481, three weeks short of her 9th birthday, 'the High and Excellent Princess', Anne Mowbray, died. In December 1964 her lead-encased body was found by an excavator driver on a building site in East London, two miles from where she, as the wife of the younger son of a king, had been laid to rest in Westminster Abbey. When Henry VII's building works on his fine new Lady Chapel commenced at the abbey in 1502 it was necessary to move Anne's coffin temporarily to the Convent of the Minoresses near the Tower of London, where her mother had been living for several years, but for some reason she was never returned to the abbey.[6] Medical examination revealed she was a red-haired, well-formed, relatively healthy little girl with incipient tooth decay, who had escaped fractures and perhaps most infections of childhood.[7] Her fortune remained with her husband, but shortly afterwards Edward IV manipulated the rules again, so that if the boy also died young without heirs, the Mowbray inheritance would go to the king and his heirs male and still not revert to Anne's blood relatives.

The vast Mowbray widows' holdings of Anne's grandmother, the Dowager Duchess Katherine, together with those of her mother Elizabeth Talbot, fourth duchess, which would have come to Anne eventually, were upon their deaths to go to her widower for his lifetime and only then revert to Lord John Howard, although those of Elizabeth Talbot had already been significantly depleted by the king as part of her daughter's dowry settlement.[8] Bearing in mind the boy was still only 8, while Howard was at least 57 and his son Thomas was by then in his late thirties, if the prince led a normal life span the Howards would not come into the inheritance for another two, possibly three, generations.

*The Chronicle of Crowland Abbey* records that by 1482 Edward IV was 'a man of such corpulence and fond of boon companionship, vanities, debauchery, extravagance and sensual enjoyments'.[9] Lord Howard was at home in Stoke by Nayland when news arrived at Tendring Hall that the king was seriously ill. He left for London on 7 April 1483, arriving on the 9th. His accounts show he paid for a boatman to row him to Westminster Palace, where he arrived shortly before the once-upon-a-time blond, handsome, six-foot-three superhero died, nineteen days short of his 41st birthday; dangerously overweight and mentally worn down.[10] The cause of death is not known, although Thomas Basin, the former Bishop of Normandy, was convinced he had overdone it with the fruit and vegetables.[11]

First in the king's funeral procession on 17 April came the clergy, then Lord Howard immediately before the bier with the royal coffin draped in cloth of gold. After the service at Westminster Abbey the procession left for Syon Abbey, where they would break their journey to Windsor overnight, 'and the Lord Howard, the king's bannerer, rode next before the forehorse bearing the king's banner upon a courser trapped with black velvet with divers escutcheons of the king's arms, with his mourning hood upon his head'.[12]

The absent new king, Edward V, was only 12 and had lived mostly at Ludlow Castle since 1473 as nominal President of the Council of Wales and the Marches, in the care of his maternal uncle, Anthony Woodville, Earl Rivers. Also absent was the boy-king's only surviving paternal uncle, Richard, Duke of Gloucester, then living in the North with his wife, Anne Neville (the widow of the Prince of Wales killed at Tewkesbury) and their only child, 9-year-old Edward of Middleham. From 1472 onward, Richard of Gloucester, then aged 20, had gradually become established as the most important citizen in northern England, governing the country north of the River Trent, and appointed Lieutenant of the North in 1480. If fate should deal him a hard blow he was a young man with a great deal to lose.

What motivated Richard of Gloucester to intercept his nephew the king's retinue on 30 April while on its way to London will not be examined in detail here; at the time Richard claimed it was to save the boy from his mother, Queen Elizabeth's family – the Woodvilles – whom he believed wished to control the new young king and were trying to turn him against his uncle of Gloucester. The Council decided Richard was to be Protector until the boy's coronation and thereafter it would be for Parliament to decide whether the arrangement should continue throughout his minority.[13]

According to Polydore Vergil, writing some decades later, the two Howards, father and son, were present with the Protector at a meeting of the Council called at the Tower for 13 June, nine days before the revised date for the boy's coronation. Here, under the direction of the Duke of Buckingham and without any sort of trial, Lord Hastings was dragged outside and beheaded, either over a log or a plank of wood. The reason was unclear, but even though Hastings was one of his own main supporters, Richard knew he had been completely loyal to his late brother and at the end of the day would possibly have put up a fight for the rights of his son. There is, however, a consideration that in his capacity as Lord Protector and High Constable of England, Richard of Gloucester could use his discretion if he believed treason was being committed, or about to be.[14]

There was an urgent need to get the queen and her younger son out of Westminster Abbey, where they had taken sanctuary since news broke of the king being intercepted. Lord Howard's accounts show that he and his son Thomas hired eight boats, which they may or may not have filled with armed men, and made for Westminster where, says *Crowland*, Gloucester had ordered them and the aged Archbishop Bourchier to assure Queen Elizabeth that if she let them take her boy to be with his brother, now lodged in the Tower in preparation for his coronation, he would be safe.[15]

Thereafter events moved quickly, beginning with the resurrecting of the old rumour that had been causing great merriment among the French for decades, namely that Edward IV was really the son of Cecily Neville and an archer by the name of 'Blancborgne', conceived when she and the Duke of York were posted to Rouen. Soon there followed the amazing revelation of the Protector lately receiving information that his brother's marriage to Elizabeth Woodville was bigamous, in that before he married her he had entered into a binding pre-contract of marriage with Lady Eleanor Butler, née Talbot, which, if true, meant Edward IV's children were illegitimate. Since Lady Eleanor, an aunt of the late Anne Mowbray, had died in 1468, the accusation could be neither confirmed nor dispelled.

On 23 June the Duke of Buckingham addressed the Lord Mayor of London, the Aldermen, chief citizens and councillors at Guildhall setting out the position of the children of Edward IV. As there had been no verification of their illegitimacy, his lobbying for their removal from the succession was illegal. On the 25 June the Lords at Westminster were asked to consider who should rule now the princes were disqualified. Buckingham assured his audience that after a great deal of consideration he had reached the conclusion that the only viable candidate would be Richard of Gloucester, he being the only one who could prove his legitimate descent from the late Richard, Duke of York, and thus back to Edward III. He thought Gloucester might accept the throne if petitioned fervently enough, then left their lordships to think it over.

The assembled lords were men of their times, used to subterfuge and violence, but there was also fear. Hastings, who had appeared to be high in the Protector's favour, had been executed without trial. Pragmatism seemed the only way forward; if they were not going to be able to stop Richard, they would have to go along with him if they wanted to survive.

In what must have been a fine piece of theatre, the Lords of the Council having 'consulted their own safety', as Domenico Mancini subtly put it, met at Richard's mother's home at Baynard's Castle near the Tower and proceeded to invalidate his brother's marriage to Elizabeth Woodville and declare all their children illegitimate and the young king 'a proved impostor', all of which was illegal in the absence of an enquiry.[16] Gloucester then 'reluctantly' accepted the Council's petition, was declared King Richard III and rode to Westminster Hall to take his seat at the King's Bench. Standing at his right hand was the man who within forty-eight hours he would make Duke of Norfolk in a new creation.

# Chapter 3

# The Duke of Norfolk

Rather than being a high-ranking policy maker, Lord John Howard standing beside King Richard III at Westminster Hall on 26 June 1483 was an experienced, well respected and reliable diplomat, administrator and member of the Council who had worked his way up from relative obscurity to the lowest rung of the peerage. Two days later he was catapulted to the very top of the ladder of the nobility as Duke of Norfolk in a new creation. He was also awarded a large part of the old Mowbray inheritance denied him by Edward IV. In addition, his son Thomas was created Earl of Surrey.

The days of the Protectorate and the subsequent short reign of Richard III are the grey areas in John Howard's life story. Were the portion of the Mowbray inheritance he received and the granting of the dukedom of Norfolk rewards for services Richard III expected to be rendered? Are some historians justified in associating the Howards with the disappearance of the Princes in the Tower?

The original 1397 creation of the dukedom of Norfolk had expired with Anne Mowbray's father and technically the second creation for Prince Richard, Duke of York before his marriage to her was entirely new and need not have been restored to Mowbray heirs, who could have been granted a dukedom of a different title. With the boy having been declared illegitimate, if King Richard wished to restore the Norfolk dukedom to John Howard there would have been no need for either of the princes to come to harm. However, historian Helen Castor believes Howard supported the usurpation 'from the first' in order to secure what was his rightful inheritance, and sees his son Thomas as being amongst those arresting and carrying out the execution of Hastings.[1]

There is no evidence from the time that either of the Howards were suspected of causing the princes any harm, but in 1844, when editing the second volume of the Howard Household Books, John Payne Collier drew attention to an invoice of 21 May 1483 for wood and nails for making beds and sacks of lime delivered to the Tower, which he thought looked suspicious.[2] Little was made of this until 1964 when Melvyn J. Tucker claimed to have linked all the parts of the puzzle of the princes' disappearance and suggested that, as Constable of the Tower, John Howard would have had access to the boys and was preparing to hide them away.[3]

The weaknesses in the theory include it not being known for sure whether Howard *was* already acting constable in May and June; also, it was still early days in the unfolding story, and the younger prince would be in sanctuary in Westminster for another three weeks. According to *Crowland* the boys were seen some time later, while Anne Crawford, who puts forward the theory that the word 'Tower' refers not to the Tower of London but to a private property, hence the items appearing in private accounts, believes the Howards' involvement with their disappearance 'inherently unlikely'.[4]

The new duke was made hereditary Earl Marshal 'by girding him with a sword and putting on the cap and golden circlet and delivery of the golden rod'; a similar rod or baton of gold with ebony finials at both ends had been given to his grandfather Thomas Mowbray in 1397. The Earl Marshal's baton of the same design is still carried by the Dukes of Norfolk on ceremonial occasions, as by his descendant Edward Fitzalan-Howard, the eighteenth duke and current Earl Marshal, at the coronation of Charles III in 2023.

As Earl Marshal and High Steward, John Howard oversaw the coronation and celebrations of Richard III from 30 June–7 July 1483. In the procession on the afternoon of Saturday 5 July, Thomas Howard, Earl of Surrey, bearing the sword of state, walked between his father on his right and the Great Chamberlain Buckingham on his left, immediately in front of the king.[5]

Unsurprisingly, in view of the chaos within her family, King Richard's elderly mother, Duchess Cecily, was absent from the banquet that followed at four in the afternoon in Westminster Hall, but her sister, the four-times widowed Dowager Katherine, who by then was in her eighties and had been titled Duchess of Norfolk for fifty-eight years, attended and shared a variety of dishes with the Lady Margaret Beaufort, who had carried the new Queen Anne's train.

When 20-year-old Catherine of Valois gave birth to a son at Windsor on 6 December 1421, her husband, King Henry V, was in France, where eight months later, on 31 August 1422, just before his 36th birthday, he died of dysentery, never having seen the child who succeeded him as Henry VI. The widowed queen lived at her son's court at Windsor until the late 1420s when she left to take up residence in one of her own establishments. Included in her entourage was a man named Owen Tudor, a distant descendant of old Welsh nobility, variously described as her late husband's friend and servant, or as being the keeper of Queen Catherine's household. He possibly came from the Tudors of Penmynydd, Anglesey, and rose to the position of squire of the body to Henry V after the Battle of Agincourt in 1415.

Whether Owen Tudor and Queen Catherine had married in secret before or after the act in 1428 forbidding the remarriage of a dowager queen without the king's consent, or indeed had married at all, their children's legitimacy was not widely questioned at the time. Of their several children, Edmund and Jasper Tudor were the eldest. Incredibly, the situation went unchecked until 1437 when Catherine was forcibly separated from Owen and their children and sent to Bermondsey Abbey where she is believed to have died in childbirth aged 35. Owen was hounded, imprisoned in the notorious Newgate gaol from where he escaped, only to be recaptured and imprisoned at Windsor, but was subsequently pardoned. His sons Edmund and Jasper were placed in the care of Katherine de la Pole, Abbess of

Barking, where they remained until 1442 when their half-brother, Henry VI, began taking an interest in their welfare, taking them into the royal household and conferring earldoms on both within a decade: Edmund of Richmond and Jasper of Pembroke.

Lady Margaret Beaufort, born in May 1443, was a great-granddaughter of John of Gaunt and his mistress and eventual third wife Katherine Swynford, and therefore a great-great-granddaughter of Edward III. Gaunt gave his offspring with Katherine the name of Beaufort, taken from one of his estates in France. Margaret's father, John Beaufort, first Duke of Somerset, died when she was a year old; being a girl, Margaret could inherit his fortune but not the title. After the annulment of her first marriage she was placed under the guardianship of King Henry VI's half-brother Edmund Tudor, who in 1455 made her his own wife when she was 12 and he 24. In August 1456 he was captured by the Yorkists and imprisoned at Carmarthen Castle in Wales, where on 3 November, only a year and two days after his marriage, he died of plague, leaving 13½-year-old Lady Margaret seven months pregnant. Her brother-in-law, Jasper Tudor, took care of her at Pembroke Castle where her only son Henry Tudor was born on 28 January 1547.

In June 1472, Lady Margaret, a Lancastrian born and bred, married for the fourth and last, time. The groom was northern Yorkist magnate, Thomas Stanley, which enabled her to return to Edward IV's court and hopefully secure the repatriation of her son, who was living in exile. Her case is a good example of how the Wars of the Roses divided families but also sometimes enabled them to hedge their bets by having a spouse in either camp. At the time of Richard III's coronation, Margaret Beaufort was 39, her only son was 26 and had been living under the protection of the Duke of Brittany since the Lancastrian defeat at Tewkesbury twelve years earlier, where the last of the male Beauforts died, leaving Margaret as the sole survivor. Devoted to the son she last saw when he was 14, her hopes that Edward IV would let him come back home were dashed with the king's premature death.

The reign of Richard III lasted only two years and two months. The young brothers in the Tower had disappeared in 1483 and rumours began spreading that they had come to harm. What happened to them is still not known and open to speculation and it is by no means certain that skeletons found in the Tower in the reign of Charles II and now interred in Westminster Abbey really are their remains.[6] After the coronation, John Howard, the new Duke of Norfolk, was home by mid-August inspecting his vast holdings in his local area. His inheritance had also brought wider flung possessions, which he set out to visit mid-September, including Chesworth House near Horsham in Sussex where, three generations into the future, the discovery of unseemly behaviour by one of his great-granddaughters would be the cause of huge embarrassment and present a very real danger to the Howard family.[7] The king's further grants of more manors and then the death of Duchess Katherine in September, made John Howard the greatest landowner in East Anglia.

Henry Stafford, Duke of Buckingham had been one of King Richard's greatest supporters, but in September he joined forces with the Lancastrian John Morton, Bishop of Ely and Lady Margaret Beaufort to replace him with Henry Tudor, on condition Henry married Elizabeth of York, the true heiress of the House of York if her brothers were dead. The endeavour failed, with Tudor fleeing back to exile in Brittany and Morton to Flanders. Lady Margaret, who had conspired with the Princess Elizabeth's mother, the former Queen Elizabeth, through secret messages and had partly financed the endeavour, was stripped by Parliament of all her titles and estates, which, however, was not as devastating as it might have been, with Richard having her assets transferred to her husband, Lord Stanley.[8]

On 2 November 1483, 28-year-old Buckingham was beheaded in Salisbury market place for treason. His eldest child, 5-year-old Edward, would meet the same end on Tower Hill nearly four decades later. After Buckingham's death, John Howard held more land than any other magnate in the country; he was in his late fifties, elderly for those times, a man of vast wealth with many business interests and numerous estates to run.

The Parliament which had been postponed because of the rebellion eventually met in January 1484, and the passing of the Act of Titulus Regius ('royal title') explained officially the circumstances of the accession of Richard III and it is from this that detail of the happenings of 1483 may be gleaned, including the dubious evidence for the bastardisation of Edward IV's children.[9] In February the Howards, with other leading nobles and clergy, swore an oath of loyalty to Richard's son, Edward of Middleham, who had been created Prince of Wales and Earl of Chester at York Minster on 8 September the previous year. But on or about 9 April, a year after the death of Edward IV, the boy died at Middleham Castle aged 10, leaving his parents frantic. Not only was it the loss of a beloved only child, but also of a future king for whom there were few acceptable alternatives. Eleven months later the boy's mother, Queen Anne, also died.

Henry Tudor had hopes of taking the crown and at Rennes Cathedral on Christmas Day 1483 swore to come back again to claim the kingdom and marry Elizabeth of York, but his effort of 1484 also proved fruitless. However, by late autumn times were changing. King Richard had intended to transfer the leading Lancastrian, John de Vere, the Earl of Oxford, from prison in Calais to British soil where he could be closely watched, but he escaped from Hammes Castle with his jailor and was able to rendezvous with Tudor. This was a huge bonus, as he had the extensive military experience Tudor, and what little remained of the Lancastrian faction, lacked.

On 1 August 1485 Henry Tudor set sail with a small army of followers, some of them Yorkists, augmented by 3000 French mercenaries, making landfall six days later on the Welsh coast near Milford Haven in Pembrokeshire, the home territory of his childhood. Although the droves of Welsh supporters he hoped would come flocking to him failed to materialise, he pressed on into England knowing there might never be another chance. The Duke of Norfolk was also on home territory, preparing himself shortly to be moving to Bury St Edmunds, the designated rallying point under his banner for Yorkist East Anglian nobility and gentry and their recruits.

On the 19th King Richard left Nottingham for Leicester thirty miles away and camped on the 21st at nearby Market Bosworth, which was cutting it fine, but he was confident Tudor was still some distance away. In six weeks' time the king would be 33, five years older than his enemy, but had so much more experience of fighting and warfare that to him the outcome must have seemed a foregone conclusion: provided that those with him remained loyal.

The Yorkist battle plan was for John Howard and his son to lead the vanguard of about 3000 men, roughly one third of the king's total. Once the men he had brought from East Anglia were delivered to Richard he had fulfilled his obligations; at about 60 years of age he need not have fought, or at least could have opted to take a less prominent part. Like the numbers involved and the precise location, the actual actions in the battle are often unclear and were not recorded in detail by contemporaries, or accounts have been lost.[10]

What is known is that it was barely dawn on Monday 22 August 1485 when Henry Tudor and his army, commanded by Howard's kinsman Oxford, appeared sooner than anticipated, leaving Richard's army with no time to hear Mass, which would have greatly unnerved many of them. For some time the complete loyalty of the Stanley brothers had been a nagging doubt; after all, Lord Thomas's wife was Henry Tudor's mother. But they were problematic for Tudor as well, for neither his stepfather nor his step-uncle, William Stanley, had declared for him yet, and on the field of battle anything could happen. In the ensuing encounter, that lasted about two hours, the two vanguards engaged, led by the Howards for Richard and Oxford for Tudor, but the Earl of Northumberland and his contingent stood by, as did the Stanleys, who entered the fray only in the latter stages on Tudor's side when they saw Richard was in trouble.

The elderly Duke of Norfolk and his son fought bravely, and tales of him coming face to face with his opposite number, his cousin Elizabeth's son, in the midst of the mêlée of Bosworth are probably true. Tradition has it the men on their warhorses charged at each other and Oxford lost his shield. Norfolk slashed him across the arm but then his own visor fell off. Oxford slashed at Norfolk's helmet but desisted from finishing him off because of the advantage of being twenty years younger, but immediately Norfolk, his face exposed by the loss of the visor, was killed by an arrow through the skull.[11]

This scenario seems rather too neat; John Howard being killed by an unnamed third party rather than by a fairly close blood relative seems just too convenient. Yes, the two men were related and in years gone by had got on well and enjoyed hunting trips together, and during his incarceration in Calais, Norfolk had helped out Oxford's mother and his wife financially, but in the heat of battle it was every man for himself. If Oxford did kill Howard, not only would it be in self-defence, but it would have demoralised the duke's men, which after all, was one of the main purposes on the field of battle that day. Both were men of their times and knew and accepted that kill or be killed was the foremost rule of the game.

King Richard, probably knowing his premier soldier was down, and guessing Northumberland was not going to come to his assistance and the Stanleys would follow whoever looked like winning, seized upon his only chance. Living in times when the death of the leader of one side meant the termination of the battle and victory for the other, Henry Tudor, with a small number of supporters around him, was kept back from the worst of the action, but Richard charged and managed to cut down his standard bearer, William Brandon. It was all to no avail; he seems to have got close to his nemesis, but as Polydore Vergil wrote, 'Richard III was killed fighting manfully in the thickest press of his enemies'. His corpse was treated shamefully; stripped and thrown naked across a horse, it was taken for burial at the church of the Grey Friars in Leicester where his remains were found in 2012.[12]

The old soldier John Howard's body was treated with more respect, and travelling via Northampton and Cambridge finally came home to East Anglia. Hitherto his family had been laid to rest in Stoke by Nayland in Suffolk, but for the first Howard Duke of Norfolk it was to be at Thetford Priory in Norfolk, near the last two Mowbray dukes. Presumably his tomb would have been of the finest workmanship, but, like so many others, was destroyed after the dissolution of the monasteries and nowadays his possible initial place of burial is a sad spot tucked away in the now roofless but once beautiful church of the priory and marked only by an information card. It seems likely that at the dissolution his remains were removed to Framlingham Church by his grandson. The Howard tombs there were opened in 1841 and remains included those of an older man with severe wounds to the front of the skull, consistent with having been struck by a battle axe rather than pierced by an arrow.[13]

John Howard, Duke of Norfolk was a man of his times who had a long life well lived. Of Tendring Hall, which seems to have been his preferred residence, nothing now remains. It had been in the possession of his mother's family since the late thirteenth century and the Howards kept its name even though Alice had been the last of her line. Favouring his home territory to the showy excesses expected of the court whenever he was able, he nevertheless was a man who enjoyed his luxuries and home comforts. Inventories for possessions he took to stave off the discomforts of being at sea on the Scottish campaign of his later years record luxuries for his ship's cabin such as books, tapestries, feather beds, carpets, fine tableware and silver bowls, including his 'silver pyssing bowl'.[14] He was fond of music, reading and playing chess, and the fact he sent his son to school indicates recognition of the value of an academic education in addition to the traditional grounding he himself had experienced as a boy in the care of his Mowbray relatives.

A talented businessman and brave soldier, unlike many of his contemporaries he remained loyal to the same side throughout the Wars of the Roses; for a man like him, death at Bosworth would have been preferable to being taken prisoner. The sad blemish on John Howard's story is that, like others, he took the side of a usurper against a king, a decision made worse by the fact that Edward V was just a child of 12, and his reputation has thus been tainted (although not in his own lifetime) by the suggestion that he and his son might have caused harm to the boy and his brother, of which there is no proof.

# Chapter 4

# Rehabilitation

Norfolk's son, Thomas Howard, Earl of Surrey, by then aged 42, had sustained serious wounds on the Bosworth battlefield and rather than be captured and face an ignominious execution, or be left at the mercy of those waiting to pick-over the bodies of the dead and dying, implored Sir Gilbert Talbot to finish him off. Instead, Talbot had him removed to safety, from where he was taken prisoner and incarcerated in the Tower for the next three-and-a-half years.[1]

His father was posthumously found guilty of treason, the dukedom revoked and assets seized. Lucky to be spared the death penalty, but convicted of treason and attainted like his late father, Thomas Howard forfeited everything and could not inherit nor pass assets on; this applied to the whole family except for his wife's own properties.[2] His incarceration, however, although alarming, was not necessarily uncomfortable, for he had a very generous allowance of £8 a month to cover board and wages for three servants.[3]

In 1487, two years after the Battle of Bosworth, the Yorkists produced a 10-year-old pretender to the throne, Lambert Simnel, claiming he was Edward Plantagenet, the son of Edward IV's brother George, Duke of Clarence, executed for treason in 1478. During the chaos caused by Simnel's supporters, Thomas Howard was offered an opportunity to escape from the Tower and fortunately had the good sense not to take it, reasoning he still had the potential to work his way into Tudor favour.[4] It was a wise decision, for Henry VII did indeed recognise Howard's potential as a soldier and administrator, and in March 1489 he was released, his attainder reversed and some, but not all, of his lands and properties restored. In May the earldom of Surrey was restored to him, but not his late father's dukedom.

His three decades of service as a loyal servant of the fledging Tudor dynasty began with his appointment as one of a number of senior magistrates upholding the laws of the forests north of the River Trent. In May 1490 he was appointed Vice-Warden of the East and Middle Marches on the borders of Scotland. After destructive 1496 and 1497 incursions into England by the young James IV of Scotland, Thomas Howard was one of those who negotiated a Treaty of Perpetual Peace, sealed by James's betrothal to Henry VII and Elizabeth of York's eldest child Margaret Tudor, then aged 7. Surrey, however, also had a marriage closer to home to arrange.

In 1497, only four months after the death of Elizabeth Tilney, his wife of twenty-five years, Surrey, then aged 54, obtained a dispensation from the Pope to marry her first cousin, 20-year-old Agnes Tilney, the girl destined to be the Howard matriarch for over three decades, and whose brother, Sir Philip Tilney, was in his service. Among Agnes's stepchildren were the heir, Lord Thomas, older than her by about four years, Lady Elizabeth, whose daughter Anne Boleyn was not yet born, and Lord Edmund, whose daughter Katherine Howard would be born nearly a quarter of a century later.

Surrey continued to prove his loyalty and abilities to Henry Tudor to such an extent that in 1499 he and his young wife were recalled to court and in 1501 he was appointed to the position of Lord Treasurer, one of the Great Offices of State. He was also entrusted with a number of diplomatic missions including the negotiations for the marriage of Arthur, Prince of Wales to Katherine of Aragon, who on 14 November 1501 were married in St Paul's Cathedral. Arthur had had his 15th birthday in September, while Katherine would be 16 in December. The cause of the prince's death the following April is still a mystery, but, except for the usual unsubstantiated mutterings about poison, there was no serious suggestion of foul play.

On 11 February 1503, Queen Elizabeth died on her 37th birthday, after the birth of a girl, Catherine, who survived only a few days. King Henry, in a quandary over having to send Katherine of Aragon back to her parents and return the enormous dowry, thought he might then marry his daughter-in-law himself, but when her parents recoiled at the suggestion he sought and was granted a papal dispensation for the widowed princess to marry his younger son Prince Henry when he grew up.

In June the late queen's eldest daughter, already referred to officially as Queen Margaret, began her journey to her new life in Scotland in the care of the Earl of Surrey, the leader and main organiser of the glittering procession, accompanied by his wife Agnes, who by now was about 26 years old to his 60 and had already borne him several children. At York the young queen appeared 'richly arrayed in a gown of cloth of gold with a rich collar of precious stones and a girdle reaching down to the ground made of spun gold. The Countess of Surrey [Agnes Howard] carried her train'.[5]

The sight of Margaret and King James romantically riding into Edinburgh together on one horse was very popular with the people, despite the fact the bride-to-be was only 13, whereas the groom was 30 and already father of five children by four different mistresses. On 8 August the marriage was celebrated with great splendour in Holyrood Abbey with Surrey giving Margaret away and the rites performed by the Archbishops of Glasgow and York. Within days, however, Margaret was writing to her father that, 'my lord of Surrey is in great favour with the king here and he cannot bear to be without his company at any time of the day'. This young girl, so very far from home, goes on to complain about Howard's attitude towards her, 'and if he [her chamberlain] speaks anything on my behalf, my Lord Surrey speaks to him in such a way that he dares speak no further'.[6]

Thomas Howard's career continued to flourish and little-by-little his father's old lands were restored to him and new ones added, with a large parcel of Norfolk manors in 1507 including Kenninghall village between Norwich and Thetford.[7] In 1509 he was an executor of the will of Henry VII who died on 21 April aged 52 and who, in his last days, had restored to him all but the actual dukedom of Norfolk, which he possibly had been intending to do in the near future.

Until he reached 18 in late June, the new King Henry VIII's grandmother, Lady Margaret Beaufort, was to act as regent, based at Richmond Palace. Attending and advising her there were Lord Privy Seal, Bishop Richard Fox and Lord Treasurer, Thomas Howard. However, newly liberated from his father's ever watchful eye, Henry moved fast, marrying his brother's widow Katherine of Aragon on 11 June, being crowned on the 24th and celebrating his 18th birthday on 28 June. His grandmother, who just might have exercised some influence over the teenage king, died the following day aged 66. The beginning of a new reign might have been seen as an appropriate occasion for the restoration of the Norfolk dukedom to a now elderly man who had shown exemplary loyalty to the Tudor dynasty for the past twenty years, but it was not forthcoming.

The late Henry VII's tasks first and foremost had been to stabilise England and the economy after thirty years of civil war, and from him Henry VIII inherited a healthy treasury. Unlike his father, however, Henry the younger with plenty of money to hand, no overwhelming sense of responsibility and fancying himself as a modern-day Henry V, was actually looking for the thrill of conflict abroad, particularly with France, the traditional enemy. This, and the encouragement from the rising star Thomas Wolsey, is what the more circumspect of his advisors like Thomas Howard were going to have to deal with.

The Earl of Surrey was never a favourite of Henry VIII, but his second son became a great friend and encouraged Henry's dreams, to such an extent that even Wolsey was alarmed, writing to Richard Fox on 30 September 1511 that Edward Howard was actively encouraging Henry to go to war with France's ally James IV, and his (Fox's) presence at court was imperative: 'Mr. Howard urges the king against the Scots, by whose wanton means his Grace spendeth much money, and is more disposed to war than peace. Your presence shall be very necessary to repress this appetite.'[8]

On 7 April 1512 the king appointed Edward Howard admiral of a fleet of eighteen ships, including the *Mary Rose,* carrying 3700 mariners and soldiers, to patrol the Channel and the Thames estuary. In spite of the whole enterprise ending in disaster, in March 1513 he was appointed Lord Admiral of England, Ireland and Aquitaine.[9] For some reason Henry and Wolsey considered his limited previous experience and disappointing performance were sufficient to allow Edward Howard to lead the next endeavour against a large French fleet then being mobilized.

Already time was of the essence and the French fleet must be blockaded. Howard would be responsible for everything from the state of the ships to the ordering, delivery and replenishing of supplies and, most important, as Lord Admiral, needed to have sufficient understanding of his situation to be able to decide what strategies were viable. In short, if he thought his 1512 experience had been challenging, his upcoming task would in all probability be a nightmare, which is what it was from the very start, with such helplessness and desperation coming through in his letters to Henry VIII and Wolsey that it is difficult not to feel sorry for him.

Within three days of leaving the Thames estuary for the Kent coast he was writing to Henry VIII from the *Mary Rose*, 'Sir, For God's sake have your Council send us victuals'.[10] His decision to attack the French fleet in the harbour at Brest proved fatal. In the exchange in the afternoon of 25 April, when from small boats he attacked their heavily armed flagship, he was wounded and fell into the water in full armour, which dragged him to the bottom. He was 36.

The position of Lord Admiral immediately went to Edward's elder brother, Lord Thomas Howard, who, although not a seasoned sailor, possessed the ability quickly to assess and evaluate a situation such as that which met him on his arrival at Plymouth in the face of mutiny. He wrote to Wolsey, 'I have here found the worst ordered Army and the furthest out of rule that ever I saw... Scribbled in great haste on the *Mary Rose* at Plymouth at half past eleven on the night of 7 May'.[11] King James IV graciously sent commiserations to Henry VIII on the death of Edward Howard, asking that they be received in the spirit in which they were sent, 'We are truly sorry ... through acquaintance we had of his father, that noble knight who conveyed our dearest companion the Queen to us.'[12]

By 1512 James IV had been on the throne of Scotland for nearly a quarter of a century, was in his late thirties and had earned praise at home and abroad as a cultured and educated monarch; a true Renaissance prince. He had continued to unite the various factions in his country to an extent that had not been seen before, and was building one of the most sophisticated fleets in the world. He was, though, being provoked by Henry VIII who considered him to be his vassal. The Treaty of Perpetual Peace between Henry VII and King James had been a good move for both countries; Henry VIII, on the other hand, itching to fight the French as soon as possible, viewed their ally the King of Scots in a different light. The preamble to a Subsidy Act (an alteration to taxation) that came before the English Parliament in 1512, had added insult to injury, showing scant respect for the Treaty by declaring James to be 'the very homager and obediencer of right to your Highness'.[13]

When full-scale war against France became a certainty in 1513, Lord Treasurer Thomas Howard, Earl of Surrey was to remain at home as one of the chief advisors to Katherine of Aragon, the designated regent for Henry in his absence. Perhaps his time in the limelight was almost up. Should King James opt for a full invasion while Henry was away in France with a large army and some of the best equipment, England could be overwhelmed by France's ally the Scots, and as a consequence the Howard family facing blame and ruin. The position in which Surrey found himself was an insult to his abilities and decades of faithful service, but being the man he was, he determined to ready the north of England for what he anticipated would be a full-scale invasion from north of the border.

# Chapter 5

# Saviours of the Realm: Flodden

On 16 August, near the French village of Guinegatte, Henry VIII and his allies ambushed French cavalry coming to the aid of the besieged town of Thérouanne, who turned their mounts and fled so fast that the encounter became mockingly known as the 'Battle of the Spurs'. Even though Henry was delighted and made the most of his victory and the resulting barrage of sycophantic plaudits, it was hardly a triumph comparable to that of his hero Henry V at Agincourt. Six days later James IV of Scotland crossed the River Tweed into England with an army estimated to number 42,000 and carrying twenty-nine artillery pieces that included seventeen heavy siege guns.

In both countries men aged 16 to 60 were eligible to fight, but Surrey had reached his three score and ten years. He was in Pontefract, about thirty miles from York, when he heard the news and on August 25 ordered that recruits from the northern counties of Northumberland, Durham, Cumberland, Westmorland, Lancashire and Cheshire prepare to assemble at Newcastle on 1 September. With these added to his own 500 men and the 1500 his son Thomas the Lord Admiral was bringing by ship, he would eventually have a force of about 26,000. By this stage about 10,000 of James IV's original 42,000 had either deserted with their plunder or gone down with sickness, but Surrey was still significantly outnumbered.

On 5 September King James was in the vicinity of Milfield Plain and Flodden Hill in Northumberland when Surrey, about twenty miles away, wrote issuing the challenge to give battle on Friday 9th. Having little food left and lacking robust tents should the army have to remain in the area until the autumn frosts began, meant he needed to get his mission over as soon as possible. The letter, although accusing James of breaking the Treaty of Perpetual Peace, was written in the very polite and deferential style to be expected of a senior English nobleman corresponding with a king.

Another letter, however, from his son Lord Thomas, was a different matter altogether. Surrey, as commander, must have been aware of it, and perhaps it was part of the strategy to make sure James was sufficiently riled to accept the challenge. The Lord Admiral wrote as though he were the Scottish king's equal, which of course infuriated him, warning that the Scots need not beg for mercy, for apart from the king himself, he intended to spare nobody.[1] In his response James politely disagreed with the warmongering accusations against him, ignored the insults and agreed to give battle on the said date. As Surrey understood it, the Scots would wait for the English Army on flat land in the vicinity of Milfield Plain.

The English herald, Thomas Hawley, Rouge Croix Pursuivant, Surrey's messenger had been intercepted some distance from the Scots' camp to preserve its exact location and would be held for the time being. The message of acceptance of the challenge was therefore carried to Surrey by James's own man, Islay Herald who, for the same reason, and as an assurance Rouge Croix would be safe, was then detained by the English in some comfort under the eagle eye of Thomas Tonge, York Herald.

Islay sent his servant back to King James assuring him he was safe and about to be released, whereupon the Scots released Rouge Croix, who rejoined Surrey who by then, with his teams of oxen making heavy weather of pulling the artillery along in the glutinous mud, had reached the village of Wooler Haugh. There he was made aware of the nasty problem that lay ahead, when his scouts reported that James had set up on Flodden Hill, not on the Milfield Plain and the steepness of the hill and marshy land at the foot of part of it left only a narrow approach as the only way the English could advance, meaning they would be walking into a death trap.

Surrey decided to appeal to James's better nature. Rouge Croix was sent back to the Scottish camp with a letter reminding him of the arrangement and that Surrey had not expected him to take advantage and was imploring him to keep to the agreement and wait for him at Milfield Plain:

> ... and by your Herald Islay you answered ... you would wait for me at the place you were at the time my message was shown to your Grace...' but instead, 'put yourself into a ground more like a fortresse or Campe than upon any indifferent ground for battell.' Written 'in the field in Wollerhaughe, 7 September, 5 o'clock in the afternoon.

It was signed by himself and eighteen of his commanders, requesting that James send a signed agreement to meet him on the actual Milfield Plain.[2]

When the letter, again written in the polite manner expected of Surrey, reached James on the morning of the 8th he was furious; detaining Rouge Croix, whom he refused to see, he sent a servant back with a verbal response that it was not up to a mere earl to tell a king what to do. Thus was the friendship forged with Surrey long ago at James's wedding to Margaret Tudor well and truly broken.

Meanwhile, a tricky and potentially deadly situation was developing. James's Islay Herald still had not returned to camp, so his servant, who had returned, suspecting foul play refused to release Rouge Croix and his servant, insisting that if Islay was not back by noon the Scots would behead them. Fortunately for all concerned, Islay rolled up in time, no doubt rather shame faced, for he had indeed been released by the English as and when promised, but instead of making his way straight back to the Scottish camp, had indulged in a heavy drinking session with his new best friend York Herald, and was rather worse for wear. It has not been possible to discover the identity of Islay Herald or whether he was killed in the ensuing battle; the last recorded holder of the post had died in 1512 and then there is a gap until the 1530s. Both Rouge Croix and York Herald survived.

That morning, 8 September, the English struck camp and crossed the River Till at Weetwood Bridge, but instead of turning northeast towards Flodden, marched north. James, whose scouts would report this, could have put a number of interpretations on the unexpected move. Firstly, was Surrey abandoning the venture, in which case James could claim a victory? But this was not in character with the man, and if retreat was his aim, why not march his men south? Secondly, if they were heading for Berwick, as they appeared to be, was it in order to take on supplies? Perhaps Scottish intelligence gatherers had found that Surrey's desperately needed food and ale supply wagons had been raided on their way from Newcastle and his men faced drinking potentially deadly rain or river water. Thirdly, could Surrey be bypassing James and marching directly into Scotland?

Surrey's actual plan, none of the above, was clever, but a huge gamble, as it would take his army into a patch of unknown territory. They would take the old Roman road known as *Devil's Causeway* as far as Barmoor, about eight miles from Wooler, and camp there for the night. This would be no mean feat for an army of over 20,000 men on their last rations as well as being exhausted from moving artillery weapons through thick mud in heavy rain that never stopped. For those not allowed the privilege of staying in the castle, it would be a cold, windy, soaking wet and hungry few hours.

At 5 o'clock in the morning on the day of the battle, the English struck camp and bore west towards the village of Branxton, which lay behind Branxton Hill, about a mile and a quarter north of Flodden. If it was suicidal to face the enemy from the flat land on the southern side of Flodden Hill, then they would face them from the north of it, with themselves on the top of Branxton Hill. For an excellent explanation of the ensuing battle, which shows how the topography played a vital part, see the L.A.B. Scotland *Remembering Flodden Project* video.[3]

Although Lord Thomas Howard's route was longer with the artillery needing to cross the River Till at Twizell Bridge, he arrived first, stunned to find that the enemy, anticipating the English plans, had at the last minute abandoned Flodden and occupied Branxton themselves and now only about a quarter of a mile of unknown terrain lay between the latter and where he was standing. His shock is evidenced by his immediate action of sending his *Agnus Dei* – Lamb of God – medallion to his father who was not far behind, the sign that he was in great difficulty and needed help immediately.[4]

King James did not attack before the whole English army was assembled, even though the three o'clock deadline was approaching. According to the *Pitscottie Chronicles* he said, 'I am determined to have them all in front of me on one plain field and see what all of them can do against me'.[5] In reality, the show of bravado could have been because he did not know where the rest of the English were, or perhaps his army was just not ready.

Denied Branxton Hill, the English were, nevertheless, on slightly elevated land, and King James, possibly, had not realised the significance of a waterlogged dip at the foot of Branxton which would quickly turn into a quagmire. Nor, it seems, was he fully aware that although the hill sloped fairly gently to the west where Lord Home and the Earl of Huntley were stationed facing Lord Edmund Howard's detachment, the downward slope facing north opposite Surrey and his son the Lord Admiral, was much steeper. Surrey had already lost Edward, his second son that year, and now waited with his first and third sons for battle to commence. His lesser-known boys to his first wife were already dead and his surviving sons with Agnes – William, Thomas and Richard – were only 3, 2 and 1 respectively. Once again the Howards as a noble dynasty could be on the brink of destruction.

At about four in the afternoon, and for the first time on British soil, battle commenced with artillery fire from both sides. The Scots soon found that guns ideal for bombarding castles were less suitable for their current circumstances, so seeing that the enemy's gunners were failing to make much impact, the English decided to turn their artillery on the Scottish pikemen.[6] Many of Surrey's men were armed with bills, or bill hooks, six-to-eight-foot-long wooden poles with metal blades at the end, almost like an agricultural tool used for chopping and trimming vegetation. Curved like a scythe so they could easily slash legs and bring horses down, and with a spike attachment, acting like a bayonet, the bill hook was a most formidable weapon enabling slashing and stabbing actions from a distance.

Its more modern version was the pike, a sixteen-foot-long wooden pole topped with a metal spike of up to one-and-a-half feet, used in tight-knit, hedgehog-like formations which were deadly when executed by expertly trained men, just so long as they moved in perfect coordination, could keep the momentum going and no man lost his footing. If not exactly James IV's secret weapon, the pike was his great hope. Lord Edmund found out just how destructive pikes could be when the lords Home and Huntley, needing to escape the English artillery bombardment, came down the western slope of the hill and led a pike charge against him. He was felled and wounded, but fortunately the Scots wanted him alive and although his men were badly scattered and some fled the battlefield, he was rescued by Lord Dacre's cavalry. Seeing their pikemen's success and being still at the mercy of English artillery, the Scots facing Surrey and Lord Thomas were directed to do the same, but here two weaknesses were their downfall: lack of knowledge of the lie of the land and insufficient weapons training.

The north-facing slope of Branxton Hill was much steeper than it appeared and perilous underfoot after prolonged rainfall. The whole point of pikemen's manoeuvres was to advance in unison and maintain momentum, but it was impossible to keep a foothold in such bad terrain so the pikes became a liability and were discarded, causing deadly trip hazards. Those who somehow reached the waterlogged dip at the bottom found themselves knee-deep in mud and stumbling over bodies. Pikemen also bore small side arms, a sword and short handled axe, both useless against the Lord Admiral's billmen, who inflicted horrendous losses upon them. When it came down to the hand-to-hand fighting which lasted until after six o'clock, the Scots were surrounded, except for on the west where Home and Huntly had stood off after their encounter with Edmund Howard and Dacre. It was carnage; the Scots battled on, but were a lost cause.

King James was caught in the jaw by an arrow and cut down by English billmen, suffering devastating arm and neck wounds, and the flower of the Scottish nobility was obliterated, often several from the same family, as well as a number of the leading clergy; of the Scottish leaders only Home and Huntley survived. It was estimated that in two-and-a-half hours of fighting 10,000 Scots and 4000 English were killed, a dreadful toll in such a short space of time that would not be surpassed until the First World War.[7]

Obviously the glory and credit for the Flodden victory would go to Henry VIII, still across the Channel basking in the glory of his own little victory, which was insignificant by comparison. His wife wrote to him, 'Your Grace shall see how I can keep my promise, sending you for your banner a king's coat. I thought to send him to you in person, but our Englishmen's hearts would not suffer [allow] it'.[8] Although James IV had been excommunicated for breaking the Treaty of Perpetual Peace, Henry VIII was granted a papal dispensation to bury his brother-in-law in St Paul's Cathedral in the manner befitting a fellow monarch, but he remained unburied, and although there grew up many stories of how the remains of James IV were desecrated over the centuries, his true fate is unknown.[9]

James's wife, Margaret Tudor, in the early stages of pregnancy, acted as regent for their 17-month-old son who was crowned James V, but in August 1514, less than a year after her husband's death and only four months after giving birth to his posthumous son, Alexander, she made a secret marriage with Archibald Douglas, sixth Earl of Angus. To many this was unacceptable and resulted in Margaret, pregnant by Angus, fleeing to England where she gave birth to their daughter, Lady Margaret Douglas. For the Howards the English victory issued in a new era of good fortune, that might, or might not, last. Thereafter, among his prize possessions at Framlingham Castle, the Earl of Surrey kept two silver-gilt cups taken from the battlefield engraved with the arms of James IV and weighing 300 ounces, which he bequeathed to Cardinal Wolsey in 1524.[10]

In a magnificent ceremony at the Archbishop of Canterbury's palace across the King's Highway from Norfolk House, Thomas Howard senior's Lambeth home, the victor of Flodden, attired in splendid crimson robes, was 'Honourably restored unto his right name of Duke of Norfolk', on Candlemas Day, 2 February, 1514, the precedence to date from the original Mowbray creation of 1397.[11] In recognition of the victory, Norfolk and his 'heirs forever' were to bear as an augmentation to their coat of arms of the upper half of a lion 'pierced in the mouth with an arrow and coloured according to the arms of Scotland, as borne by the said King of Scots', a grisly reminder of the nature of the death of James IV.[12]

Later in the year, in the eyes of one young woman, however, he was somewhat less of a hero. In the early autumn of 1514, Henry VIII's younger sister, the lovely 18-year-old Princess Mary, became a casualty of her brother's not very successful encounters with Louis XII of France when she found herself a pawn in a peace treaty negotiated by Wolsey and Norfolk, and sent abroad to become the bride of the gouty old French king already twice married and three times her age. On 10 October, the day after the wedding, in circumstances disconcertingly similar to her sister Margaret's experience in 1503, Norfolk allowed the French to discharge Mary's most experienced English attendants, causing her to complain bitterly two days later to her brother that Wolsey would never have allowed it.[13]

Among those left behind, but little equipped to fight her corner should the need arise, were two very junior maids of honour, the Duke of Norfolk's granddaughters, the young Boleyn sisters Mary and Anne. In 1515, when Norfolk was 72, the position of Lord Chancellor that would have been his final triumph was lost to him forever when the honour went to Thomas Wolsey, thirty years his junior.

In the dying hours of April 30 1517, officials, including Under-Sheriff Thomas More, were desperately trying to reason with rioters running amok through the ill-lit streets of London. Traditionally, the eve of May 1, the feast of St Joseph the Worker, was a time of revelry for artisans and labourers, but in 1517 the camaraderie turned to violence in the City, when as many as 2000 people, including apprentices and journeymen, attacked immigrant settlers in their homes and businesses. It was the ugly climax to a situation that had been brewing for some time and of which the authorities were well aware.

After curfew, Alderman John Mundy had come upon a crowd of youths in Eastcheap having a mock fight with wooden swords and being cheered on by a large crowd. He ordered them to disperse, but emboldened by safety in numbers and a few too many tankards of beer, they questioned his authority, whereupon he tried to march their spokesman off to jail. As they dragged their friend from his grasp, the cry of 'Prentices and clubs! Prentices and clubs!' went up and rioting broke out. Nobody was killed, but it was severely dealt with.

Grafton's *Chronicle* paints a disturbing picture of Norfolk's son, Lord Edmund Howard, who appears to have supervised the executions of some of the of the rioters, who 'were executed in the most rigorous manner, in the presence of Lord Edmund Howard, who showed no mercy but extreme cruelty to the poor younglings [youngsters] in their execution'.[14] On or about 22 May the remainder of the 300 arrested were led in procession to Westminster Hall in the manner of men about to be executed, that is barefoot and clad only in their shirts and with halters around their necks. The wrongdoers, some of them barely into their teens, were brought in and immediately threw themselves on the ground crying for mercy.

In a carefully choreographed performance Wolsey, Norfolk and others then fell to their knees and began pleading with the king on the prisoners' behalf. The Venetian diplomat, Nicolo Sagudino, acknowledged that Henry and Wolsey's pre-arrangement and preparation of the spectacle of the pardon had been extremely well done, but was horrified that bodies, or in some cases just bits of those already executed, remained on the gibbets for weeks.[15]

In May 1521, by then almost 80, an exceptionally old man for the times, Norfolk was assigned the nasty task of presiding over the treason trial of his own son's father-in-law, Edward Stafford, Duke of Buckingham, the son of the Buckingham executed by Richard III. Being descended from Edward III meant that Stafford was carrying a massive millstone around his neck at a time when Henry VIII was becoming obsessed about having no legitimate son. A disgruntled servant Buckingham had dismissed told the authorities he had spoken of stabbing and deposing Henry and listened to prophecies of his death, which led to him being charged with treason. At the end of the trial at Westminster Hall, as Buckingham was brought to the bar to learn his fate, the assembled worthies' attention was fixed upon Norfolk, who appeared to be not fully focused. Eventually he recovered himself sufficiently to utter the terrible verdict. Then, before the assembled courtroom, and on the brink of passing the death sentence, he broke down in tears.[16]

Were they crocodile tears, or was this simply an old man who had just about had enough? In his eight decades he had lived through so much, but now, as he was approaching the end of his years, he was becoming overwhelmed by circumstances beyond his control and fearful for the future of his dynasty and country in the increasingly bizarre world of Henry VIII. In December 1522 Norfolk resigned as Lord Treasurer to be replaced by his son Thomas, Earl of Surrey and retired to his castle at Framlingham in Suffolk, where he died on 21 May 1524. Immediately the chamber of state, great hall and the other vast rooms were draped in 440 yards of costly black material embellished in gold with his escutcheons of arms, as was the chapel where his coffin would lie before the altar for a month, and which he had always kept 'prince-like for he had great pleasure in the service of God'.[17]

On June 22 the coffin bearing the duke's life-sized wax effigy was mounted on a bier which bore 100 smaller wax figures of heraldic beasts and hooded weepers. It was transported the twenty-four miles on a chariot drawn by horses bedecked in black with six gentlemen walking alongside to the Priory of Our Lady, the Cluniac monastic house in Thetford, Norfolk. One of the most important of the East Anglian monasteries, Thetford Priory was the last resting place of his father John Howard and the third and fourth dukes of Norfolk of the original Mowbray creation. There followed 400 hooded torch bearers, in turn followed by 500 nobles on horseback and in their turn by numerous chanting clergy, many joining the procession as it passed through their towns. Among the lesser mortals walked a contingent of apprentices from London, a reminder of Norfolk begging for their lives in 1517.

The procession arrived at Thetford the next day and the funeral commenced at five o'clock the following morning. As the Bishop of Ely sang Mass, a mounted knight wearing the late duke's armour and carrying his battle axe, blade head down, entered the church; walking beside him and wearing the distinctive heraldic uniform of Carlisle Herald was Thomas Hawley, a face from the past, formerly Rouge Croix Pursuivant, who had carried the Howards' messages to James IV at Flodden.[18] Dr Matthew Mackerel, abbot of the Premonstratensian abbey of Barlings in Lincolnshire, then preached a sermon on the text 'Behold the lion of the tribe of Judah triumphs' from Revelation 5:5, which, it was said, so terrified the congregation that some mourners fled the church.

After the sermon, the bishop consecrated the new vault and the duke's staves of office were broken and thrown into the grave. 7-year-old Lord Henry Howard standing beside the new vault would have had no inkling that his grandfather would be the only Howard to be laid to rest there. Less still could anyone have foreseen that only a dozen years hence, on the orders of the king, Dr Mackerel would suffer a hellish death, and not long after that the great priory itself would lie in ruins.[19]

To most of the thousands of onlookers who had lined the route of Thomas, second Duke of Norfolk's spectacular funeral procession it would have seemed that his prolific dynasty was unassailable. He had been succeeded by his eldest son as third duke, and had also left several other surviving children from his two marriages. His grandchildren included the captivating young Anne Boleyn, who at the time of her grandfather's death had already been two years at the court of Henry VIII and would ultimately, it could confidently be expected, make a very good marriage. Anne's cousin, Lord Edmund's little daughter Katherine Howard, one of the latest additions to the family, was about 3 years old and thriving. What could possibly go wrong?

## Chapter 6

# A Great Matter

When his sister Mary's husband expired in early 1515 after a few months of marriage, English Henry, then 24 and famed for his good looks, learning and athletic prowess, was suddenly faced with Francis I as King of France, an equally accomplished young man of 20. An even younger leader appeared just over twelve months after Francis in the shape of a 16-year-old nephew of Katherine of Aragon and grandson of Ferdinand of Aragon and Isabella of Castile, through whom he was recognised as the first King of Spain, Carlos I. In 1519 he succeeded his paternal grandfather as head of the House of Hapsburg, who since 1508 had also been Holy Roman Emperor, and was elected to the same position, becoming the Holy Roman Emperor Charles V, and is frequently referred to as 'the Emperor'.

In the eighteenth century Voltaire described the Holy Roman Empire as 'not holy, not Roman and not an empire'. It had been created in AD 800 by the coronation of Charlemagne, King of the Franks as 'Roman Emperor' over territories that had once been the western part of the old Roman Empire. In the second quarter of the sixteenth century its cohesion was threatened by Lutheranism which would cause a religious divide.[1] Francis I, the Emperor and the Papacy in Rome would be at odds with Henry VIII on and off for the rest of his life.

Thomas Wolsey, born about 1473, the son of butcher Robert Wolsey of Ipswich, entered the service of Henry VII in 1507, becoming Almoner to his successor in 1509, and from then on swept all before him. By 1514 he was Archbishop of York; a cardinal's hat followed in 1515, the same year he achieved the position of Henry VIII's Lord Chancellor, dashing the second Duke of Norfolk's hopes. For much of the time, Henry VIII had complete confidence in him, but, as would any man in his position, on the way to the top Wolsey made a lot of enemies. He also amassed a great fortune, to which the surviving portion of his palatial masterpiece at Hampton Court still bears witness. The historian David Starkey says of Wolsey that he was Henry VIII's creature, for whom 'nothing [was] too big or too small or too dirty'.[2] By 1527, when he had held enormous power for twelve years, it remained to be seen how the cardinal would acquit himself, and what form his master's response would take, should he find himself faced with a potentially insoluble problem.

Of Katherine of Aragon's several pregnancies since her marriage to Henry in 1509 only one child survived, the Princess Mary, who was 10 in 1526, the year her father became infatuated with the woman who would change their lives. He was 35; it was very much a male dominated world, so, in spite of there being no legal barrier to his daughter succeeding him, he longed for a legitimate son. Alas, his wife, now 41, had not been pregnant for seven years, losing her last baby a few weeks before her husband's mistress, Bessie Blount, gave birth to a son he named Henry Fitzroy, 'son of the king', and later created him Duke of Richmond and Somerset. Bessie had been replaced in the royal affections by Mary Carey, née Boleyn, and now it was Mary's younger sister's turn. These sisters' parents were Sir Thomas Boleyn and Lady Elizabeth Howard, a daughter of the late Flodden duke and his first wife, Elizabeth Tilney.

The date of birth of the third Duke of Norfolk's niece, Anne Boleyn, was not recorded, but it is likely that by 1526 she was somewhere between 19 and 25. Anne has not gone down in history as being a great beauty but was captivating in a *je ne sais quoi* sort of way that set her apart from other ladies of the court. George Wyatt, using information passed down from people who had known her, revealed 'albeit in beauty she was to many inferior, but for behaviour, manners, attire and tongue she excelled them all'.[3] Anne Boleyn was an educated woman, articulate and sometimes opinionated, who knew all about the king's brief dalliances with the ladies. While she could not completely rebuff his amorous attention, she declined Henry's bed, and in so doing made herself more desirable than ever to a man not used to being refused anything. With the sovereign becoming so thoroughly smitten by one of their own, an interesting time was beckoning to the Howard clan.

Henry VIII's marriage breakup is often referred to as a divorce, but Katherine of Aragon had been a faithful and worthy consort, so what he really needed was an annulment on the grounds there had been an impediment to their marriage before it ever took place. That old standby claiming one of the parties had been pre-contracted to someone else was not possible in his case, but in 1527, confident he had found a quick and foolproof way out, he proposed to Anne Boleyn. Henry thought the perfect solution to his dilemma lay in the Bible itself no less, when it revealed to him why God had seen fit to give him a healthy son out of wedlock but none within it. The key was in the Old Testament Book of Leviticus, 'If a man shall take his brother's wife, it is an unclean thing ... they shall be childless'.[4] The term 'childless' was conveniently interpreted for him by a leading scholar of Hebrew as meaning without sons.

Henry's case rested on whether Queen Katherine's brief first marriage to his elder brother had been consummated. Even though they had both been young he was banking on it being readily accepted that it had, meaning the papal dispensation granted by Pope Julius II enabling Katherine to marry her brother-in-law was an error that needed to be rectified at once. It soon became obvious, however, that all was not as clear cut as he hoped, with Katherine appalled at the suggestion, and Wolsey realising the case needed to be put before the Pope. Thus was the scene set for Henry VIII's 'Great Matter' to become excruciatingly complicated and drag on for years: a problem at last that Wolsey just might not be able to fix.

Meanwhile, the third Duke of Norfolk was beset by ongoing marital difficulties of his own. His first wife, Anne of York, a daughter of Edward IV, died in 1511, pre-deceased by their four children. Lord Thomas Howard, as he then was, took as his second wife Lady Elizabeth Stafford, daughter of the third duke of Buckingham, who was only 15 and had been in love for nearly two years with her father's ward Ralph Neville, fourth Earl of Westmorland about the same age as herself, whom she was due to marry at Christmas 1512. Buckingham tried to persuade Howard into having one of her younger sisters, but being nearly 40 and having no son and heir, he needed a wife able to bear children sooner rather than later.[5]

The Howards' marriage would prove to be a nightmare for both of them. The eldest of their surviving children was Henry 'the Poet Earl', born about 1517, he who later so despised the 'new erected men'. By 1527, or earlier, the duke had taken a certain Bess Holland as his mistress and lived with her openly at his fine new house at Kenninghall in Norfolk, an ultra-modern red brick mansion with over 70 rooms,[6] where his wife continued to live in great distress in a *ménage à trois* under the same roof for some years, calling Bess 'a bawd, a drab, ... a churl's daughter, which was but washer of my nursery eight years'.[7]

Following an illness, possibly dysentery contracted when posted to Ireland in 1520, Norfolk had a condition which had an adverse effect on his bowels for the rest of his life; there are letters in which he describes the unfortunate consequences in some detail. In the late 1520s he appears to have been so dangerously ill that the king sent his own physician, Dr Butts, to Kenninghall to treat him, for which he was very grateful and wrote to Wolsey that without the doctor's expertise he would have died.[8] Recovery was slow, and soon afterwards the duke was struck down by shaking, the telltale sign of the dreaded sweating sickness, which in his already weakened state he was lucky to survive. Little detail remains, but this was during the 1528 widespread outbreak of the disease and his stepmother Agnes confided to Wolsey she thought Norfolk had been struck down owing to poor housekeeping, or as she put it 'default of keeping', in his fancy new home.[9]

Papal legate Cardinal Lorenzo Campeggio finally arrived in England in October 1528 to hear Henry VIII's case, but it was not until 31 May 1529 that the legatine court at last began proceedings at Blackfriars, the great monastery beside the Thames. Some of the witnesses, however, were allowed to testify elsewhere, among them 'Agnes, widow of Thomas late [second] Duke of Norfolk', who gave her age as '52 or more'. What the redoubtable Duchess Agnes was doing in Norfolk in the summer of 1529 is unclear, but on 16 July, a Friday, in Thetford Priory's Church of St Mary, in the presence of Sampson Mitchell, canon of Chichester, a John Fletcher and her chaplain William Molyneux, she began giving her deposition.

We can have no idea whether she was torn between loyalty to Queen Katherine or support for her own family, but there is no reason to believe Agnes was not telling the truth when she said she clearly remembered Katherine arriving from Spain to be Prince Arthur's bride. Soon afterwards she had been one of the attendants who accompanied the newlyweds to their apartments in 1501 for the traditional bedding ritual, saw them put to bed and left them there, assuming their union would be consummated. The document of her deposition records what she remembered and had assumed happened at the time.[10] Three days later Mitchell was already back at Blackfriars to place her statement before the legatine court, and three days after that the cardinals Campeggio and Wolsey adjourned the court for the summer. It never reconvened.

In October a letter from Pope Clement VII informed Henry that the dispensation of Pope Julius II, had actually *allowed* for the possibility the marriage had been consummated and was perfectly sound.[11] By the time it arrived, however, Thomas Wolsey was out of favour and in deep trouble. Apart from not securing an annulment, a series of other diplomatic failures had angered Henry and it appeared the cardinal's time was up and he was about to join the rapidly expanding club of those Henry had once held close, but who would find no mercy from him once they had outlived their usefulness.

Henry, late in 1520 or early 1521, for security reasons had written in his own messy hand to Wolsey that he should 'make good wache' on a group who resented him, possibly including the Norfolks. Now those very same people's assistance was required in getting rid of him.[12] On 17 October Wolsey was forced to surrender the chancellorship and stood accused of *praemunire*, that is, working with a foreign leader, the Pope, to resolve a situation which should be determined in his own country. At 6 o'clock that evening at York Place, his riverside palace in Westminster, Wolsey surrendered the Great Seal to the dukes of Norfolk and Suffolk, both of whom hoped to profit from his demise. However, the coveted post of Lord Chancellor went to neither Norfolk nor Suffolk, but instead to Sir Thomas More.

October 1529 saw all Wolsey's property officially declared forfeit. In the hope of ingratiating himself with the king and detracting from those who accused him of amassing vast wealth and living far above his station, he had already given Hampton Court over to him. The same month saw the unedifying spectacle of the excited human magpies Henry VIII, Anne Boleyn and her mother Elizabeth (Howard) Boleyn picking over Wolsey's possessions at York Place, which would soon become yet another royal palace. One has to wonder whether they purloined the 'Skotish' pots left to him by the Flodden Duke, which by then Wolsey had owned for five years.

On 9 December Eustace Chapuys, the recently installed Imperial Ambassador, wrote to Charles V that he had received an invitation from Norfolk to take supper with him at a house near his, the ambassador's, lodgings and on arrival had found the duke and the other guests playing cards. Being December, we can be sure that in the luxurious rooms there would have been roaring fires, plenty of the very best quality candles burning, the finest tapestries keeping out the savage winter draughts and gorgeous vessels and dishes of gold and silver set out for the choicest food and drink they were about to enjoy. Greetings were exchanged and Chapuys proceeded to work the room, picking up titbits of information and gossip for the Emperor.

When Norfolk at last got the ambassador on his own he began by flattering his relatively new acquaintance, 'the Duke and I went to a corner of the hall and there, leaning against a sideboard, began to exchange civilities, the Duke saying a number of flattering things about my person and services to Your Majesty, and I reciprocating in the same strain'. After various items of business had been discussed the duke had become rather coy, teasing that he wanted to 'make a revelation', only he feared he could not be sure Chapuys would keep the information to himself.

We can picture Norfolk attired in his costly furs and velvets, the firelight and flickering candles picking out his thin features and slim frame as he leaned a bony hand upon the elaborately carved sideboard. Here stood a man full of pride in his ancestry, probably inwardly sneering at the new-made men in the room, while suffering the indignity of having to fawn around this jumped-up foreigner to get him to bring Charles V around to siding with Henry. But if he could achieve that, what then might the future hold for the Howard dynasty?

At last he came to the point, which was to request the ambassador to sound out Charles V to see if he would support the annulment. Chapuys 'remonstrated strongly against such a proposition' and insisted the union with Anne Boleyn could never take place, to which Norfolk replied, 'I believe that neither time nor counsel can deter the king from his determination'. The two of them left about midnight, Norfolk insisting that he and his entourage see the ambassador home, on the way telling him the good news that he had been put in charge of Fitzroy's education and had hopes his own son would befriend the boy.[13]

A few days later there was another letter. Diplomat Thomas Boleyn, of less noble stock than his wife Lady Elizabeth Howard, had been created Viscount Rochford in 1525, when Henry VIII was involved with his daughter Mary. Chapuys now informed his master he had been ennobled again, this time to the earldoms of Ormonde and Wiltshire, with his son George taking his old title Viscount Rochford, giving them status more appropriate to the family of a future queen consort. The day following, the king 'gave a *grand fête* in this city, to which several ladies of the Court were invited, among them ... the two duchesses of Norfolk, the dowager and the young one, the Lady Anne taking precedence of them all, and being made to sit by the king's side'.[14]

So, by the end of December 1529 Henry's passion for Anne Boleyn was stronger than ever, as was his long-suffering wife's determination not to give in to his demands for a separation, not only for her own sake but also for Princess Mary, who would be bastardised and lose her place as Henry's successor should her parents' marriage be annulled.

In spite of appearances, not everyone would have slept soundly after King Henry's December 1529 *grand fête*. For one thing, Duchess Agnes had a hugely worrying problem: her daughter, Lady Katherine, and son-in-law were treading a very fine line with the king. This particular Katherine Howard was born ten years or so after her parents' 1497 marriage. In 1521, when they were both 14, she married Rhys ap Gruffydd, whose grandfather Sir Rhys ap Thomas, had helped Henry Tudor when he landed at Milford Haven in 1485 and had subsequently been made a leading administrator in Wales.

It was expected his son, Sir Gruffydd ap Rhys, would follow in his footsteps, but he pre-deceased him in 1521, so when Katherine's grandfather-in-law died, her 17-year-old husband expected to follow him as Chamberlain and Chief Justice and thus effectively governor of the region. However, Henry VIII instead appointed 36-year-old Walter Devereux, Lord Ferrers. The couple were determined not to go quietly, with Rhys eventually arrested and summoned to London. Instead of lying low and being thankful her husband had not been harmed, so far, nor had been forced to forfeit any of his extensive lands and properties, Katherine continued the fight.

For Lady Katherine's half-brother, the third Duke of Norfolk, fortunes at this stage were mixed. He had been made President of the Privy Council, but by early February 1530 his niece Anne Boleyn had not spoken to him for nearly a month.[15] One event that was favourable to the Howards, however, was that 13-year-old Henry, Earl of Surrey began fulfilling his father's dream by becoming a companion and mentor at Windsor Castle to the king's son, Henry Fitzroy, Duke of Richmond and Somerset, then aged 11.

With no progress towards an annulment and suspecting it was not likely there would be, Henry VIII began looking for a different approach. William Tyndale's *The Obedience of the Christian Man and How Christian Rulers Ought to Govern* sowed the seed in his mind that a ruler is accountable to God alone, and with the *Collectanea satis copiosa* ('The Sufficiently Abundant Collections') claiming to demonstrate, after exhaustive research by many experts and scholars, that the Pope was *not* supreme in spiritual matters, he began to think he might indeed take his Great Matter into his own hands.[16]

After his fall from grace Wolsey had been living quietly at Esher in Surrey, but was pardoned in February 1530, causing anxiety for Norfolk who had been keen to bring about his downfall and feared reprisals should the cardinal now be restored to favour. Although Archbishop of York since 1514, Wolsey had never been enthroned, nor had he even bothered to visit that great northern city with its colossal Minster. That oversight was immediately rectified when rising star Thomas Cromwell conveyed Norfolk's message advising the cardinal to prepare himself to leave as quickly as possible for the journey north, or else, which he did on 5 April.

When Wolsey reached the archbishop's fine residence of Cawood Castle ten miles south of York things seemed to be looking up considerably, but it proved to be a false sense of security. By the time he had settled in and sent word to London requesting his grand ecclesiastical robes be sent on, which angered the king enormously, he was already under suspicion of working with foreign powers.

Wolsey was arrested on 4 November at Cawood and charged with 'intrigue against the king, both in and out of his kingdom', in other words *praemunerie*. He set out for London under armed guard to be tried for treason, which carried the death penalty, on a journey taken in short stages because of his poor health. Mercifully, on the way he died of natural causes at Leicester Abbey on the 29 November 1530 aged 57 and was buried without a monument. The splendid black marble sarcophagus he had prepared for himself remained unused, but was not wasted and now sits on Horatio Nelson's tomb in St Paul's Cathedral.[17]

## Chapter 7

# Times of Change

Henry VIII's fifth and longest Parliament, known as the 'Reformation Parliament', first assembled on November 3 1529, sat through nine sessions and was not dissolved until 14 April 1536. Henry and Thomas Cromwell, who had been Cardinal Wolsey's secretary and most senior advisor, used Parliament to intimidate the Church and question the Pope's power in England. On 11 February 1531 Convocation granted Henry VIII the title of 'singular protector, supreme lord, and even, so far as the law of Christ allows, supreme head of the English Church and clergy'. Later in the year Katherine of Aragon was sent from court and for the rest of her life would be refused access to her daughter.[1]

As patriarch of the Howard family, Norfolk was already embarrassed by his wife's support of Katherine of Aragon and poor opinion of Anne Boleyn, for which she was sent from court,[2] but his standing with the king was further compromised in the autumn of 1531 when his half-sister's husband, who had been given his freedom due to ill health, became embroiled in further dangerous activities. In a foolish move he had changed his name to Rhys ap Gruffydd fitz Urien, in memory of an ancient Welsh dynasty, enabling his enemies to persuade Henry he intended to declare himself Prince of Wales and unite with James V of Scotland against him.

Rhys, not yet 25, was convicted of treason and executed in December 1531. With his death as a traitor his vast possessions were forfeit to the crown; some were restored to his son Griffith (c.1524–1584) but not until the 1550s. Historian Ralph Griffith sees Rhys's execution as an act of judicial murder based on charges devised to suit the prevailing political and dynastic situation.[3] Next to nothing is heard of Rhys's grieving mother-in-law, Duchess Agnes, at this time, although it is likely that it was in 1531 when her stepson Lord Edmund Howard was posted to Calais that one of his younger children, another Katherine Howard, went to live with her at Chesworth House near Horsham in Sussex.

To her mother's horror, Norfolk's daughter, Mary Howard, became one of Anne Boleyn's maids of honour and it appeared she may be chosen to be Fitzroy's bride. Meanwhile, Mary's brother Henry, now 14, still at Windsor with Fitzroy, in April married his fiancée Frances de Vere. When Sir Thomas More resigned as Chancellor in May 1532 after reforms of the Church he could not accept, Norfolk, like his father before him, must have been living in hope, but More was succeeded by Thomas Audley, Speaker of the House of Commons, an avid supporter of Henry's attempt to secure an annulment.

Still wary of a complete break with Rome, Henry hoped he could win over Francis I into influencing the Pope in his favour and on October 11 1532 he and

Anne Boleyn, recently created Marquess of Pembroke in her own right, sailed to Calais with a contingent estimated to number well over 2000 persons. It is believed that it was during the return voyage, or in Dover, they finally fully consummated their relationship. Anne became pregnant almost immediately and remained well, which had to be good news, but now Henry had to move forward as fast as possible if his son – after all he had been through it would surely be a boy – would be born to an indisputably legal wife.

It is thought that he married Anne Boleyn in secret in London, possibly on 25 January 1533, which in the eyes of the Pope made him a bigamist. Thus Henry was looking urgently to replace Archbishop Warham of Canterbury, who had died the previous August, with a man who accepted the repudiation of Katherine of Aragon, would readily promote him as the head of the Church in England and bring the Great Matter to a rapid conclusion.

Cambridge don, Thomas Cranmer, had supported Henry's wish for an annulment and had suggested opinions should be sought from leading university theologians throughout Europe as to whether it was acceptable for a man to marry his deceased brother's wife, which had eventually produced the *Collectanea Satis Copiosa*. In January 1532 he was appointed ambassador to the court of Charles V in the forlorn hope he might be able to persuade him to support the annulment of his aunt's marriage, but had no success.

While travelling with Charles in Italy, Cranmer received a letter dated 1 October 1532 bringing the news that he was to be appointed the new Archbishop of Canterbury, but for the time being must keep the news to himself. This must have been an enormous shock to him, as it would be to others when it became public, for his position as Archdeacon of Taunton was of significantly lower status than any of his predecessors. He did not arrive in England until the beginning of January and was not made aware of the king's marriage until after the event. He did, however, move the situation on rapidly, and on Wednesday 9 April the Duke of Norfolk led the high-ranking delegation informing Katherine of Aragon that henceforth she was to be styled Princess Dowager – in other words, as Prince Arthur's widow – and Henry VIII was now married to Anne Boleyn.

Queen Anne's first coronation procession was planned for 29 May 1533. Her Lord Chamberlain, Thomas, Lord Burgh of Gainsborough Old Hall in Lincolnshire, had been very recently bereaved when his eldest son and heir had died young leaving a childless widow, Katherine Parr, who now found herself unwanted and surplus to Burgh family requirements.[4] Norfolk's wife, who should have taken a prominent role in the coronation, still declined to be associated with Anne Boleyn. Therefore, arriving at the Tower for the traditional stay before a coronation and dressed from head to foot in the finest jewels, fabrics and furs, Anne was assisted instead by her step-grandmother Agnes, the 'old' Duchess of Norfolk, with Lord Burgh helping to bear the weight of the train by supporting it in the middle for her.

On Saturday 31 May, about five months pregnant, Anne Boleyn made her way from the Tower to Westminster Hall through the city packed with curious onlookers, not all of them well-wishers, Her Chamberlain and Duchess Agnes were again present, at the very centre of the pomp and splendour, which would continue the next day at the coronation in Westminster Abbey.[5] Norfolk was absent on a diplomatic mission to France trying to persuade Francis I to cancel his upcoming meeting with Pope Clement VII; his mission failed and on 11 July when Clement again ordered Henry to repudiate Anne Boleyn and take Katherine of Aragon back or face excommunication, Norfolk was ordered home immediately.

At Greenwich Palace on the afternoon of 7 September 1533 Queen Anne was delivered of a healthy child, a step-great-granddaughter for Duchess Agnes. Henry VIII and the Howard/Boleyn family would have been devastated, but Anne had conceived easily and had a trouble-free pregnancy, so surely more children would follow and, God willing, they would be boys. Of course any disappointments had to be played down, and three days later baby Elizabeth was christened in great magnificence at the nearby Church of Observant Friars in Greenwich, with Duchess Agnes and other members of the queen's family taking prominent roles in the proceedings:

> The old Duchess of Norfolk bare the child in a mantle of purple velvet, with a long train held by the earl of Wiltshire... The dukes of Suffolk and Norfolk were on each side of the Duchess ...The Archbishop of Canterbury was godfather, and the old Duchess of Norfolk and the old Marchioness of Dorset godmothers.[6]

However, in spite of their prominent position at the christening, all was not going well for the Howards; Norfolk had failed to manipulate Francis I against the Emperor and the Pope, and then his niece failed to produce a son and heir to ensure the survival of the Tudor dynasty. However, in November, still very much against the wishes of her mother, Norfolk's daughter Lady Mary Howard married Henry Fitzroy; they were both 14. By and large the life of the Howard matriarch, the Dowager Duchess Agnes, was running smoothly. One of her step-granddaughters, Katherine Howard, Lord Edmund's daughter, now in her early teens, was more than likely still living with her full time while her father remained at his post in Calais.

When the Reformation Parliament reconvened on 15 January 1534 for its fifth session, its main task was to consolidate the religious reforms, convince the public they were lawful and introduce severe penalties for those who refused to accept them. Many, such as the late Archbishop Warham, having seen developments since 1531, had fretted over where it would all end. By 1534 there could be no doubt, with the king, Cromwell, Audley and the Duke of Norfolk all working to enforce and protect the changes. But their task was a hard one; as Richard Rex has said 'the politics of 1534 were the politics of bravado not of assurance'.[7] The fact that every adult could be required to swear an oath of allegiance to the new order, and the horrific punishments inflicted on those who refused, merely showed how insecure, as yet, the reforms really were.

The king would be 43 in June; even if a son should be born in the next year or so he would need to live at the very least another twenty years to avoid a minority rule, a thought to greatly concentrate the mind of a man whose Plantagenet grandfather

Edward IV, whom in many ways he physically resembled, had died at only 40 and his Tudor father, Henry VII, at 52. But problems ran deeper, for in the privacy of their apartments away from the artificiality of the court, all was not well with Henry VIII and Anne Boleyn.

Seven years was a long time to have waited for wedded bliss, and the precious son and saviour of the Tudor dynasty that would have made it all worthwhile had turned out to be a daughter. Anne's volatile temper and the fierce arguments between them were, for a man used to having his own way, becoming tiresome and approaching the intolerable. Her relations with her uncle were also shaky; one of her old flames, Henry Percy, told Chapuys that in front of others she had used such shameful words to the Duke of Norfolk 'as one would not address to a dog', causing him to leave the room in indignation, muttering under his breath that she was 'the great whore'.[8]

The Act of Supremacy of 3 November 1534 made the king the 'Only Head of the Church of England on Earth so far as the Law of God allows'; thus he replaced the Pope in England.[9] Both Sir Thomas More and John Fisher, Bishop of Rochester, already in the Tower since April for refusing the Act and Oath of Succession disinheriting Princess Mary in favour of Anne Boleyn's children, refused the Oath of Supremacy; the Treasons Act which followed close on its heels ensured they remained there. The Carthusian Order, who called themselves 'Christ's Poor Men', were a silent, solitary, self-sufficient order, often coming from a prosperous background and were respected by the people who, despite the brothers being a silent order, could turn to them for help and advice. If Henry VIII could win these men over to his far-reaching reforms it would be a tremendous stepping stone in the right direction for him.

On a typical country road between the small North Lincolnshire town of Epworth and the village of Owston Ferry, beyond a wide grass verge and long hawthorn hedgerow lies Low Melwood Farm. Memories jotted down and tales told by Victorian and Edwardian children playing in the farm buildings reveal that hidden among them they found the entrance to the mysterious 'secret tunnel' traditionally said to link the farm and the Old Rectory in Epworth. Such a structure, however, would have been over two miles long, virtually impossible to build, or keep secret, and would have served no purpose whatsoever. In reality, what they saw was probably ruins of the crypt of a church under a group of long demolished or repurposed religious buildings, all that remains of the Axholme Charterhouse, the Low Melwood Priory of the Carthusians founded by Thomas Mowbray, the original Duke of Norfolk in 1397.[10]

Augustine Webster, who had become the prior in 1531, set out in February 1535 to meet Robert Lawrence, prior of Beauvale Charterhouse in Nottinghamshire with whom he was travelling to the Capital to meet John Houghton, prior of the London Charterhouse. They never came back. The Carthusian Order was in a quandary over the reforms and, although there was no question of their loyalty to Henry as king, like More and Fisher they balked at having to take the Oath of Supremacy. Having arrived in the Capital, the three priors requested a meeting with Cromwell with the view to discussing the possibility of some sort of compromise. They and a Bridgettine monk called Richard Reynolds from Syon Abbey were arrested and sent to the Tower on Cromwell's orders.

At their trial on 28 April before the Duke of Norfolk they all pleaded not guilty to treason; on 4 May Norfolk, his nephew George Boleyn, 15-year-old Henry Fitzroy and a great many of the court, some in jocular mood, were among the spectators 'openly and quite close to the victims' when the priors and Reynolds were hanged, drawn and quartered.[11] These men of God, who had done no mental or physical harm to anyone, had been tied to hurdles behind horses and dragged through the filthy streets of London from the Tower to the place of public execution at Tyburn, where Marble Arch now stands. Still wearing their habits, they were hanged until semi-conscious then cut down and while still alive castrated and, still breathing, gutted like animals at an abattoir before being beheaded and chopped into quarters to be displayed around the city, including above the gates of the London Charterhouse itself.

The shock effect on the population would have been profound and deterred many who, for the sake of their conscience, might otherwise have risked defying the Oath, but Henry was not yet done with the monks of the London Charterhouse. In all, between 1535 and 1540, eighteen Carthusian brothers were brutally killed, all except Lawrence and Webster being of the London house. Their persecution and the vile manner in which they died has to be one of the lowest acts of the whole of the reign of Henry VIII.

In June, Bishop Fisher was charged with treason and found guilty of denying Henry VIII was the Supreme Head of the Church in England and beheaded on Tower Hill. The Duke of Norfolk was among those involved in the trial of Sir Thomas More, where he was found guilty on 1 July under the Treasons Act and beheaded five days later. Others made sure they were seen to be loyal; but just where did the Duke of Norfolk stand? He, a religious conservative, witnessing all he had known and believed in being undermined opted for pragmatism and, in the hope his mortal soul could face the consequences, decided to allow his conscience to toe the line.

# Chapter 8

# Choler and Agony

Eustace Chapuys received news from Katherine of Aragon's apothecary in December 1535 that she was in decline and suffering severe abdominal pain. On the 30th he appeared at court seeking permission to visit her at Kimbolton Castle near Huntingdon, where she had been held since May 1534. The response from the king was so convoluted and vague Chapuys did not know what to make of it, but took a risk and went to her anyway.[1] For Katherine's sake he had told her Henry was sorry to learn of her illness, but confessed to Charles V it was a white lie, since to him the king had seemed delighted at the prospect of her death. On 5 January she seemed to be improving and he left, but two days later she died, aged 51.

On 24 January 1536 Henry was taking part in a great joust at Greenwich which Queen Anne, pregnant again, did not attend. She was spending a quiet day with her ladies when her Uncle Norfolk arrived with the shocking news Henry had suffered a fall and his massive horse had rolled on top of him, leaving him concussed for two hours. With awful irony it might be seen as rough justice, for five days later, while Katherine of Aragon was being interred in Peterborough Abbey as Princess Dowager, Anne Boleyn suffered a miscarriage, which she blamed on Norfolk having been clumsy in his delivery of the bad news. Chapuys, although no friend of the duke, dismissed this as nonsense:

> The said Concubine wished to lay the blame on the Duke of Norfolk, whom she hates, saying he frightened her by bringing the news of the fall the King had six days before [she miscarried]. But it is well known that is not the cause, for it was told her in a way that she should not be alarmed or attach much importance to it. Some think it was owing to her own incapacity to bear children, others to a fear that the King would treat her like the late Queen, especially considering the treatment shown to Mistress Semel a lady of the Court, to whom, as many say, he has lately made great presents.[2]

Flirtatious courtly love was a peculiar phenomenon that had developed over a number of centuries. It was an entertaining game that was supposed to know its boundaries but had all the potential within the close-knit and rumour-mongering community of a royal court to go disastrously wrong. For a third party trying to engineer someone else's quick downfall, a few innocent words of courtly love in tandem with The Treasons Act of 1534 were a real gift; after all, 'I love the Queen' could mean whatever an accuser wanted it to mean. Mark Smeaton, a 23-year-old musician and singer in Anne Boleyn's service, would have been known to her, but not of sufficiently high rank to be considered a friend or confidant. On 29 April an inappropriate exchange of words was said to have passed between them and although she seems to have made little of it, walls in Tudor palaces definitely had ears, and by the end of the day Cromwell had been made aware of the conversation.

Sir Henry Norris was one of those men who had had a good life in the service of Henry VIII since his youth, acquiring land, property and influence. As Groom of the Stool, the senior member of the group of trusted attendants of the privy chamber, the king's private apartments, he assisted him with his ablutions after using his velvet-seated commode, then the height of luxury. Norris became a close confidant and would have seen himself as being secure for life as long as he continued to please, toed the line and kept out of trouble.

Opinions vary as to his age, putting his birth sometime between 1482 and the mid-1490s. Historian Eric Ives believed it possible that when Queen Anne had asked courtier Sir Francis Weston if he knew why Norris's wedding with Madge Shelton had stalled he had replied, foolishly even if only meant in jest, that all was not what it seemed, for when Norris came to Anne's apartments, as he was permitted to do as long as others were present, it was not for the love of Madge at all, but to be near the queen herself.[3]

On 30 April, the day following her exchange of words with Smeaton, and in the hearing of others, Queen Anne, who should have known better, asked Norris why he did not go ahead with the marriage and then told him what she thought. She claimed he was waiting for dead men's shoes 'for if ought comes to the king but good, you would look to have me'; a throw-away jocular comment perhaps, but perfect ammunition for anyone with the all-encompassing Treasons Act at their fingertips. Poor Norris was horrified, and seeing his future suddenly and violently cut short, insisted he had never ever harboured such an outrageous thought.

At the May Day jousts Henry VIII in all his glittering majesty was being affable to everyone and Anne was seated in splendour as the queen consort; but Smeaton, already in Cromwell's custody, was about to endure as many as four hours of torture before being broken into confessing to adultery with the queen. When a message arrived from Cromwell, Henry left the joust with the minimum of fuss taking with him Norris, destined for the Tower, and never saw Anne Boleyn again. Soon the queen herself was in the great fortress, escorted there by her own uncle.[4]

Many would not have believed any of the fabricated accusations against Queen Anne of at least twenty instances of adultery, including incest with her brother George, complete with fictitious dates and graphic details. She was also accused of having on several occasions discussed the king's death with Sir Henry Norris, Sir Francis Weston and Sir William Brereton.[5] On 15 May, the Duke of Norfolk, as Earl Marshal and acting Lord Steward for the trial of his own sister Elizabeth's son and daughter, pronounced them guilty of treason, considerately informing his niece that the king might be merciful and commute the penalty from burning, the usual punishment meted out to women for treason, to beheading.[6]

On 17 May the men were beheaded on Tower Hill. Smeaton, being socially inferior had to suffer the horror of watching the others die in order of seniority beginning with George Boleyn. Two days later on Tower Green, aged somewhere between 29 and 35, Anne Boleyn had her head removed with one blow by an expert swordsman brought over from Calais. Her body was hastily buried under the floor of the Tower's church of St Peter ad Vincula, where her brother already lay. Her little daughter Elizabeth had already been declared illegitimate and soon would be struck from the succession like her half-sister Mary.

Eleven days after his second wife's execution Henry VIII married 'Mistress Semel', the mysterious lady mentioned by Chapuys in February as being the recipient of gifts. The ambassador would not realise it at the time, and did not have the name quite right, but his was the first recorded mention of Jane Seymour.[7] Her brother Edward Seymour was a Gentleman of the Privy Chamber, so was well known to the king, but their father apparently less so; Sir John Seymour of Wolf Hall in Wiltshire was prominent among the gentry but was not of the nobility.

Other problems for the Howards were developing thick and fast. Henry VIII's sister Margaret was 47 in 1536. It was thirty-three years since Norfolk's father, then Earl of Surrey, and his wife Agnes had accompanied her to Scotland for her wedding to James IV. Lady Margaret Douglas, her daughter of her second marriage, was now 21 and at the English court. Hopefully Jane Seymour would give Henry his long-awaited sons, but failing that, with both of his daughters declared illegitimate and struck from the succession, potentially Lady Margaret was next in line, so the choice of husband for her required some serious planning. All of which went gloriously awry when Henry discovered she had promised herself in marriage to one of the Duke of Norfolk's young half-brothers.

Born in about 1511 when his father was 68 and Agnes in her mid-thirties, this Lord Thomas Howard was part of the group of young close friends at court that included Lady Margaret, Norfolk's son the Earl of Surrey and his wife Frances de Vere, and Henry Fitzroy and his wife Mary Howard, Surrey's sister. Nevertheless, the king took drastic action and sent both Lord Thomas and Lady Margaret to the Tower.[8]

Only seven weeks after Anne Boleyn's execution, 25-year-old Lord Thomas Howard was found guilty by Act of Attainder, meaning there was no trial, and accused of being 'led and seduced by the Devil, not having God before his eyes' and 'attempting to interrupt and impede the succession to the crown', for which he was sentenced to death for treason. Lady Margaret became ill, promised never to see Thomas again, and was transferred from the Tower to Syon Abbey. With her son in the Tower in the summer of 1536 under sentence of death, Duchess Agnes already had enough problems, but her daughter Katherine Rhys was again causing concern.

At some stage, not too long after the 1531 execution of the husband to whom she appears to have been genuinely devoted, Katherine had remarried. The choice of husband was almost certainly made by the Howard family to remove her from the troubles in Wales. Henry, Lord Daubeney seems not to have been a particularly likeable man; a London agent of the Lisle family disliked him so much that he wished he might die childless 'as I trust he shall do, and that shortly'.[9] He no longer held extensive estates, had no high standing at court and no great fortune to speak of. In other words, he was just the ticket for a rebellious young woman whose family needed her to slide into obscurity.

By 1535 Katherine was writing to Cromwell complaining about her husband and seeking a divorce, which was granted by an ecclesiastical court in 1536. She did not remarry, and from then on appears to have stayed close to her mother, both emotionally and geographically. Bizarrely, when Daubeney was created Earl of Bridgewater in 1538 she took his title, and it was as Countess of Bridgewater she would find fame during a notorious scandal at the beginning of the next decade. One of the few positive factors showing at least a chink of light at the end of the tunnel for the Howards in the summer of 1536 was Norfolk's son, Henry, having become the father of a healthy boy the previous May.

Another positive, although about to be shattered, was that despite her mother's reservations the duke's daughter, Mary, and her husband appeared to be well suited and both enjoying good health. However, Lord Husee had been correct when he revealed in a letter to Lord Lisle on 18 July 'My lord of Richmond is very sick', for five days later Henry Fitzroy, Duke of Richmond and Somerset, died at the very time the Bill to remove Anne Boleyn's daughter Elizabeth from the line of succession was going through Parliament.[10] He was 17, and his death brought a whole new can of worms into the life of the Duke of Norfolk.

For the time being Henry VIII had no wish to make his son's death widely known, so charged Norfolk with the task of burying him in the Howard tomb at Thetford, in secret and with no ceremonial. On the last day of July the body set out from London on a plain cart with two understated attendants following at a distance. Unfortunately, it was so 'secret' that Chapuys was already writing about it on 3 August before the wagon had even reached its destination, while the following day the Bishop of Tarbes, who had been hoping to see Norfolk on diplomatic business, casually mentions in a letter that the duke had gone off home to bury his young son-in-law.[11]

As the Howards already knew only too well, Henry VIII could be dangerously capricious. The burial of his son had been carried out as he ordered, with no pageantry or ceremonial to draw attention to the identity of the deceased, but it would have been advisable for them personally to have supervised the arrangements more closely. The king had very quickly been informed that his son's funeral had been a shabby affair, and obviously his death had not remained secret.

When news arrived at Kenninghall on 5 August that Henry was furious, Norfolk was terrified. In the space of two-and-a-half months a niece and nephew had been executed for treason, a half-brother was languishing in the Tower found guilty of treason, his feisty half-sister was in the news again for all the wrong reasons, his estranged wife, living apart from him for two years continued to write endless letters to Cromwell about how badly he treated her, including beating her when she was pregnant, which he always vehemently denied, and now he stood accused of giving a disrespectful burial to the king's only son.

A very frightened man, Norfolk rewrote his will, and then, in desperation, at about ten o'clock that night he wrote to Thomas Cromwell:

'This night at eight o'clock came letters from friends and servants all agreeing that the King was displeased with me because my Lord of Richmond was not buried honourably... I ordered both the Cottons [George and Richard Cotton, members of the late Richmond's household] to have the body wrapped in lead, but it was not done, nor very secret ... I trust the King will not blame me undeservedly. It is further written to me that a bruit [rumour] doth run that I should be in the Tower of London. When I shall deserve to be there Totynham [Tottenham] shall turn French.'

He signed off, 'Saturday at 10 at night, 5 August, with the hand of him that is full, full, full of choler and agony.'[12]

The next morning Thomas Howard, now in his sixties, set out for London fearing he was leaving home for the last time; but capriciousness, by its very nature, can work both ways, and when the duke arrived at court expecting to be escorted to the Tower, apart from Henry not being exactly overjoyed to see him, nothing happened. So, still shaken, he went back home to Kenninghall, not quite as full of choler and agony as he had been when he left.

## Chapter 9

# The Northern Rebellions

The *Valor Ecclesiasticus* was a survey instigated by Thomas Cromwell involving visitations of all the country's churches and monasteries to assess their value and interview the clergy about their income. This nationwide survey, begun in January 1535 and required to be complete by the end of May, was carried out by often poorly qualified commissioners, some willing to be more than a little economical with the truth.[1]

Following the Act of Supremacy, the monasteries could no longer come under the protection of the Pope, but as soon as Henry VIII had the results of the *Valor Ecclesiasticus* he knew exactly what was going to happen to them. The initial blow came with the Act of Suppression on 8 June 1536 which would close the smaller houses and give their valuables and properties over to the king. Fundamental beliefs that had been inculcated into people all their lives had already changed, or were banned, and now the smaller monastic houses were to be despoiled; but would it eventually apply to all of them? And, ultimately, where would the hundreds of parish churches stand?

The dissolution of the monasteries must have seemed like witnessing pillage and plunder at the hands of an invading foreign power. There had been corruption, but many had not been nearly as corrupt or mismanaged as painted by Cromwell's commissioners, and in the less affluent North, at a time when there was an urgent need for economic reform, they were an integral part of everyday life, which was a major factor in the mayhem that was about to follow.[2]

However, a fair portion of the nobility and those in authority, including religious conservatives like the Howards, whom we might expect privately in their own minds to have questioned the destruction of shrines and holy relics and would have been appalled by the sale of monastic land and buildings, would soon be falling over themselves petitioning Cromwell in order to grab a piece of the action and, as Norfolk said, 'Where others speak, I must speak'. Once the spoils were acquired, either gifted by Henry VIII or more likely purchased or rented from him, there was an economic killing to be made from the ready source of excellent quality building materials including the lead on the vast roofs which was worth a fortune, as well as from the extensive lands, lesser buildings and fish ponds that could be sold off piecemeal.

In Howard's case his Mowbray ancestors had been founders and generous benefactors of monasteries, for example the magnificent Byland Abbey in Yorkshire, since the twelfth century, so maybe he soothed his religious conscience by telling himself that on their behalf he was entitled to a large share of the spoils. He was, however, out of the picture, still lying low at Kenninghall. Becoming anxious he would be left out of the unseemly land grabbing, on 16 September he wrote to Cromwell, 'Help me, for my old service, to be advanced, as soon as those that have yet little served his Highness, to have farms [rents] for term of years'.[3] How it must have grated on his pride to see the enrichment of those upstarts currently close to the king, especially the low-born Cromwell himself, to whom he was having to grovel, while there was he, a duke, after decades of service to the Tudors cowering out of sight and out of mind following the Fitzroy funeral fiasco.

Less than five months after Anne Boleyn's death, the king's peace, and his confidence too, were severely battered by the uprising that began in Lincolnshire, a large county with the prospect of over fifty religious houses facing dissolution, and spread incredibly quickly. Eventually becoming known as the *Pilgrimage of Grace* when it spilled over into Yorkshire, it developed into a movement involving tens of thousands of Henry's subjects ranging from the great and ancient noble families to the most humble labourer.

Although its many causes had been simmering for some time, the Lincolnshire Rising was not a rebellion against the king personally, but rather against clergymen such as Archbishop Cranmer, and certain of Henry's advisors, especially those of humble origin like Thomas Cromwell and Richard Rich, Chancellor of the Court of Augmentations responsible for the allocation and disposal of the monasteries' assets. These men were perceived as leading their monarch astray by encouraging him in the 'new' religion and egging him on to destroy the monasteries and raise taxes. Bearing in mind the bloody destruction of those who had already challenged Henry VIII, it was brave but naïve of the common people to expect him even to listen to their demands, let alone accede to them.

On 8 September 1536, Louth Park Abbey in the Lincolnshire Wolds was suppressed, relieved of its valuables, and its lands granted rent-free for his lifetime to Anne Boleyn's former Chamberlain, Lord Burgh of Gainsborough. On 1 October, the Vicar of Louth, Thomas Kendall, preached an inflammatory sermon, putting his parishioners in fear for the future of their beautiful and beloved parish church with its many treasures and, their great pride and joy, its magnificent 295-foot spire that was only twenty years old. Rumours spread. The next day the Bishop of Lincoln's Registrar arrived to carry out an inspection of the clergy to determine whether they were conforming to the new rules in religious teaching. Villagers seized him, and the Lincolnshire Rising had begun.[4]

The following day, the Commissioners of Subsidy, headed by Lord Burgh, were convening in nearby Caistor for the purpose of assessing the new taxes, and faced with 3000 rebels they fled, but some local gentry were captured. Lord Burgh escaped, abandoning his wounded servant to die, and immediately wrote to Henry VIII with an account of what was happening.[5] October 4 saw the Bishop of Lincoln's Chancellor lynched at Horncastle and two days later the rebels marched on the city of Lincoln; some local gentry joined them, most of them claiming later it was out of fear for their lives. The rebels had been seizing articulate and influential men they needed to be their 'captains', one such being a visiting Yorkshireman in his mid-thirties.

The Humber Bridge linking Yorkshire and Lincolnshire was opened in 1981. For many years it was the longest single-span suspension bridge in the world and straddles the river more or less between the points where one of the main Humber ferries would have operated in Tudor times. At the beginning of October 1536 Robert Aske, a Yorkshire lawyer heading south for business in London, crossed into Lincolnshire by the Hessle to Barton-upon-Humber ferry. On the 1¼ mile crossing the ferrymen told him of how the commons at Castre [Caistor] had taken prisoner the commissioners and the bishop's ordinary or commissary, and how the churches were to be destroyed and ornaments taken away.[6]

The lawyer's plan was to take a detour in order to visit the home of his sister, Julian, and her husband, Thomas Portington, at Sawcliffe village.[7] He had hardly ridden two miles out of Barton, however, when at the village of South Ferriby he was stopped by local men who forced him to swear to their oath 'to be true to God and the King and the commonwealth [the people]' and then let him go. Arriving at Sawcliffe he found his brother-in-law had been called to Caistor on the king's business and, as Lord Burgh had already written to Henry VIII, was among those taken by rebels.

About an hour before dawn the men who had confronted Aske earlier, turned up at the Sawcliffe house demanding he go with them. At Caistor he had talks with Sir Thomas Moigne, Member of Parliament for Lincoln, whom the commons had taken from his house at Willingham and forced to be one of their captains. Although they had taken Aske against his wishes, he found he sympathised with the rebels' cause and helped them draft a petition to the king, which they sent to Windsor on 9 October, professing their loyalty but entreating him to make widespread changes, including reinstating the monasteries and getting rid of Thomas Cromwell and his like.

Henry VIII had not understood the impact of the suppression of the monasteries on the common man; much less did he care. The Lincolnshire rebels were desperate and very brave, but expectations that his eyes would suddenly be opened to their misery were unrealistic. Soon there were thousands of them and Henry and his advisors seem to have been totally unprepared, with no sort of contingency plan in place for such an eventuality. He threatened them with an army of 100,000 which was all nonsense, as so many men would take an age to recruit and be impossible to equip; the only standing army was based in Calais and he had little reserves in the way of weapons and armour.

The Duke of Norfolk's own half-brother, Lord William Howard, appears on a very long emergency list of the names of persons who are ordered to supply men against the northern rebels, and the numbers required of them, which appeared on 7 October, but three days later Lord William was appealing to Cromwell to write to Duchess Agnes, for without his mother's help he would be unable to raise the requisite 100 men.[8]

It must have cost Henry VIII dear to admit that the only man who had any chance of putting down a major revolt was the Duke of Norfolk, who was summoned on the 7th. The Bishop of Carlisle, with whom Norfolk dined, later told Ambassador Chapuys that he had never seen the duke so animated as he was at the news that he was to be back in favour.⁹ It might have crossed Henry's mind that some of the rebels' demands for the halt of religious reform and the removal of certain leading advisors were what Norfolk himself wished for. He did, however, command the duke's sons, the Earl of Surrey and his younger brother, to stay on call in their own area and not accompany their father north.

Norfolk, still on his way, wrote to London of having too few men to face the rebels and was reduced to asking around to see if other commanders could have a sort of 'whip round' and let him have 400 bows and 500 sheaves of arrows because he had not been able to get any for love nor money.¹⁰ But suddenly the effort they had all put in seemed to have been for little purpose, for between 11 and 12 October the Lincolnshire resistance began to melt away.

On the 11th, Henry's immediate reply to the rebels' demands had arrived at Lincoln. The royal response was a great disappointment and surely struck great fear into them. Hopes dashed, they were reviled by the king as 'the traitours and rebelles in Lincolnshire', in a response that consisted of nothing more than severe reprimands and threats. The herald who carried the papers told Thomas Moigne, their unwilling 'captain', to read it out. The royal rant commenced with Henry expressing his incredulity at the common people of Lincolnshire having the effrontery to dictate to their sovereign as to whom he should appoint or dismiss as his ministers, or how he ought to deal with matters of religion and state. But Moigne deliberately missed out the sentence he thought would further inflame the situation:

> How presumptuous then are ye, the rude commons of one shire, and that one of the most brute and beastly of the whole realm, and of least experience, to find fault with your Prince, for the electing of his Councillors and Prelates ...¹¹

The king's message concluded with a warning: they were to return home, not assemble in groups, and hand over the perpetrators, or he would send the Duke of Suffolk to deal with them.

Lincolnshire was calming down, but what was developing in Yorkshire was a very different matter. Robert Aske abandoned his trip south and back in Yorkshire rallied the people of Beverley, imploring them to be true to 'God, the King, and the commonwealth' and 'to maintain the Holy Church'. The revolt known as *The Pilgrimage of Grace* was aimed at restoring the old faith and re-establishing those monasteries already closed. The rebels' red and gold banner depicted the five wounds of Christ, a symbol forbidden under the 'new' religion, and the call spread like wildfire. On 19 October Henry instructed the Duke of Suffolk at all costs to prevent them uniting with the Lincolnshire rebels who might already be regrouping:

> ...if it appear to you by due proof that the rebels have since their retires from Lincoln attempted any new rebellion, you shall, with your forces run upon them and with all extremity destroy, burn, and

kill man, woman, and child the terrible example of all others, and specially the town of Louth because this rebellion took his beginning in the same.[12]

By October 20, with the rebellion fast spreading into the counties of Cumberland, Lancashire and Westmorland, Norfolk saw that with rebel numbers already estimated at over 30,000 his only option until reinforcements arrived was to negotiate with them and stop them making for the Great North Road and London. In a difficult situation and knowing others would be only too eager to accuse him of disloyalty, he wrote to the king begging him to understand he had no other choice.

Six days later, with the king's army of about 7000 lined up behind him, he was estimated to have faced as many as 23,000 rebels at Scawsby Leys near Doncaster, who agreed to disperse their army and nominate two representatives to travel to Windsor to put their grievances before the king. They were too trusting. They had the advantage of numbers, while Norfolk, short of men and weapons, was merely stalling for time. Thomas Howard, a conservative in religion, loathing many of Henry's advisors, and to some extent of the same mind as the rebels, on this day might have changed the course of history had he thrown in his lot with them.

On 17 November representatives of the two sides again met in Doncaster, the rebels refusing to disperse unless given a general pardon, which, again playing for time, Henry eventually offered on 6 December to those north of Doncaster, with the proviso they lay down their arms and disperse immediately. Robert Aske, putting his faith in his sovereign, accepted his invitation to court at Christmas.

The Duke of Norfolk went home to Kenninghall but by 16 January 1537 was already heading north with extensive instructions, including the tracking down of anyone who had lapsed since being pardoned and any monks and nuns who had tried to return to closed monasteries.[13] A new rebellion in the northern counties of Cumberland and Westmorland led by Sir Francis Bigod was a failure. Robert Aske, confident in Henry VIII's promises, which included having Queen Jane crowned at York, called for the commons to ignore Bigod, assuring them the king would understand their very difficult situation.

Norfolk declared Martial Law and Bigod's rebels were soundly defeated at Carlisle on 16 February 1537, but it was all Henry VIII had needed to justify the terrible retribution he was already intent on wreaking, including upon people supposedly pardoned for the outbreak in Yorkshire and not involved at all in the new disturbances. The Duke of Norfolk, so far removed from the harsh lives of the ordinary people, but at the same time having some beliefs in common with them, showed some understanding of those about to receive the ultimate punishment:

> God knows they may well be called poor caitiffs [despicable people; cowards] for at their fleeing they lost horse, harness and all they had upon them, and what with the spoiling of them now, and them so marvellously sore in time past and with increasing of lords' rents by inclosing... this border is sore weakened and specially Westmorland the more pity they should so deserve and also that they have been so

sore handled in times past which as I and all other here think was the only cause of this rebellion.[14]

Sadly, compassion from a man who strove to please his king at any price could only ever be skin deep. On 22 February, the day after he spoke of pity, his latest orders from Windsor, were to:

> ... cause such dreadful execution to be done upon a good number of the inhabitants of every town, village and hamlet ... as well as by the hanging up of them in trees as by the quartering of them and the setting up of their heads and quarters in every town, as shall be a fearful warning.[15]

Commencing his grim task two days later, Norfolk sneered that among those unwillingly involved in the rebellions by being taken by rebels against their will the common saying was, 'I came out in fear of my life, I came forth for fear of the burning of my house and destroying of my wife and children', which he saw as 'such [a] small excuse'. Those to be executed were selected by the advice of the council and gentlemen of the area.[16]

It seems to have been something of a lottery as to who would die and who would be spared. So many noblemen and gentlemen of Yorkshire had joined the Pilgrimage of Grace in the autumn that Henry could not execute them all. Therefore they were divided, somewhat arbitrarily, into two groups – those who were to be forgiven and restored to office and favour, and those who were to be executed, many on framed-up charges of having committed fresh acts of rebellion after the general pardon.[17] Norfolk did the job on the northern counties efficiently, including executing over seventy in Carlisle alone, but even he stopped at the quartering, which was brought to Henry's attention when women tried to remove bodies for burial, and the king was angry they had not been mutilated and the quarters nailed up in public places.

In all, 216 who took part in the Lincolnshire and Yorkshire risings were executed, although Norfolk thought that to be only a fraction of those who deserved it. Several lords and knights perished along with six abbots, thirty-eight monks and sixteen parish priests. Rebels in 'brute and beastly' Lincolnshire where it had all begun and where there had been no pardons granted, were picked out for special attention.[18]

Inevitably, Sir Thomas Moigne's October 1536 meeting with Robert Aske at Caistor, described as 'friendly' had been reported to the king, while his incomplete reading of the message to the rebels in Lincoln, however good intentioned, made him a marked man. While many of the Lincolnshire gentry who had been held by the rebels against their wishes were pardoned, the unfortunate Moigne was taken to London, then returned to Lincoln where he stood trial on 6 March. As a lawyer he defended himself and thirty others; all were found guilty and faced hanging, but he was hanged, drawn and quartered there the following day. He is thought to have been about 27 years old and left a wife and young children.[19] Thomas Kendall, the

Vicar of Louth whose sermon had been the catalyst for the uprising, suffered the same fate on 25 March at Tyburn.

Barlings Abbey near Lincoln survived the first Act of Suppression because it was one of the larger religious houses, with an annual income of over £200; its abbot was Dr Matthew Mackerel, the cleric who had preached at the funeral of the third Duke of Norfolk's father at Thetford in 1524. It is not known whether he had acknowledged the royal supremacy, but he cannot have been posing many problems or would not have been appointed Suffragan Bishop of Lincoln in 1535.

According to Mackerel's own account given on 20 October 1536, which is similar to those of other nearby houses such as Bardney Abbey and Kirkstead, under threat he provided food and lodging for a large number of rebels on the night of 4 October. The next day they tried to persuade him to join them, he refused, but learning that by Friday several gentlemen had been coerced, he took more food and on Saturday sent six of his canons with still more.[20] Within days the rebellion collapsed and by Sunday, 15 October, he and his six brethren were already lodged as prisoners in Lincoln Castle; he and the six canons were hanged, drawn and quartered at the end of March 1537.

On 24 March the Yorkshiremen Robert Aske, Lord Thomas Darcy and Sir Robert Constable of Flamborough were sent to London, ostensibly for talks with the king. They had actively discouraged support of Bigod's rebellion but that would not save them. On 2 June Francis Bigod was hanged at Tyburn; on June 30 Lord Darcy was beheaded on Tower Hill. Robert Aske and Sir Robert Constable suffered the horrendous slow deaths of being hung in heavy chains, Constable on 6 July over the walls of Hull and Aske on the 12th over the walls of Clifford's Tower in York Castle. The executions were witnessed by the Duke of Norfolk:

> On Friday, being market day at Hull, Sir Robert Constable suffered, and doth hang above the highest gate of the town, so trimmed in chains, that I think his bones will hang there this hundred year. And on Thursday, which shall be market day, God willing, I will be at the execution of Aske at York. Grace's pardon notwithstanding.[21]

The humongous task that now lay ahead for Norfolk was to remain in the North and restore some sort of normality.

# Chapter 10

# A Birth, a Death and a Betrothal

The Earl of Surrey, Henry Howard, headed back to the delights and irritations of the court at the beginning of August 1537. As he made his way to Hampton Court he would have had good reason for feeling trepidation as to what sort of reception he was going to get. Already for some months there had been disparaging remarks from the Howards' detractors that their services in the North had not been without a certain amount of self-interest. Surrey's father and his father before him, having had wide experience of administering the area, led to rumour that Norfolk, temporarily in charge and based at York, expected to become the permanent chief administrator of a newly constituted body, almost a local prince; a position, it was said, he hoped would eventually pass to his son, then aged 20.

Livid and humiliated at having been forced to explain to Henry VIII why Surrey, ordered to remain at Kenninghall at the outbreak of the rebellion, had gone to him in the North without permission, Norfolk would have welcomed the opportunity to face his accusers.[1] But it was Surrey, young, stressed and brimming over in equal measure with pride in his ancestry and contempt for lesser mortals, who was about to face them now. Whoever it was that tried his hand at goading him in public soon had his mouth shut for him when the fiery young earl snapped and punched him in the face.[2]

It might have given Surrey a brief moment of satisfaction, but there was an awful price to pay for the flouting of protocol. Shedding blood within the confines of a royal palace was a very serious offence, punishable by having the right hand – the sword hand – cut off in a very painful and nasty public ceremony including the cauterisation of the stump and, bizarrely, the beheading of a live cockerel.[3] His father, serving in the North and unable to get to see him, was mortified at the thought of his son and heir losing his sword hand at such a young age.

Surrey languished in jail at Windsor while behind the scenes Lord Chancellor Audley was successfully working to pull strings on his behalf and he was freed after only a couple of weeks. In spite of all he had done quelling rebellion during the past year, and ever aware that rumour is always more potent and destructive when the subject of it is absent, Norfolk still failed to be recalled to court, with Henry asking him to remain in the northern shires keeping the peace until a new body, the Council of the North, could be set up in York. His hopes of leading that council, if indeed he did harbour any, were dashed when the presidency went to the Bishop of Durham, Cuthbert Tunstall.[4]

Norfolk was back in London when news came from Hampton Court on 12 October that Jane Seymour had given Henry VIII a healthy, legitimate son and heir, twenty-eight years after he came to the throne. According to contemporary accounts, her tortuous labour lasted anything from thirty to more than fifty hours, but in spite of her torment she seemed to be doing well, but 'at eight at night' on October 24, the Duke of Norfolk wrote a frantic letter from Hampton Court to Cromwell bidding him to get there as soon as possible:

> My good lord I pray you to be here tomorrow early to comfort our good master, for as for our mistress, there is no likelihood of her life, the more pity, and I fear she shall not be on lyve [be alive] at the time ye shall read this.[5]

He was right. Jane Seymour, no more than 29 years old, who had been Henry VIII's third wife for less than eighteen months, died just before midnight, possibly of puerperal fever.

A week later, the duke's young half-brother Lord Thomas, who had endured appalling conditions in the Tower for the past fifteen months, succumbed to fever. His body was returned to his mother, the Dowager Duchess Agnes, with instructions to 'bury him without pomp', which she did at Thetford Priory, close to his father. The remainder of 1537 would of course have been sorrowful for Agnes, but apart from what appeared to be an inconsequential spot of trouble when she discovered the music teacher Henry Manox was becoming over-familiar with young Katherine Howard, an infringement of protocol she believed she had soon nipped in the bud, her household appeared to be running well.

The twenty-seven months between the death of Jane Seymour and Henry VIII's next marriage was the longest period between his coming to the throne in 1509 and his death in 1547 he was without a wife, and is sometimes put down to his great grief at losing her. This, sadly, is not strictly true, as the hunt for a new wife began within a week, with Cromwell writing to Duchess Agnes's son, Lord William Howard, then in France, 'The King is little disposed to marry again, but some of his Council have thought it meet for us to urge him to it for the sake of his realm'. One possible candidate was Mary of Guise, Madame de Longueville, 'of whose qualities you are to inquire, and also on what terms the King of Scots stands with [her]'. Lord William wasn't to return without ascertaining this, but the English interest in her was to be kept secret.[6]

Cut up as Henry was over losing Jane Seymour, subsequent correspondence suggests that he quickly rallied and by Christmas was seriously smitten. In a letter at the end of December, just over eight weeks since Jane died, the French ambassador was writing to Francis I that Henry '... is so amorous of Madame de Longueville that he cannot refrain from coming back upon it'.[7] In May 1538, however, it ceased to matter anymore, as Mary of Guise married his nephew and went on to become the mother of Mary, Queen of Scots. The task of finding Henry VIII an attractive, enthusiastic and nubile spouse was not going to be an easy one. The traditional political barriers to taking a foreign princess to wife were further exacerbated by the break with Rome. Added to that, it could be said that so far he had hardly shown himself to be a loving and steadfast husband.

On 12 March 1538 Henry's court painter, Hans Holbein the Younger, spent three hours in Brussels with the 16-year-old Duchess of Milan, making preparatory sketches of her face and hands. The portrait in oil on oak was completed in London. Born Christina of Denmark she was a niece of the Emperor Charles V, and a great-niece of Katherine of Aragon. Married to the Duke of Milan in 1534 as part of a political alliance when she was only 12 and he 39, at 13 she was a widow. Wearing her widow's weeds for the portrait with little in the way of distraction, the viewer's eyes are taken straight to the face, which is gently refined and rather pretty. There is an almost Mona Lisa type enigma about her faint, shy smile and a hint of rather attractive dimples in the cheeks. And now this lovely teenaged widow was supposed to be looking forward to the prospect of becoming Henry VIII's fourth wife.[8]

Henry was enchanted, but the idea was always a non-starter. Apart from her beautiful portrait, Christina is well known to lovers of Tudor history as the astute young lady who is supposed to have said something to the effect, 'If I had two heads, I would happily put one at the disposal of the King of England'. No doubt apocryphal, the yarn does, however, perfectly catch the state of Henry's current reputation. In happier circumstances Christina would probably have fulfilled his dreams of having healthy sons: she remarried in 1541 and bore three children in three years before her husband's untimely death at the age of 27. In retrospect, it is a pity that only a few years later another young girl, nearer home and of approximately the same age as Christina, would not manage to slip through the deadly marriage net cast by Henry VIII.

In the midst of his search for new love, Henry's former mother-in-law Elizabeth Boleyn, Countess of Wiltshire, the Duke of Norfolk's sister, died at the beginning of April 1538 in her early sixties and was buried in Lambeth's Church of St Mary, where her ledger stone was found in 2018. The cause of death is not known, although the month before her daughter Anne's fall in 1536 she was reported to be 'sore diseased with the cough, which grieves her sore'.[9]

It is likely that it was at some stage in 1538 the Dowager Duchess Agnes and her household relocated from Chesworth House near Horsham in Sussex to Norfolk House in Lambeth, available to her for her lifetime through the terms of her late husband's will. She would have moved periodically between the two properties throughout the past decade or more, but the latest move, this time with the majority of her household, but excluding the musician Henry Manox, appears to have been intended to be more or less permanent. Unfortunately, soon there were new incidents of inappropriate behaviour between some of her female charges and the male employees, but, again, the old lady admonished everybody and was satisfied that the perpetrators had been sufficiently chastised, and doubtless were thoroughly ashamed of themselves.

Holbein the Younger's portrait of Thomas Howard, third Duke of Norfolk painted in 1539 when the duke was 66 hangs in the Queen's Drawing Room at Windsor Castle.[10] The Venetian ambassador described him as 'small and spare in person', thus the portrait's three-quarter-length format cleverly gives him a more imposing presence than in reality.[11] Norfolk, wearing the Order of the Garter, holds in his right hand the Earl Marshal's gold baton with its ebony finials, and in his left the white staff of Lord Treasurer. As with the Christina of Denmark portrait, the background is plain, concentrating the viewer's attention on the subject, but unlike Christina, whom Holbein depicted looking out towards the viewer, Thomas Howard has adopted the more usual stance, turning slightly to his right, his eyes not engaging ours.

His clothing is sumptuous: a dark, velvet surcoat deeply edged and lined with lynx fur, worn over a garment with only the red silk sleeves exposed. He wears a black hat and his hair is covered by a coif of black material. The Royal Collection notes that 'a salmon pink preparatory layer, which Holbein used on other portraits at this date, gives warmth and life to Norfolk's face' and notes 'the unnerving realism of Norfolk's expression'.[12] The realism, which truly is unnerving, shows the clean-shaven and lived-in face of a weary man now into his old age who, despite his best efforts to please, never managed to endear himself to his king, or attain the top position he, and his father before him, so coveted. Here is a man burdened with a young, sensitive and volatile son and heir and even now, in the increasingly uncertain world of Henry VIII, at this late stage in his life Thomas Howard could yet come to grief.

The violence against the monastic community continued. The Church had held about one third of the land in England, formerly taxed by Rome, with that revenue now running into Henry VIII's coffers. Almost 400 monasteries had already been dissolved; the Suppression of Religious Houses Act 1539 would seal the fate of the remaining 550 or so, which included all the larger ones. Quite apart from the destruction of magnificent buildings, the loss to English history and culture was hideous.

The Duke of Norfolk had fretted in 1536 that his absence from court would hamper his chances of getting his hands on the spoils, but subsequently had done rather well. On 3 November 1537, only ten days after Jane Seymour's death, while trying to point out to the king he needed to be on the lookout for a new wife, he had taken the opportunity to broach the subject of certain monastic properties he fancied, which eventually paid off, to be followed by others, so that his accounts for 1538 and 1539 show very healthy returns. A property the duke wanted, indeed needed, was Thetford Priory, the location of the last of the Mowbray and first of the Howard ducal tombs. With the remains of his first wife, Henry VIII's aunt, Anne Plantagenet, and Henry Fitzroy also there, he hoped to reach some sort of compromise that would treat the priory as a special case, or at least allow its impressive church to remain standing.

Agreeable at first, Henry soon changed his mind, so it had to go and was surrendered by the last prior in February 1540. In July Norfolk acquired it and its extensive lands and properties for a very reasonable price. Eventually, suspecting the future was uncertain but hoping that the parish churches would be safe, he decided to move the occupants of the Howard family vault to the Church of St Michael the Archangel at Framlingham. Today the craggy ruins of Thetford Priory, largely constructed of local flint, are impressive, but the places where Norfolk's father and grandfather's elaborate tombs once stood in the long disappeared beautiful priory church are a sorry sight.[13]

Still a Catholic at heart, by 1539 Henry decided religious reforms should go no further, and in some cases be reversed. A split was developing, with himself, Stephen Gardiner, Bishop of Winchester, and the Duke of Norfolk on the conservative side of the divide, ranged against the reformers led by Cromwell and Cranmer wanting to push on further. In the summer Norfolk came into his own, in June introducing a bill into Parliament which was passed as The Six Articles Act. Known as 'the whip with six strings', it was long, harsh, and rather like going back to having Catholicism but without a Pope, and put reformers in the sort of precarious situation the conservatives had once experienced. The English people in general were now walking a very fine line: the penalty for leaning too far towards Rome, or conversely too far towards extending the reformed faith, was death.[14] On a happier note, Norfolk's income was increasing substantially, and, much to the relief of all concerned, by the autumn it looked as though Henry VIII had found himself a fiancée at last.

Nominally the leader of the dukes and princes who had elected him as Holy Roman Emperor, Charles V, also Charles I of Spain and Archduke of Austria, was having to come to terms with the spread of religious reform, especially in the German states, which had the potential to divide and weaken the status of the Empire. A new entity called the Schmalkaldic League, a federation of German leaders in sympathy with the Reformation, had emerged in the early 1530s and one member, Duke William of Cleves, was currently in dispute with Charles over the neighbouring Duchy of Guelders.

Here an opportunity presented itself to the English diplomats still searching for a new queen. Duke William's eldest sister, Sibylle, was married to John Frederick I, Elector of Saxony, the head of the Schmalkaldic League; the good news was she had two unmarried sisters. In the spring of 1539 Hans Holbein once again set out with instructions to paint a prospective bride as accurately as possible. This time, however, it was a double commission, as the king wanted to see likenesses of both the Cleves girls, Anna and Amalia. It was the portrait of Anna Von Kleve that made his heart skip a beat, and negotiations for their marriage continued through the summer of 1539. With the treaty signed on 4 October, the wedding of the two complete strangers was to follow in December. Once again Henry could not praise Holbein's skills enough, while Thomas Cromwell, who had overseen the negotiations, was delighted with the outcome.[15]

The arrangement was good: if Charles V, now allied with the French, attacked England, the Duke of Cleves and his allies would stir up trouble in the Empire forcing him to divert his resources. The downside was that, although Henry could hardly wait for the girl half his age to step out from Holbein's lovely portrait into his ample arms, this treaty binding him to a fourth and foreign marriage would herald the first and only time Henry VIII committed himself to wedlock without already knowing his future wife. In the case of Anne of Cleves, he had never even met her.

## Chapter 11

# Lord Edmund Howard

Norfolk's brother, Lord Edmund Howard, was the fourth child of the future second duke's 1472 marriage to Elizabeth Tilney. When called upon to take part in the jousting at Henry VIII's coronation celebrations at Westminster Palace in 1509 he was 30, older than some of the 'fresh young gallants' but hopefully still young enough to get himself noticed by the teenage monarch. He put on a very good performance but, unlike his elder brother Edward, failed to establish himself in the new king's inner circle of close friends.

As the third son of the then Earl of Surrey, Lord Edmund could not expect a legacy of any significance when his father died, and like many younger sons might have opted to support himself by following a career in the Church. Whether it was his father, who must have helped support him thus far, rapidly heading towards his three-score-and-ten years that galvanised him into action is not known, but in early February 1511 Edmund enrolled as a law student in London's Middle Temple.[1] He left after barely two weeks, when the call came from the royal court to make himself available for the celebrations marking the birth of a son and heir to Henry VIII and Katherine of Aragon, and would never return to his studies. This time the king himself, now 19, would take the starring role in the jousting on 12 and 13 February as '(Sir) Loyal Heart'. The baby, named Henry for his father, died nine days later.

Sadly, thereafter Lord Edmund was tolerated but not encouraged by his young, egotistical king who saw himself as already being a wise and powerful ruler, as well as the supreme performer in all he undertook. In the informal language of today we would say that Lord Edmund, being not fully cognisant with the 'rules of the game', well and truly messed up. Accounts of the joust reveal that what Edmund had failed to grasp was that no matter how talented you were, you just did not sing sweeter, wrestle harder or joust better than Henry VIII, especially when he was showing off in front of a large crowd.[2]

It had failed to dawn on Edmund why, even though the expert jousters like his own brother-in-law, Thomas Knyvett, and the king's best friend, Charles Brandon, all came within a whisker of beating Henry, somehow they always lost to him in the end. Edmund Howard, on the other hand, kept riding hell-for-leather towards Henry, more than once knocking him to the ground with his lance, to the horror and, in some cases surely, the diplomatically hidden amusement, of the spectators.[3] At a similar but lower key event a few months later, Edmund's brother and brothers-in-law were again invited to take part, but he was sidelined.

Lord Edmund's division was the only section defeated by the Scots at Flodden in 1513. Although he was brave and sustained significant wounds, afterwards he briefly found himself in an unenviable position facing possible disciplinary action when a furious Henry VIII received a letter accusing Edmund of allowing his men to desert the battlefield, a situation that had been out of his control.

When in 1514 his father, by then restored to the dukedom of Norfolk, accompanied the king's sister Mary to France for her wedding, Edmund went with him. He had been given £100 from the treasury to kit himself out in magnificent garb for the celebratory joust, but although a very large sum it was nowhere near adequate and the king failing to reimburse him for the difference only added to his increasing debts, which in the following fifteen years would totally overwhelm him.[4] At some stage he was appointed Justice of the Peace for the county of Surrey, charged with keeping law and order and dealing with those who flouted it, but his achievements were mixed and he had to answer to the authorities for his failures on more than one occasion. In 1517, as we have already seen, he was accused of extreme cruelty at the executions following the Evil May Day Riots.

Lists showing participants in the 1514 voyage to France in the entourage of Princess Mary Tudor do not show Edmund as being accompanied by a spouse, but some time before the 1517 riots he had married Joyce, or Jocasta, Leigh, née Culpeper, a widow with five children, whose father and late husband had left her very comfortably off. Joyce's mother Isabel's first husband was Richard Culpeper, a wealthy Kent landowner. The widow Isabel next married Sir John Leigh (or Legh), while shortly afterwards her daughter Joyce, then aged about 12, married his younger brother Ralph Leigh.

Ralph Leigh, the father of Joyce's five children, had died in 1509, leaving her more than able to provide for them, but Edmund Howard's out of control and ever-accumulating debts and poor management eroded her inheritance to such an extent that both her Culpeper and Leigh relatives stepped in to try to stop him completely ruining her. With Joyce he is believed to have had six children, including the most famous of the many Katherine Howards of the Tudor period, born around 1521. By the time his little daughter Katherine was 6 or 7, Lord Edmund was in such dire straits he was forced to remortgage Joyce's properties, while at the same time borrowing heavily from friends or getting them to stand surety for his debts – a hugely flawed arrangement, as some would find to their cost. By this stage he was in such a mess he was actually hiding from his creditors and dreading the knock at the door.

A small part of a letter of 1527 from Edmund Howard to Thomas Wolsey is often quoted, and when taken out of context does not elicit much sympathy from the reader. As ever, Edmund is bemoaning his troubles and asking for help in finding a way of alleviating his money problems. He claims that, though willing, he is unable to 'dig and delve'; in other words, manual labour is beneath his dignity, he being the son of a duke. Today we would probably advise him that beggars cannot be choosers and, for the time being at least, he should take whatever employment he can get, but in his times making such a radical move as to be actually labouring like the common man would have completely alienated a nobleman like himself from his class and those who had the real wherewithal to assist him, should they feel so inclined.

The letter in its entirety, however, is long and rather moving, showing an almost broken man by then in his late forties and nearing the end of his tether. He admits hiding to escape his creditors and needs desperately to provide for 'my poor wife and our ten children'. He pleads that he cannot be accused of heinous crimes such as treason, murder, felony, rape, extortion or bribery; his only crime, he insists, is being in debt. He is so desperate he would willingly go on the king's forthcoming expedition to the 'new found land' and wonders if Wolsey could help him with that:

> ... for now I do live a wretched life ... and nothing have I to live on ... to find me my wife and our children meat and drink... And Sir, I have nothing to lose but my life... I beseech your Grace to pardon me for this my bold writing, but very poverty and need forceth me this to do... Written with the hand of him that is assuredly yours. Edmund Howard, knight.[5]

Poverty, of course, is relative, and in reality this son of the higher echelons of the nobility probably had some way to go before he faced the terrible fate of being the father of a starving, poverty-stricken family living below the breadline in a decaying hovel.

Also, at this stage it could have been an exaggeration to claim he still had ten of his children and stepchildren living at home to provide for. Nevertheless, for the children of a man of few means where the very concept of conspicuous consumption was a large part of the passport to success, such a life of uncertainty must have been grim. A little girl like Katherine Howard and the other younger children must have been aware of their parents' anxiety, but their situation became even worse when their mother died in 1529. Shortly afterwards their father married the widow Dorothy Troyes, who died within a year.

On St Nicholas's Day at the beginning of December 1531, Lord Edmund arrived in Calais where he presented to the Vice Treasurer a letter from his sister Elizabeth's daughter, Anne Boleyn, thanking him for his kindness 'to my Lord Edmund'. In effect, rather than a thank-you note, it was more of an order that Edmund should be treated well. His niece, then still the king's mistress, had possibly pulled strings to secure him a job and enable him to escape his creditors. The Comptroller of Calais, responsible for financial arrangements and supplies within the Pale had died in 1530 and it was agreed in April 1531, none too wisely, that Lord Edmund, famously hopeless with money, was to replace him.[6] Between April and his arrival in Calais in December, Edmund's Lambeth household had been closed down and his children settled elsewhere. It could have been at this point that Katherine Howard was placed in the care of the Dowager Duchess of Norfolk, her step-grandmother.

In the spring of 1532 Edmund's half-brother, Lord William Howard, asked Cromwell to intercede with the king regarding his brother's debts, to which he seems to have agreed. Edmund's letter of thanks in May 'To my wellbeloved friend, Mr. Cromwell' reveals a tale of woe similar to his letter to Wolsey five years earlier. Though he is 'highly kinned' he is 'as smally friended as man may be', and claims to have been so beaten in the world that he 'knows what a treasure is a faithful friend'.[7]

At some time during or shortly after 1532 he married yet another wealthy widow, which begs the question just what could it have been about Edmund Howard, a man whose financial management was widely known to be disastrous, that kept attracting those rich women to him? Perhaps he was a very attractive man, or it might have been an attempt on their part at social climbing, but it must have been obvious by that stage that although he was the Duke of Norfolk's brother, he was gaining little from him in the way of either financial or moral support. The latest spouse, Margaret Jennings, née Mundy, was the widow of London merchant and Alderman Nicholas Jennings who died in 1532, and daughter of the Alderman Mundy whose attempts to arrest curfew breakers had sparked the 1517 Evil May Day riots.[8]

It comes as no surprise that Lord Edmund Howard's time in Calais was not an overwhelming success; in September 1534 Cromwell had to send out two assistants to help him deal with illegal exporting.[9] The job was not well paid either and hardly sufficient to cover his expenses let alone allow him to begin paying off his debts, which continued to haunt him. In the summer of 1535 Lord Husee was writing to Lord Lisle, 'I am told my Lord Edmund hopes to be here [London] in the court with the King or the Queen, and have a better living. It is said the commissioners shall reform many things at Calais'.[10]

A positive aspect, if it can be called that, was that having the Channel between Edmund and his creditors put the burden of those debts on the shoulders of people who had tried to help him. Poor John Shookborough, who had stood surety for him some time before he left for Calais, found himself under arrest because he could not pay when Lord Edmund's creditors pursued him, demanding their money there and then, forcing him to appeal to Cromwell for help:

> On Thursday morning last I waited upon you at the Austin Friars. I saw you at mass there; went with you, when mass was done, to Dormer the alderman, with many other suitors, but did not dare speak to you. As I went into the city I was arrested as surety for Lord Edmund Howard for 26l., [£26] of which I have paid 10l. and have five years' payment for the rest. I am surety for more, and dare not go abroad in the city. I pledged a damask gown and a good coat for 5l., which I shall lose if I do not pay the money tomorrow night. If you would lend me the money, I will leave my gown in your hands, and pay you before Lady Day next. I have a gelding, which I will give you for your favour.[11]

Despite all his shortcomings Edmund Howard was not disliked in Calais, and in 1537, when his colleagues voted him to be mayor, he seemed to be a popular choice. Back home, however, the appointment that would have boosted both his finances and self-esteem was derided by Henry VIII, who refused to allow it. Cromwell wrote that the king would not allow 'my Lord Howard to be admitted to the mayoralty'.[12]

Among all his troubles Lord Edmund seems, for part of the time at least, to have retained a sense of humour. A letter from him to Lady Lisle, wife of the Lord Deputy of Calais, is sometimes quoted as a sign he was henpecked and abused by his wife Margaret, but the description therein of her reaction to his unfortunate medical predicament could have been intended to be a bit of fun between friends.[13] He was suffering with 'the stone' and was having problems passing water, so her ladyship stepped in with a potion, possibly one of her own concoctions, to put him out of his misery. It worked very well; too well, in fact. Edmund had 'taken it about midnight' and as a result had been able to 'void much gravel'. There was, however, an unfortunate side effect:

> But for all that, your said medicine hath done me little honesty, for it made me piss my bed this night, for the which my wife hath sore beaten me, and saying it is children's parts to bepiss their bed. Ye have made me such a pisser that I dare not go abroad, whereof I beseech you to make mine excuse to my Lord ... that I shall not be with you this day at dinner.

He informed Lady Lisle he has been told that if he eats the wing or leg of a stork he will never wet the bed again and signs off, 'All yours, Edmund Howard'.[14]

April 1538 found Lord Edmund at his sister Elizabeth Boleyn's funeral in Lambeth. There is no positive indication that he was reunited with his daughter Katherine, who might not have moved with Duchess Agnes to Norfolk House opposite until later in the year, although it is possible they went to Lambeth for the funeral.[15] Correspondence beginning the previous month shows that Lord Edmund would already have been in England when his sister died.

In March he had been called upon to answer a list of queries sent from officials in London as to the situation in the Pale, where all had not been well for some time. This would have been difficult for him with his friend Lord Lisle being the Deputy. Lord Edmund was quizzed on 'The unquietness of the King's subjects' who were suffering through lack of law and order, extortion, illegal seizing of their possessions, and the lack of the administration of justice.

In his reply of 9 March Edmund told of the differences or 'small love' between the Deputy and various officials including the Mayor and the High Marshal. As to the Mayor himself there appears to have been 'small love' between him and just about everybody. In answer to complaints by residents that the law was not being upheld satisfactorily, Edmund revealed that:

> There are many divers [different] laws and customs and the ministers have little learning. There is no one that can discuss precedents but [except for] one person which every day by 8 or 9 of the clock in the morning will be in a hard case [in no fit state] to discuss any matter of law except [unless] he be kept from the good drink.[16]

He advised that a commission be sent to investigate the shortcomings and that the laws in Calais be the same as those in England, opining that is a pity there are so few learned men there.

However, correspondence dated the same day appears to show he had already had news he was to be permanently recalled to England. Still perilously short of money, he reminded Cromwell he is a man without means and that all his assets and provisions were tied up in Calais, so if he had to vacate his position before 6 April he would incur great loss. He hoped Cromwell could enable him to return there until that date to put his affairs in order.[17]

His request, however, appears not to have been granted, for on 2 April a letter to Lord Lisle shows Lord Edmund still to be in London and attempting to put in a good word for the Deputy, although he himself will be recalled permanently, 'I am told I shall be removed from Calais'.[18] On the 18th of the month he again writes to Lord Lisle, this time from Lambeth where he may have been staying at a property of his own or at Norfolk House; at this point he had been in England for at least two weeks and might have been able to see his daughter Katherine, then aged about 17.[19] In January 1539 Edmund Howard was to have 'certain lands' given him. Where these were and where he had been living since April the previous year is not specified; he was to be succeeded in Calais by a 'Mr Bowis' (Bowes).[20]

The old saying tells us that Fortune favours the brave. Lord Edmund Howard, undoubtedly brave in battle, was a knight upon whom Fortune never greatly smiled, and died in March 1539 aged about 60.[21] That autumn his daughter Katherine, still living in Lambeth with her step-grandmother, was summoned to court to begin training for a role as one of the maids of honour to Anne of Cleves, who would shortly be arriving in England to become Henry VIII's fourth wife.

# Chapter 12

# Our Wife Agnes

When in May 1524 Agnes Tilney, second wife of Thomas Howard, second Duke of Norfolk, was widowed, they had been married nearly twenty-seven years. As was the custom, upon her husband's death the now dowager duchess would vacate the main ducal residence, in this case Framlingham Castle, in favour of the new incumbent. However, the late duke's Lambeth and Horsham mansions and lands were part of the huge settlement that came to Agnes for the rest of her life, reverting to her stepson Thomas Howard, the new third duke, only at her death.

The new duke was left the greater part of his late father's vast estates, together with some outstanding goods, such as:

> ... our great hanged bed, with cloth of gold, white damask and black velvet and browdered [embroidered] with these two letters T A [the initials of the Christian names of himself and Agnes] and our hanging of the story of Hercules made for our great chamber at Framlingham.

The bed and the magnificent Hercules tapestry would be so valuable it would be like leaving someone top-of-the-range priceless works of art today, though one has to wonder what the recipient felt about his stepmother's initial being 'browdered' all over his trophy piece. Agnes, however, was set to become an exceptionally wealthy woman in her own right for the rest of her life.

The will of Thomas Howard 'being whole of mind and of good memory' is remarkable for the enormous value of the goods he left to his wife, and is one of the few surviving documents where someone other than the ruling monarch speaks of himself in the plural:

> To our wife Agnes all manner of plate, jewels garnished and ungarnished, all our household stuff, bedding, hangings, sheets, fustians, blankets, pillows, cushions, hanged beds of gold and silk, or what other stuff that ever they be of, and all other stuff belonging to bedding and apparelling of chambers.

And on and on it went. She was also to have 'all our chapel stuff, with all manner of kitchen stuff', as well as all his clothing, all his horses and geldings with all their harness, and all his weaponry. Also to be hers were:

all our rings, jewels of gold, garnished and ungarnished and all other plate of gold and silver and silver and gilt, with all our wine, gold and silver and all our other goods and chattels.[1]

In 1524 Norfolk left an estate worth £4500 per annum, worth many millions today, and, according to his funeral monument, when he died 'he could not be asked one groat for his debt, nor for restitution to any person'. Any debts he was owed should come to Agnes to be used to pay the costs of his funeral, held on such a grand scale it put some royalty to shame. He left instructions for the constructing of his tomb before the high altar at the priory of Thetford in Norfolk to be executed by 'Master Clerke, Master of the King's Works at Cambridge, and Wassel free mason of Bury [St Edmunds], and pictures of us and Agnes our wife to be set together thereupon'.[2]

The late duke wanted 'our said wife to have and enjoy all our said goods of our bequest' and beseeched Cardinal Wolsey to be 'good and gracious' to Agnes, and make sure she received that which she was due, and hoped 'for a poor remembrance he will take our gift a pair of gilt pots called our Skotish pots'. This was a priceless legacy to Wolsey, since these 'Skotish' pots are believed to have been those belonging to James IV that were brought home by Thomas Howard from the Flodden campaign.[3]

Duchess Agnes and Sir Thomas Blenarhasset were to be the executors. One of the witnesses to the mighty duke's signature had been a William Ashby. Years later the exhausted and elderly Ashby would plead with his interrogators to leave him alone, as he had been questioned twice already and could tell them nothing more about Duchess Agnes's part in the unseemly behaviour of her step-granddaughter Mistress Katherine Howard at Chesworth near Horsham and Norfolk House in Lambeth.[4]

Agnes Tilney had been about 20 when she married the then Earl of Surrey, her late cousin Elizabeth's husband of a quarter of a century, on 8 November 1497 in the chapel of the great castle at Sheriff Hutton near York, where he was sometimes stationed while Henry VII's administrator in the North and protector of the Scottish borders. Remarriages were often rapid in those days and at 54 the earl was not getting any younger, but we might be forgiven for wondering whether Agnes was in Countess Elizabeth's service and had perhaps caught the eye of her cousin's ageing husband even before his wife's death the previous April, as by August he had already obtained a papal dispensation for the marriage needed because of the two women's close kinship.[5]

The Tilney family had lived and served as local administrators in south Lincolnshire and East Anglia since the time of the Norman Conquest. Elizabeth's father, Sir Frederick Tilney of Ashwellthorpe in Norfolk, was the eldest son and heir of Sir Philip Tilney of Boston, Lincolnshire, and Ashwellthorpe, while his younger brother, Hugh Tilney of Skirbeck and Boston, was the father of Agnes and her brother Philip. Elizabeth had been her father's heir, but part of her attraction to the Howards when she married Thomas, the future second duke, in the early 1470s would have been that as the widow of Sir Humphrey Bourchier, late heir to Lord Berners, she would be a wealthy woman for her lifetime. Her cousin Agnes, on the other hand, while coming from a perfectly respectable branch of the family, seems to have had little to bring to the marriage of 1497 that would have made much difference to the earl's assets, so this could well have been a love match, on his part at least.[6]

By the time of Agnes's marriage, twelve years after Bosworth, her new husband might have assumed he was already well on the way to the restoration of the Norfolk dukedom, but that dream would not be realised for another seventeen years. His heir, Thomas, his eldest son by Elizabeth Tilney and about four years older than his new stepmother, had been married to his first wife, Edward IV's daughter Princess Anne of York, for more than two years, making him a brother-in-law to Henry VII's wife Elizabeth of York. With Agnes, the Earl of Surrey had several more children, which he continued to father into his late sixties, including Lord William Howard, the Lord Thomas who died in the Tower in 1537 and the Katherine Howard whose marriages to Rhys ap Gruffydd and Henry Daubeney caused her mother so much anxiety.

Despite author Michael Glenne's claims that Duchess Agnes was bad tempered, malicious, petty minded with no children of her own [sic] and had spies planted in the homes of her stepchildren to store up evidence for lawsuits she planned for later, in reality her relationship with her late cousin's children and their spouses appears to have been reasonably friendly, the possible exception being her stepson Thomas's second wife Elizabeth Stafford, the Duke of Buckingham's daughter, who by birth was a significant cut above her stepmother-in-law.[7]

By 1501 Surrey was back at court with a seat on the Privy Council and in June of that year became Lord Treasurer. Through her husband's position Agnes was frequently in attendance at the court of Henry VII, and later of his successor, playing a prominent ceremonial role on special occasions. Following the marriage her husband negotiated in 1501 between Prince Arthur and Katherine of Aragon, Countess Agnes became one of that young woman's attendants. Her recollections for the legatine enquiry of 1529 indicate she may well have been in the princess's welcoming party, but she cannot have been the Duchess of Norfolk mentioned in surviving documents, as the dukedom had not yet been restored and her husband was still Earl of Surrey, while Margaret Chedworth, widow of the first Howard duke had died in 1494.[8] Thus if there was a Duchess of Norfolk present in the welcoming party, it must have been Elizabeth Talbot, Anne Mowbray's mother, the final Mowbray dowager, who lived until 1506.

We have seen that in 1503 Agnes was with her husband when he led the party escorting Princess Margaret to Scotland for her marriage to James IV, and we may be sure that when she carried the princess's train in York and danced with her at Berwick-upon-Tweed, Agnes herself would have been wearing the most sumptuous of outfits embellished with some of the fine jewels her husband would leave her in his will twenty years later.

With the dukedom of Norfolk restored in 1514, when she was about 37, the former Agnes Tilney was firmly established as one half of a very important diplomatic couple. It was as Duchess of Norfolk that she went to France with Henry VIII's sister Princess Mary later in the year who, as we have already seen, was far from happy at the lack of consideration towards her from the new Duke of Norfolk and would have much preferred to be dealing with Wolsey. When in 1516 Henry VIII and his wife finally had a baby that survived, Duchess Agnes was a godmother to the little girl, another Princess Mary

At the time of her husband's death in 1524 Agnes would have been in her late forties, bordering on elderly for the times, but was apparently in good health and certainly without financial worries, still enjoying incomes from numerous estates in Surrey, Suffolk, Lincolnshire, Essex and Sussex, as well as the continued occupancy of Chesworth House near Horsham in Sussex and Norfolk House in Lambeth. She was still required to put in appearances at court, and according to the ordinances issued at Eltham in 1526 for the proposed reform of the royal household, the Dowager Duchess of Norfolk was recorded as the first lady of the queen's (Katherine of Aragon) household after the king's sister Mary, dowager queen of France.

Duchess Agnes did not remarry, probably from choice because the taking of a second husband would automatically have put her affairs and finances into his hands, so by staying single she remained a wealthy, independent and well-connected woman in her own right, and not without influence. It is also doubtful whether her stepson, aware of the intricacies caused by the three remarriages of Katherine Neville, the second Mowbray duchess, would have encouraged his father's widow to put Howard money, lands, property and goods and chattels into the hands of another man. In 1533 Thomas Cranmer, still feeling his feet in his role as the new Archbishop of Canterbury, wrote to Agnes explaining he had asked the king for rather too many favours lately and was afraid of pushing his luck, so did she think she might, on his behalf 'cause some of your special friends' to persuade Henry to grant a licence for one of his servants to go to Calais on business.[9]

The 'old', that is dowager, Duchess of Norfolk was also an accomplished apothecary and administered her cures personally to the sick and suffering, so those living under her roof would be in good hands should they fall ill. In September 1528 she wrote to Thomas Wolsey that on 15 August, she had met some of his household, presumably near Norfolk House:

> My lord, it fortuned me as I went in procession in my parish-church on Our Lady-day, I saw Forest, your servant, alight upon his horse, and so I asked of him the question how your grace did? And he said that your grace did very well, thanked be God; and after, my servant Hogon communed with him, and he showed [said] that some of your grace's servants were and had been sick.

The area was in the grip of the dreadful sweating sickness, which in this outbreak was particularly widespread, and the duchess, offering to minister to Wolsey should he fall ill, could not resist a little dig at her stepson who, together with many in his household at Kenninghall in Norfolk, had had the 'sweat' due, she thought, to poor housekeeping, or 'default of keeping', as she put it.

She had daily experience of matters of illness, she said, and was so successful in her cures that her neighbours would send to her 'and if they be sick at heart I give them triacle and water imperial' (concoctions of spring water and herbs and spices), which according to her had saved many who had been at death's door. Hers is said to be one of the best surviving descriptions of the sweating sickness and how it was treated, and Agnes tells Wolsey that:

> The best remedy that I do know it is to take little or no sustenance or drink unto 16 hours be past... My Lord, I never saw people so far out of the way in no disease as they be in this; and about 12 or 16 hours is the greatest danger. There be some that sweateth much, and some that sweateth very little, but burneth very sore: but the greatest surety is in any wise to keep your bed 24 hours.[10]

However, as Wolsey was still trying, and failing miserably, to resolve the king's Great Matter, as long as he stayed well enough to be able to do his job, an outbreak of the sweating sickness would not necessarily have been at the top of the cardinal's list of problems.

So, in the mid-1530s, with Elizabeth Stafford banned from court, her stepmother-in-law was still the most senior of the non-royal duchesses, and a woman of great wealth and no little influence, but her life was not the indulged bed of roses we might think. In 1537 or thereabouts she would have been 60 years old and mourning the recent deaths of two of her children: Lord Thomas who died in the Tower, and his sister Elizabeth who passed away either the same or previous year.

## Chapter 13

# Chesworth and Lambeth

If Katherine Howard went to live with Duchess Agnes when her father Lord Edmund became Comptroller of Calais, the first six or seven years would have been spent mostly at Chesworth House in rural Sussex, a portion of which is still extant and is now a private residence. A substantial moated property in Katherine's day with over 200 acres, Chesworth has been described as having consisted of many parts including a large two-storeyed timber-framed range built north of the moat, aligned from north to south and stylistically of the late fifteenth or early sixteenth century. Added to this were the usual farms, barns, woodland, fishponds, bakeries, breweries, kitchens, laundries, outbuildings, stables, gardens, orchards, abattoirs and everything else required for a great household to function.[1]

Because it cannot be absolutely certain when Agnes moved her household to her Lambeth residence, some of the events in Katherine Howard's life are difficult to date and locate exactly, but for the purposes of this account it will be assumed that the final move happened in 1538 and that steamy extra-curricular activities between the young Katherine Howard and her music teacher had been at Chesworth House. However, it was to be a different liaison, at Norfolk House in Lambeth, with one of the gentlemen of the dowager's household that led to her undoing. It was also to this same fine ducal Lambeth residence that in the spring of 1540 a massive pillar of the nation – massive in more ways than one and with no knowledge of Katherine's past – would come to woo the girl who, at 19 or thereabouts, was considerably less than half his age.

Taking a walk down Lambeth's Old Paradise Street today, one could perhaps be excused for thinking that the rather romantic name somehow does not quite match the location, but in the summer of 1540 King Henry VIII visiting his new-found 'jewel for womanhood' would have told you that in his opinion Paradise was indeed to be found in this place.[2] Lambeth in Tudor times was very different from tightly-packed Westminster and the City of London, which began their eastward sprawl opposite on the north bank of the Thames with Westminster Abbey, the ancient Palace of Westminster and Whitehall Palace, the last being the former York Place only relatively recently appropriated by King Henry from Cardinal Wolsey.

By contrast, in Lambeth, still fairly rural in character, the main buildings of importance were the archbishop's residence, at that time known as Lambeth House but in later centuries as Lambeth Palace, Norfolk House itself, a house a short distance away belonging to the Bishop of Rochester and a small number of mansions of the lesser nobility. Following the south bank and the bend in the river in the easterly direction would eventually take the traveller past the fine homes of some of the members of the King's Council and into Southwark with the palace of the Bishop of Winchester, close to the southern approach to London Bridge with its ominously displayed and thought-provoking collection of criminals' and traitors' severed heads.

However, the area that concerns us here is the piece of land almost opposite Lambeth Palace enclosed now by Lambeth Road, Norfolk Row, Old Paradise Street and Lambeth High Street. This area in Tudor times was just a small part of the south bank estate of the Dukes of Norfolk, and the section on which Norfolk House stood. The area where the long-disappeared fine building that was home to the aged dowager duchess and her large household stood can be seen, thanks to the internet, to great advantage on Google Maps through the satellite and street-view facility.[3]

This historic piece of land has had a chequered history since Katherine Howard's time and is now home to a Novotel hotel, which, fronting onto Lambeth Road (in Agnes's time The King's Highway) and facing Lambeth Palace, stands on what was the site of the greater part of the footprint of the Duchess's mansion itself (see Appendix, *What Became of Norfolk House*). The current Bell Inn at the left of the Novotel was built in the twentieth century and has recently been tastefully developed into office accommodation, while to the right of the hotel and on the site of a small part of the Norfolk House footprint can be found a block of high-end apartments recently converted from the former headquarters and museum of the Royal Pharmaceutical Society of Great Britain, and behind which are two blocks of former local authority flats.

Alongside the present-day Bell Inn an alleyway, Norfolk Row, runs through to Old Paradise Street, both of which appeared after Katherine Howard's time. Norfolk Row came into use after the former Howard property was divided-up post 1575 and is mentioned as a cart way in 1610. Old Paradise Street, which in the past has been known as Paradise Row and Paradise Street, was formed in the late seventeenth century and splits what was the site of Norfolk House from what were once the extensive gardens and orchards to the south and east of it.[4]

So, standing on Old Paradise Street today with our backs to the rear of the Novotel, we would face more flats and a public recreation ground of nearly two acres, renamed Old Paradise Gardens in 2013. Previous to becoming a public space in 1854 it had been an overflow burial ground for St Mary's Church since 1703, but had once been a part of the beautiful gardens and orchards of Norfolk House, where the young Katherine Howard, probably largely oblivious to the turmoil England was undergoing in the late 1530s under the traumatic rule of Henry VIII, would have laughed and flirted with admirers, including him, in the spring and early summer of 1540. Here too she would have attended the venerable Duchess Agnes, mistress of all she surveyed, and a great deal more besides, as she took the air, accompanied by her richly attired and perfectly groomed entourage of elegant ladies and gentlemen.

Nowadays the rest of Agnes's gardens and the then open countryside surrounding the huge Howard estate are packed with buildings of every sort and size, including a rather unlovely multi-storey car park and until recently Costa Coffee's roasting works, as well as being rudely interrupted by the Victorian brick arches bearing the railway lines that terminate at nearby Waterloo Station. Nothing of Norfolk House now remains above ground, but excavations carried out in 1988 and 1990 before redevelopment of the site, revealed the foundations, and in some cases parts of the floors, of five buildings dating from Tudor times.[5]

The earliest foundations unearthed were of a stone structure of the late fourteenth century, suggesting the Howards of the early Tudor era either improved or largely replaced an earlier mansion. Katherine's grandfather, the second duke, is believed to have made significant improvements at some time between 1514 and 1520 after the restoration of the dukedom.[6] His great-grandson the fourth Duke of Norfolk, son of the 'Poet' Earl of Surrey, sold the estate after 1554, after which it was sold several times more and gradually broken up into smaller lots. Wenceslaus Hollar's 1647 *Lambeth House: Palace of the Archbishop of Canterbury, London* created over a hundred years after Katherine Howard's death, and the artist William Wyatt's reconstruction following the 1990 excavation are probably the closest we shall ever get to knowing what the house looked like.[7] From the 1990 reconstruction it would appear that the Howards' Tudor mansion followed a three-sided courtyard pattern typical of the times, which enables us now to make comparisons with surviving large houses of similar age and design, for example Gainsborough Old Hall in Lincolnshire.[8]

So what of the lady of the house herself? Verbal pictures of Duchess Agnes painted by various nineteenth- and twentieth-century authors do no justice either to the woman or her regime at Horsham and Lambeth, as is demonstrated in the following paragraph from the pen of Brenan and Statham:

> She lived a rigid, almost a conventual life, dressing in the nun-like costume of the preceding reign, wearing a hair shirt, and playing the lady abbess to a houseful of women and young girls, mostly of mean birth... Almost a fanatic in religion, she sternly closed her doors in the face of the naughty world, and while practising all the outward observances of Catholicism, blindly neglected the education and morals of her servants.[9]

A sad and dispiriting picture indeed! Fortunately, it has little substance. Agnes was not recorded as being a religious fanatic; no extant documentation makes mention of such costumes or hair shirts with regard to her, and on her tomb effigy at Lambeth she went for the full works, wearing rich robes and a massive ducal coronet that emphasises her high status among the nobility.[10] The account continues:

> As might be expected from such a character, she became the dupe of many rogues, male and female. Her bailiffs robbed her, and her women, while professing piety and devotion to her interests, were secretly of the vilest behaviour, so that the old manor-house at Horsham acquired a very bad reputation in that part of Norfolk [*sic*]. It was to such an establishment that Katherine Howard was brought

at the age of nine; it was among such poisonous surroundings that she grew to womanhood.[11]

One would love to be able to ask of the authors when and by whom was the elderly noblewoman robbed, and to point out that Agnes's mansion was not located at Horsham St Faith in Norfolk, but at Chesworth near Horsham in Sussex.

Neither at Chesworth nor at Norfolk House had Duchess Agnes taken in a 'houseful of women and young girls, mostly of mean birth', described by some authors as a frightening collection of vile beings older than the little Katherine Howard and eager to corrupt her. Although it has been a described more recently as being run along the lines of a lax boarding school for extended family and daughters of the nobility, the purpose of the residents' time with the duchess was really a course of training for their futures.[12] By working in the role of servants and attendants they would learn how to run a great house and also receive training in how to behave properly in high society and transform themselves into suitable candidates for the hand in marriage of some eligible son of a well-established family.

This arrangement was commonplace in noble houses, and here, as elsewhere, the young ladies would include members of the wider family as well as children of friends and neighbours, and it is likely Katherine would have come here in any event between 10 and 12 years of age, even if both her parents had still been living. Others, such as Katherine Tilney, would be the duchess's distant relatives engaged in more mundane tasks.

At this point, however, it is worth mentioning that there were also several high-spirited young male friends, relatives and servants living with the duchess, while others visited her home socially or in the retinues of their aristocratic employers during the day. At Lambeth it was at night, however, when the old lady was sound asleep, that some of the more adventurous among them would return to experience the delights of an altogether different sort of socialising in the young ladies' dormitory.[13]

Agnes Strickland, to whom many subsequent authors, for example Brenan and Statham, turned as a major source, in the 1840s described the aged dowager duchess as being careless over the supervision of her young charges. More than once she hints at Duchess Agnes being feeble minded, while at other times makes almost a caricature of a wicked and incompetent step-grandmother out of her:

> It was an evil hour for the little Katherine when she left the paternal roof, and the society of the innocent companions of her infant joys and cares, to become a neglected dependant in the splendid mansion of a proud and heartless relative... The duchess of Norfolk was so perfectly unmindful of her duties to her orphan charge, that Katherine was not only allowed to associate with her waiting-women, but compelled at night to occupy the sleeping apartment that was common to them all. Unhappily they were persons of the most abandoned description, and seem to have taken a fiendish delight in

perverting the principles and debasing the mind of the nobly-born damsel who was thrown into the sphere of their polluting influence.[14]

Bearing in mind that her father had been reduced to hiding from his creditors and claimed to have lived in the fear he could not even afford to feed his family, when Katherine Howard went to live with the duchess, initially at Chesworth, it could have been the first time in her young life she could count on the security of stability and routine.

The image of the step-grandmother uncaring to the point of being malevolent was still going strong well into the twentieth century. American author Michael Glenne weighed-in in similar vein to Strickland, Henry Herbert, Brenan and Statham and others in his late 1940s *Henry VIII's Fifth Wife: the Story of Catherine Howard*, a book that was, and still is, so confusing that in some libraries and booksellers it was classified as biography, and with it having an index it is easy to see the confusion, but it would have been more helpfully classified as being largely fiction.

According to Glenne, Lord William Howard visited his stepmother [sic] at Horsham, in Norfolk [sic], in a vain attempt to persuade her not to take him to a court of law. Although Glenne erroneously locates Horsham north of Norwich and over 120 miles from London, and sees Katherine as being only 9 years old in 1532, Anne Boleyn's mother somehow manages to pop in from time to time, as does Anne herself, filling Katherine's head with thrilling tales of the glamorous court in London and telling the child that she expects to become queen soon, but declaring that love has nothing whatsoever to do with it. The next year Glenne's little heroine is lifted from her accommodation with the 'coarse scullions' who delight in fouling her innocent young mind, to take centre stage with the duchess at her cousin Anne's coronation in London.[15]

Unfair and inaccurate assessments of what would really have been happening at Horsham and Lambeth are unfortunately the kind of thing that catches a reader's imagination and, repeated often enough, soon become accepted as part of the real story. The dowager's Chesworth and Lambeth abodes accommodated a respectable and wealthy household in very substantial dwellings of many rooms that were home to a large number of people, possibly far in excess of a hundred, and adorned by the plethora of luxury goods Agnes had been willed by her late husband.[16]

Aged 62 or thereabouts in 1539, Agnes would have been regarded as old for the times. Running her estates and performing her social duties as the Norfolk matriarch would have taken up much of her day and no doubt left her exhausted, as would being continually bombarded by requests for financial assistance and other favours. Katherine's mid-twentieth century biographer, Lacey Baldwin Smith, implies that the incident of Lord William asking Thomas Cromwell to write to Agnes in 1536 to help him raise a hundred men to assist in putting down the northern uprising was because, in her miserliness, she had already refused his own pleas for help. Smith could be mistaken: it was Lord William who had officially been called upon to send the men and it would require further official correspondence to his mother for the responsibility to be transferred to her.[17] Later documentation indicates a possibility that Katherine Howard was short of money, and she did admit to having borrowed to pay for trinkets, but whether that was through the duchess's thrift or the girl's own mismanagement of her allowance, we cannot be sure.[18]

However, neither advanced years nor incessant demands on her time and resources are evidence in themselves that Agnes Tilney was an unfit guardian. By criticising the duchess for having Katherine Howard sleep in the girls' dormitory, Miss Strickland, who, incidentally, was one of the first erroneously to place the town of Horsham in Norfolk rather than Sussex, was overlooking the fact that in those times of domestic overcrowding and lack of privacy, any bed at all, let alone a bed of one's own, was still a luxury beyond many people's dreams. As to bedrooms, a room of one's own was virtually unknown.

The fact that beds and bedding feature so prominently in the second duke's will shows they were items of great value, and Shakespeare's bequest to his wife of his 'second best bed', in a will made almost a century after the duke had made his, is often cited as an indicator of such. (For a remarkable list of fabulous beds the reader should see the Wardrobe Accounts of Henry VIII for 18 May 1540, which also record a gift of luxury material from him to Katherine Howard.[19])

Even in a great noble house it was usual for those other than the most senior members of the family to sleep together in one room and for more than one person to occupy a bed, as Katherine Howard did with Katherine Tilney and sometimes with Alice Wilkes. Even the Duchess of Norfolk would have her close confidantes, or bedfellows, sleeping in her own chamber, and the king himself sometimes shared a bed with his closest servants, as he would have done on many occasions with a young gentleman of the privy chamber named Thomas Culpeper, who, according to the French ambassador Charles de Marillac, 'had been brought up in the royal bedchamber service and ordinarily shares his bed', while the Imperial ambassador, Eustace Chapuys, called him 'son compagnon de lit'.[20]

As far as education goes, although Katherine Howard appears to have been nowhere near as intelligent or well-educated as her cousin Anne Boleyn, who had been 'finished' at the French court, thanks to the duchess's regime she was sufficiently accomplished and attractive enough to catch the eye and keep the interest of the king who could have had almost any woman he wanted, and was sufficiently well-grounded in the social graces and complex etiquette that enabled her to fit in well when called to court. Her manners were exemplary and always she strove to make a good impression in public; even at the moment of her death. In spite of the early twentieth-century claim, 'There is good reason to believe that, even when she became queen, she was unable to read or write; certainly not a scrap of paper bearing her autograph is known to exist, and whenever she wished to write she employed an amanuensis', she could read and write, although may not have much enjoyed the process.[21]

So, contrary to what gradually grew into the popular perception of Katherine Howard being an unpaid and morally corrupted drudge in her formative years, she was comfortable, had friends and companions of her own age and was reasonably well educated for the times. Unfortunately, it was with one of her teachers, who was broadening her education in a manner not anticipated by her step-grandmother, that her first sexual misdemeanours were committed at Chesworth House.

In all fairness, in the face of the incident with her teacher and later revelations about Katherine Howard's behaviour with another young man of her acquaintance, it has to be conceded Duchess Agnes's overall supervision of those who in their turn were supposed to be overseeing others in her care, was not as rigorous as it should have been. Nor did she deal harshly enough with the men who took advantage of the situation, but the accusation of deliberate neglect or the active encouragement of 'lightness' of character in, or the physical and moral abuse of, her young residents can hardly be levelled at her.

As the matriarch of a great family, Agnes would surely have believed it was her duty to see that no scandal of any magnitude attached to that family through anything that happened under her roof, or that her young charges' reputations were muddied, especially since her main aim would have been to see them suitably well married. But unsavoury things did happen in great houses of the times: in the late 1540s even 14-year-old Princess Elizabeth was not safe from the predatory attentions of her stepmother Katherine Parr's fourth husband, a man by then in his forties and not long married to the dowager queen.[22]

In Tudor England, abuse of young people was often swept under the carpet, as it had been before and has been since, but attitudes were different then and what today would be labelled as abuse was in those days much more of a nebulous area, often with the abused in no position to complain or fight back. Agnes's stepson, the head of the family, could have told her something about that. The elderly Norfolk had a mistress, Bess Holland, but also either had access to, or knowledge of, the charms of other young ladies, as a letter to Thomas Cromwell written in June 1537 amply demonstrates, even though it might have been written partly in jest.

The duke was in Yorkshire and wrote from Duchess Agnes's old base at Sheriff Hutton Castle that the monastery at Bridlington had just been scoured of its valuables and that two boxes of 'gold stuff' taken from the shrine of St John of Bridlington were on the way to the king in London in the care of a certain Tristram Teshe, for whom he would like Cromwell to put in a good word when he arrived. If he could see his way to supporting Teshe, there would also be something in it for Cromwell himself, for if ever he needed lodgings in York he would be sure of a welcome at Tristram's house and 'if ye lust not to dally with his wife he hath a young woman with pretty proper tetins [breasts]'.[23]

Nevertheless, it does seem that, in spite of what would appear to have been Agnes's best efforts, the piece of land in Lambeth, where the Novotel Waterloo now lies, was, in the late 1530s, the scene of unseemly goings-on: a world of secret midnight feasts, stolen bedroom keys and young men availing themselves of the forbidden delights of the maidens' bedchamber.

# Chapter 14

## The Maidens' Chamber

In many ways a poor relation, having inherited little or nothing from her debt-laden father, Katherine would understand she was not of the highest standing within her extended noble family but would always have been very much aware of being a Howard and that the dynastic needs of that family must always come above everything else. As was the norm, there would be no exhaustive searching for a love match when it came to finding her a husband – he would represent just another useful alliance, and if they came to love each other it would be a welcome bonus. When Henry Manox the music teacher became infatuated with her, the young lady, by then probably 15, let him know that there were limitations to the liberties he may take, and she could never marry him, although he appears to have lived in hope.

In general, the time of Katherine's birth is said to be between 1521 and 1525, with most historians leaning towards the former, making her about 19 when she married Henry VIII and 21 when she died, which is what will be assumed in the following narrative. *The Spanish Chronicle*, however, put her age at 15 when she first crossed Henry VIII's path at the end of 1539 or beginning of 1540, making her 16, possibly still 15, when they married and no more than 18 when she died; historians Josephine Wilkinson and the late Joanna Denny also see her as being very young.[1]

The more we think about it, however, Katherine Howard's actual age ought to determine how her behaviour is assessed and to what degree she should be censured for it. Could Strickland be right that 'Katherine, unfortunately for herself, while yet a child in age, acquired the precocious charms of womanhood, and before she had even entered her teens, attracted the attention of a low-born villain in the household of the duchess, named Henry Manox'.[2] Was she a precocious teenager, or an innocent girl of no more than 12 or 13, possibly less, when Manox, more than likely not short of sexual experience, sought to seduce her? If that were the case, would she know how to deal with him? And if not, would she, as a young girl, feel too embarrassed and ashamed to seek the help and protection of an adult? To whom would she naturally turn anyway?

Could Katherine have talked about her problems with the duchess, who would probably be a fairly remote figure, and not as we imagine a loving and listening grandma of today should be like? And how would a girl, even of 14 or 15, have fared in a world then always ready to blame the female for having enticed the male, where women were regarded as the weaker willed and more lustful of the species? There was also the long established and very convenient belief that if a woman said 'no', she probably meant 'yes', while, no matter how much she may have resisted her attacker, if a raped woman became pregnant it was believed she had enjoyed the experience, or as it was rather coyly put 'had given interior consent'. When Duchess Agnes caught Katherine Howard with Henry Manox, it was the girl who 'received two or three blows' from the old lady.

Of course there is no proof that Katherine was barely into her teens or was used against her will, and according to Manox he was surprised at the liberties she allowed him to take when they met in secret in the duchess's chapel at Chesworth; but her age has to be taken into consideration before she is condemned outright as being a very bad girl. If born in 1521 she would have been 15 in 1536, the year Manox said he had first been called to the mansion, rather old to be starting music lessons, although she could have had other teachers before him.[3]

Returning to Manox himself – Agnes Strickland's 'low born villain', was possibly a member of a prosperous family from Stoke by Nayland and might have entertained hopes of marrying Katherine, but his background remains foggy. Authors Brenan & Statham described him as being 'a loutish youth, attached in some manner to the household' at Horsham St Faith in Norfolk [sic].[4] However, although not necessarily 'low born' he appears to have been short on charm, sadly lacking in common sense, and probably too old to be considered a youth.

The fact that Manox and another teacher by the name of Barnes were brought in by the Duchess to teach Mistress Katherine Howard to play the virginals has always been taken to mean he taught music as a living rather than doing it as a favour to a neighbour, but that is not necessarily so, and he remains something of a mystery and deserves further investigation. Not to be put off by anything as trivial as lack of evidence, but at the same time sympathising with Katherine, Henry William Herbert writing in 1856 rails against him and 'his sort' who are:

> ... from the dregs of society, not gentlemen from innate instincts, education, or high feeling, and yet raised by their art, and by their position as instructors, to a certain station of equality among gentlemen, and to terms of intimacy with their pupils, their standing in the community was anomalous, their influence was almost invariably evil, and themselves, for the most part, thorough profligates and villains. This Manox had become intimate with the unlucky child, at Horsham, the country place of the duchess, in Norfolk [sic]; and, though he had not seduced her, which her tender years forbade, he had obtained a fearful degree of intimacy with her; [and] had brought her to consent to a clandestine correspondence with him.[5]

Clandestine correspondence was the very least of it. Mary Lascelles (or Lassells), one of the duchess's chamberers, remonstrated with the musician, warning that the Howards would kill him if they knew what he was up to with Katherine.

Some while later Mary would reveal how he had laughed in her face that day, boasting of his familiarity with the noble girl and going into coarse detail as how, by touch alone, he would know the most intimate part of her body 'among a hundred others'. Herbert relates that, devastated when she found out '... although the poor child answered in her shame and indignation that she cared not for him ... she went [taking Mary Lascelles] in search of the virginal player, to the servants' hall of Lord Beaumont, where she found and upbraided him for his infamy'.[6]

This account, written over 300 years after the event, presents a problem. By the time of the supposed meeting, Katherine had moved to Lambeth and Manox appears to have found work nearby; would a girl who might have been too embarrassed or afraid to complain about him in the privacy and familiarity of Chesworth really be brave enough, after a relatively short time at Norfolk House and its environs, to take herself off to where she, a niece of the Duke of Norfolk, behaved like a fishwife in the home of a far lesser nobleman? Strickland, Herbert, Brenan and Statham, and Smith all claim that it was not in Katherine's nature to remain angry for long, and state that soon after her outburst she was seen walking with Manox in the Duchess's gardens at Norfolk House.[7]

The name of Beaumont also needs to be questioned, since the second viscount had died in 1507 and Beaumont titles were not revived until well after Katherine's death. Her biographer, Lacey Baldwin Smith, calls Manox's new employer Lord Bayment, but this name has also not been possible to trace in this connection. Katherine's half-sister Isabel Leigh, a daughter of Katherine's mother's first marriage, had married Sir Edward Baynton, vice-chamberlain to Anne Boleyn and Henry's subsequent wives, in 1531, so he might be the connection, but this is not proven.[8] Henry Herbert says that Manox went on to become a musician at Henry VIII's court, for which there is no evidence, and he could be confusing him with Katherine's Norfolk House romantic interest, who *did* go King Henry's court when Katherine became queen, but not as a musician, and with disastrous consequences.

Upon the move to the Lambeth mansion, with its close proximity to royal palaces and grand houses of the nobility, even though she was of no great importance, Katherine Howard's social sphere would have expanded considerably and it was not long before she is said to have made the acquaintance of a reasonably well-born member of her Uncle Norfolk's entourage. And with him our various early historians continue their lively exercises in creativity, making Francis Dereham a dashing cavalier and 'a gentleman pensioner of the Duke of Norfolk, who maintained a band of these daring desperadoes, fierce profligate hangers on, the last remains of the feudal retainers of the middle ages'. Dereham is seen as being 'a bold, handsome, insinuating man, an especial favourite of the old duchess, and a distant blood relation of the family'.[9] It is possible that Dereham's grandmother, whose name is unknown, was a sister of the duchess's father Hugh Tilney, making Francis and Duchess Agnes first cousins once removed.[10]

Francis Dereham moved into the dowager's service at Norfolk House, and was soon enjoying a romantic liaison with Joan Ackworth, one of the girls from the maidens' chamber, where he seems to have become very free and easy with the other women accommodated there, for as Katherine was to claim later, 'he kissed me as he did many others'. Dereham appears to have occupied the post of Duchess Agnes's Gentleman Usher, of less importance than the Steward of the Household, but with control over many of the staff including all cooking and waiting staff of the kitchens, and the cleaners, including the chamberers who were responsible for the bed chambers and dormitories.[11]

There would have been two dormitories at Norfolk house, male and female, located some distance apart. The females' supervisor was one Mother Emmet who would oversee their welfare and make sure they were behaving themselves. Mother Emmet is a mystery. She, who technically should have known everything that was going on and would have locked the dormitory at night and sent the keys to the duchess, appears not to have been called to give evidence during Katherine Howard's later troubles, although it is possible she may have died in the meantime or her evidence has been lost.

Meanwhile, his position of Gentleman Usher would have allowed Francis Dereham legitimate access to the young ladies' dormitory, or the 'maidens' chamber' as it was called. When Katherine's involvement with him began and ended is not known for certain, but Dereham – whose blatant and shameless night time visits to her were for him, initially, just another illicit assignation after he tired of Joan Ackworth – seems inadvertently to have become seriously smitten.

She would have been neither the first nor the only troublesome girl ever to live at Norfolk House, as she herself pointed out under interrogation later, but, rightly or wrongly, Mistress Katherine Howard was subsequently painted by her fellow inmates as being the most daring among them, who persuaded others to steal the dormitory keys from the duchess as she slept, or even stole them herself, although how she let herself out of a locked room in order to do so is a question that remains unanswered.

Later, after her former life was revealed, Katherine told Archbishop Cranmer that she had never stolen the keys nor asked anyone else to do so, although at her request and that of others the doors were sometimes left unlocked. She did not explain why, and it was then, she claimed, that Dereham 'ordered himself very lewdly', but she insisted not at her request or with her consent. Presumably Dereham would have had access to keys, and his noisy adventures under the bed covers with Katherine initially shocked and embarrassed some of the other girls in the maidens' chamber, although eventually 'broken winded' Dereham's 'puffing and blowing' became something of a joke, except for Katherine Tilney and sometimes the bewildered Alice Wilkes, who were Mistress Howard's bedmates at the time.

While we might defend Katherine's relationship with Henry Manox as having happened when she was possibly little more than a child inexperienced in the ways of the world and, even if she wished, unable to do much about it, with Dereham she was older, knew what she was doing, and was well aware from previous experience that Duchess Agnes would be outraged, so making excuses for her latest behaviour does present something of a challenge.

When news of Katherine's adventures with Francis reached the slighted Manox, although by then he possibly was betrothed to someone else, or even married, he tried to bring the couple's misdemeanours to the duchess's attention through the vehicle of an anonymous letter, which he left on her pew at St Mary's Church across the road from Norfolk House. Unfortunately, the outcome was not what he had expected, for the old lady misunderstood and fell into a mighty rage with her girls as a whole when she got home, rather than realising he was referring specifically to Dereham. However, later on the duchess did confide to his friend, Robert Damport, she suspected it might have been referring to one of her employees named Hastings and a different young lady, whose identity remains unknown.[12]

For Manox to have discovered the Dereham liaison, some news of unseemly behaviour in the maidens' chamber, must have been leaking out, but perhaps it was not understood just how serious it was. It all seems to have been naively regarded as silly, childish antics by some senior members of the family, with Katherine's uncle, Lord William Howard, describing the girls as 'mad wenches' and telling them to stop falling out among themselves, while his lively sister Lady Bridgewater, seeming not to be too worried that the late-night shenanigans could ruin Katherine's reputation, was more concerned that she was not getting enough beauty sleep. Three years later Katherine's roommates Joan Ackworth and Alice Wilkes revealed under questioning that Lady Bridgewater knew there was socialising in the dormitory at night.[13] But even if the adults did not realise the full extent of some of the girls' behaviour, it does seem odd if the implication is that they had laughed about the young people meeting unchaperoned so late at night, and had not ordered Mother Emmet to tighten up on security.

Francis Dereham later insisted that Katherine Howard had entered into a pre-contract of marriage with him, that is, a verbal agreement, which would have been a brave thing to do on both their parts without her family's knowledge. If the promise did take place this was binding enough, provided the union was subsequently consummated, for them to be considered husband and wife in the eyes of the Church, and they did address each other as such, although Dereham said it was to quieten his jealous enemies who were saying he had no chance with a noble girl like Katherine, another sign that their relationship was known about outside the confines of Norfolk House. Was she pressured into the relationship by Dereham, or enjoying having a bit of fun with him to while away the tedium of life with the dowager? Under interrogation later, Katherine admitted calling Francis 'husband' to make him look good in front of his friends, but firmly denied ever making a binding agreement of marriage with him.[14]

No firm conclusion seems ever to have been reached as to why and exactly when the relationship between Francis Dereham and Katherine Howard ended. According to Katherine herself it was almost a year before she left Norfolk House for the court, which places the height of their romance – those '100 nights' spoken of later by Mary Lascelles – towards the end of 1538 or the beginning of 1539, although the 100 nights could have been spread across a longer period. They do not seem to have had a particularly acrimonious falling out, since Dereham had later been devastated by the thought of her leaving home when she was called to court in autumn 1539, and could not bear to stay at Norfolk House once she had gone.

It is known that the duchess chastised Dereham and her step-granddaughter with blows after she caught them fraternising much too closely. This would have been the second time the girl had been found in the arms of one of the duchess's employees and the old lady well and truly vented her anger. In Agnes's defence, apart from lashing out at Katherine she appears to have given the errant Francis a jolly good smack as well. If their affair cooled after that, then her attempts to bring Katherine back to the straight-and-narrow would have been successful. As happens so often in Katherine Howard's story, without knowing exactly when the duchess took up permanent residence at Norfolk House or what happened where and when, this can only be conjecture. Accurate context and chronology are all, and throughout this particular story, at times both are rather murky.

Whatever Katherine Howard's arrangement was with Dereham, once the excitement and glamour of life at the court of Henry VIII had beckoned her, the distraught Francis found himself in the same situation as the forgotten music teacher before him and so took himself off to Ireland to ponder his future and engage in what later was claimed to be a form of piracy. Later Katherine would claim, '... all that knew me and kept my company knew how glad and desirous I was to come to court', and it is not too difficult to believe that a young woman who, as far as the wider world was concerned, had hitherto lived a rather mundane and sheltered life in some respects, would be so excited and overwhelmed by the approaching glitz and glamour and the possibilities and opportunities her new appointment could bring.[15] An alternative interpretation as to why Katherine was so eager to leave Norfolk House for the court has been put forward by historian Retha Warnicke, who sees her as having been younger than is generally thought and anxious to escape sexual abuse by both Manox and Dereham.[16]

## Chapter 15

# Mistress Katherine Leaves Home

Waiting for the traffic lights to change at the junction of the Albert Embankment, Lambeth Palace Road and Lambeth Road, with Lambeth Bridge and the Thames ahead, it might be difficult to conjure-up a picture of the ageing larger-than-life monarch being ferried to the landing stage at Lambeth Stairs in the late spring and early summer of 1540 on his way to Norfolk House. Yet the red brick main gatehouse to the Archbishop of Canterbury's palace almost opposite Katherine Howard's home is much as it was then, and the tower of Duchess Agnes's local church, St Mary-at-Lambeth, is still standing.

The main body of the church, however, including the chancel where Elizabeth Howard, Anne Boleyn's mother, was laid to rest, and the Howard Chapel where the Dowager Duchess Agnes built her fine tomb and once found the letter from Manox on her pew, was rebuilt in Victorian times with so little thought for its important historic links that it is not now possible to point out where the remains of those fine Howard ladies lie, or to say whether they had already been moved to another location. Today the present Howard Chapel is used as a bookshop within the deconsecrated church, which is now home to the Garden Museum.[1]

In June 1540 Henry VIII was 49 years old, about six-foot-one in height, his large head covered in a white coif under a jaunty velvet bejewelled hat sporting exotic plumes. In spite of his great girth, inflated by excessive weight and exaggerated by heavily padded fashionable clothing, he was still an awe-inspiring figure. He was, though, plagued by grotesque, suppurating and malodorous ulcers on his once-splendid legs, thought to be painful reminders of the long-gone thrills of the joust.

Why, people began to ask, was the king bothering to have himself ferried across the river, late at night sometimes, to an old lady's house, when he had over fifty sumptuous houses, hunting lodges and palaces of his own? The answer was very simple: he was in love, and his old heart was all aquiver at the thought of the pretty little teenager awaiting him at Norfolk House. Unfortunately, as the letter from the religious reformer Richard Hilles to his colleague Henry Bullinger reveals, she was not his latest wife, whom he had married as recently as January:

> The courtiers observed the King to be taken by another young lady of very diminutive stature whom he now has ... it is a certain fact that ... many citizens of London saw the King very frequently in the daytime, and sometimes at midnight, pass over to her on the Thames in a little boat.[2]

Eight months earlier, in the autumn of 1539, the Duke of Norfolk would have been happy to find that two of his young female relatives and one of his wards had been offered some of the coveted places in the household then being assembled for Henry VIII's latest intended, Anne of Cleves, who was due to become the new queen the following December. On 22 November, Norfolk's late brother Lord Edmund's daughter, Mistress Katherine Howard, a great-niece Mistress Catherine Carey (Mary Boleyn's daughter) and his ward Mistress Mary Norris, whose father Henry had perished with Anne Boleyn in the 1536 scandal, appear almost at the bottom of the list of the great and good who were to be rehearsed and primed for their roles at the grand reception for the bride's arrival in England.[3]

Although often stated as fact, whether or not Norfolk had been able directly to influence the choosing of the young ladies is debatable. Never a favourite of the king and having been beset by serious troubles that had threatened his standing throughout the decade, he was in any case still occupied on the Borders when Henry VIII's fourth marriage was being arranged and while his subsequent relationship with Katherine Howard was developing.

What is fact is that the Howards knew only too well that close association with King Henry could mean the kiss of death. Young Katherine's summons to court, therefore, ought to have rung alarm bells with some of the family, and probably did, although it was always useful for a noble family's fortunes to have a pretty young thing at the monarch's beck-and-call. Suggestions that the choice of Katherine was a deliberate set-up with the aim of ensnaring the king into another Howard marriage have not taken into account that at the time Henry was in love with the Holbein portrait of Anne of Cleves, was expected to be delighted with the real thing and would have eyes for no other woman, at least for the time being.

If the king should eventually tire of his latest wife and start taking rather more than a harmless and fleeting interest in one of the young ladies of the court, there would be very little anyone could do about it, for it would be a brave man, and a foolhardy one, who would seek to challenge Henry VIII over the suitability of the object of his latest infatuation. Surely, though, Katherine's kinsmen could not have anticipated that Henry would so quickly put aside his latest spouse.

The true story of how and why Katherine was chosen from among the young ladies of the nobility may never be known. Although of fairly low standing within the Howard hierarchy itself, as a grandchild of the second duke and largely brought up by his wealthy widow, she certainly had the credentials to put her on the shortlist. As to personal attributes, we know Henry preferred to be surrounded by good-looking people, so it is a safe bet that Katherine was attractive, although the French ambassador described her the September following her July 1540 wedding, as being of small stature and graceful rather than beautiful.[4]

Of the few likenesses traditionally said to be of Katherine Howard, none can be confirmed. It is unlikely she sat for a portrait before her marriage, and any Henry VIII might have commissioned of her would have been destroyed at her downfall. The Royal Collection cannot confirm that their Holbein miniature is her likeness, although the sitter wears jewellery believed to have been passed down from Jane Seymour, while a Holbein portrait of a young woman in a black dress is now suggested as being of Jane Seymour's sister Elizabeth, who married Cromwell's son, Gregory. For the purposes of this book I have decided to include the Metropolitan Museum of Art's portrait of a young woman of about Katherine's age and a photograph of a mannequin wearing Pauline Loven's reconstruction of the cloth of silver dress she wore at Lincoln in August 1541.[5] Agnes Strickland, from a Holbein drawing at Windsor, now thought to be of someone else, dismissed Katherine as looking more like a Flemish peasant than a queen, with 'the countenance of an unintellectual little romp trying to assume an air of dignity'.[6]

The Edwardian authors Brenan and Statham come to the rescue again and enlighten us as to what they see as having happened to bring Katherine to her sovereign's attention, and, as with works of their contemporaries, their presentation of the 'facts' still remains in the public perception even today. Unfortunately, in the absence of concrete evidence, and it would seem of not having managed successfully to sort into proper order what evidence there actually was, as becomes abundantly clear later on in their rendition of the story, they appear to have decided to improvise as they went along, with Duchess Agnes coming to Lambeth from Horsham (sadly yet again placed in Norfolk) to consult the duke about her properties:

> The fine old mansion of the Norfolks at Lambeth was hers for life, and thither accordingly she repaired, borne in a horse-litter, beside which rode her beautiful niece [sic], the latter's hazel eyes opening very admirably, we may be sure, at the sights and sounds of London. They had not been many hours installed in the Lambeth mansion when the Duke of Norfolk came to pay his respects to his stepmother ... It was the first time that Norfolk had seen his niece since her infancy, and he may well have been struck by the beauty which, all unknown to him, had grown up in the retirement of Horsham... She probably went to live with the Dowager Duchess of Norfolk at the latter's dower-house of Horsham St. Faith's, [sic] four miles north of Norwich, about the beginning of 1531.[7]

According to our historians, Brenan and Statham, Norfolk and his Catholic cronies could not wait to come up with a cunning plan to flaunt his lovely niece before the king. The official documentation confirms that Katherine was called to the court in late 1539 to be trained as a maid of honour, but they state it was not until June 1540 that Henry VIII himself appointed her to serve the queen, who had no idea what he was up to and 'welcomed her destined successor with equanimity'.

So far this account could be seen as being no more than a bit of silly fun, but the writers were doing students of history no favours by putting across as established fact what they only surmise could have happened. In their scenario, in the few weeks between the so-called new appointment in June and her marriage to the king at the end of July, Katherine Howard would have needed to move with the speed of a very accomplished whirling dervish to achieve what they attributed to her. The Great Ladies, that is the senior attendants of Anne of Cleves, including Henry's daughter Princess (Lady) Mary and Lady Margaret Douglas, the latter rehabilitated following the fiasco with Lord Thomas Howard, are supposedly falling over themselves to pay court to this previously unknown girl 'or rather to "the Lady Katherine", as she was now called'.[8]

The pretty maid of honour's late father was of lower rank than an earl, and there are no documents to show Henry elevated her status, so she was definitely not 'Lady' Katherine. The account continues that the fine ladies supposedly told her that Cromwell was standing in the way of her marrying the king so, egged on by her Uncle Norfolk, she worked her charms on Henry until Cromwell was brought down. Cromwell did indeed fall from grace and was executed in the summer of 1540, much to the satisfaction of the Duke of Norfolk, but where is the evidence to show that Katherine 'exerted herself to the utmost to carry out these promptings'?

Henry Herbert makes some remarkable claims in his tome of 1856, but now and then shows feelings of sadness about the Howard girl whom he refers to as 'poor child', 'unlucky child' and 'unhappy child', whom he does not see as being capable of the subterfuge of which others have accused her,

> No proof can be adduced of this tradition [the rumoured attempted ousting of Cromwell by Norfolk and Gardiner by insinuating Katherine into the Court to influence Henry]; Katherine Howard does not appear to have possessed the talents implied by the supposition of such a scheme, if she had the will, which is doubtful, nor was she of a jealous or intriguing disposition.[9]

We cannot know whether in late 1539 those few Howards already aware of Katherine's somewhat soiled reputation among her fellow residents at Horsham and Lambeth felt any trepidation at the prospect of the girl's royal employers finding out about her imperfect past. As long as she remained relatively unimportant on the periphery of the court, her behaviour before she went there could have remained secret, and she might well find a suitable husband there, but if the Howards as a family had discussed the pros and cons of trapping the king into marrying one of their own candidates, Katherine Howard would have been a risky first choice.

Duchess Agnes was interrogated less than two years hence as to what degree she had coached the girl on how to make herself attractive to Henry, and what particular garments and adornments she had purchased for her, but neither of those actions would necessarily be an indicator of plotting. Once Katherine was called to court it would have been Agnes's duty to make sure her step-granddaughter's appearance and manner were as pleasing as possible in such exalted company, but whether she went as far as actually pimping Katherine seems unlikely.[10] Whatever the circumstances of the choice of the young woman had been, in late 1539 Mistress Howard left the relative security of Duchess Agnes's Lambeth home for the gilded snake-pit that was the court of Henry VIII, and the rest, as they say, is history.

Owing to poor weather in the winter of 1539 making crossing the Channel out of the question for his new bride, Henry VIII did not marry Anne of Cleves until early January 1540. She had been expected to arrive towards the end of November, so although the document listing the members of the future queen's household dates from the third week of the month, the maids of honour could have been at court two weeks prior to that.[11] Whether or not Katherine had broken up with Dereham approximately a year beforehand, as she later claimed, we cannot be sure, but for him, and for the duchess, there were several other changes at Norfolk House at about the same time.

Edward Waldegrave, another frequent visitor to the maidens' chamber, and possibly a relative of Manox, left to join the household of Prince Edward, then just over 2 years old; Joan Ackworth married a member of the Bulmer family and moved to York; while Mary Lascelles, who had challenged Manox over his unacceptable behaviour with Katherine, married and moved to Sussex. The duchess herself did not become part of the new Queen Anne's household, and Dereham, of course, having convinced himself that his future was with Katherine Howard, remained devastated.

# Chapter 16

# 1540: Two More Wives

Katherine Howard and her fellow maids of honour would have been among the huge outdoor welcoming party for Anne of Cleves assembled at Greenwich on the freezing cold afternoon of 3 January 1540, where all the magnificence of Henry VIII's court was on show, from the breathtaking materials of the principal characters' clothing to the cunning design and appearance of the temporary buildings erected specifically for the occasion. The French ambassador Charles de Marillac, invited to the celebration, as was his Imperial counterpart Eustace Chapuys, wrote to Francis I that town criers had been busy drumming up public support for the new queen's welcome, so crowds were large and the omens were good.[1]

Because of the bad weather, Lady Lisle had to host Anne and her entourage in Calais for longer than expected and had found her to be kind, good natured and easy to please.[2] Now, at Greenwich, the moment of truth had finally arrived. Henry's future queen, escorted by the dukes of Norfolk and Suffolk and a huge retinue, was less than five miles away. However, the king himself, riding out with his own glittering escort to meet his bride, was in very low spirits, for unbeknown to the onlookers, he had already met her, and it had been far from love at first sight. De Marillac, who knew nothing of Henry's dilemma, described the event at Greenwich as being:

> ...well conducted with marvellous silence and no confusion, to the number of 5,000 or 6,000 horses. The dukes of Norfolk and Suffolk were with the said lady five miles from Greenwich and the King went to meet her on the way. She was clothed in the fashion of the country from which she came, and he received her very graciously and conducted her into his house at Greenwich to the chamber prepared for her.[3]

But all was not what it seemed. Three days earlier, unable to wait any longer to meet the lovely young woman in the Holbein portrait, Henry had ridden out to Rochester where Anne was breaking her journey.

In spite of his challenging experiences with women thus far, Henry VIII was still something of a romantic at heart and had decided to complicate matters by appearing in disguise as a messenger bringing her a gift of welcome from her fiancé. Anne, who, according to a later account was near a window watching a bull-baiting at the time, barely acknowledged the tall, ageing, overweight man who had come into her room, and when he took her in his arms and tried kiss her, she was appalled.

Even worse, the Holbein portrait appears to have flattered the bride-to-be, although she seems to have been pleasant enough in appearance, and the later accusations of poor hygiene and lack of grooming were probably maliciously made and embellished to place the blame for the failure of the marriage upon her. De Marillac, after seeing her at Greenwich and knowing nothing of the Rochester incident, told his master Francis I:

> She looks about 30 years of age, tall and thin, of medium beauty, and of very assured and resolute countenance... She was clothed in the fashion of the country from which she came. She brought 12 or 15 ladies of honour clothed like herself – a thing which looks strange to many.[4]

The unnamed Member of Parliament excitedly glimpsing the arrivals at Greenwich who penned, 'O what a sight was this to see so goodly a Prince and so noble a King to ride with a fair lady of so goodly a stature and so womanly a countenance' obviously was hugely over optimistic.[5]

Whatever the true circumstances of their first meeting, it was not a good start and Henry decided there and then he was not at all attracted to Anne, never would be and was pleading with Cromwell to find a way out, which with the wedding planned for Twelfth Night, less than seventy-two hours away, and England still in need of the alliance with Cleves, could not be done. So, on the morning of 6 January 1540 King Henry VIII and Anne of Cleves were married at Greenwich Palace, with Mistress Katherine Howard and the other maids of honour assisting her with her dress, which again was in the fashion of her own country.

Katherine's new tasks were similar to those she had performed for Duchess Agnes, but in the royal palaces everything was larger, more sumptuous, even more regimented, and for a novice it would all have been breathtaking. Before Anne of Cleves arrived, her new household, as borne out by Katherine's colleague Anne Basset's 22 December letter to her mother Lady Lisle, would have been assembling for training at the Palace of Whitehall, formerly Wolsey's York Place, still undergoing its transformation into the largest palace in Europe, which it remained until its destruction by fire in 1698.

For Katherine all of this would have been a culture shock. Norfolk House was big, but by comparison the royal palaces were massive. The young maids of honour were required to provide their own gowns and Duchess Agnes fulfilled her obligation to Katherine with garments which were expensive, attractive and tasteful, but not so elaborate as to outshine the queen. The maids were entitled to board and lodging at court, and received a salary of £10 per year; in overall charge of them was Mrs Stoner, Mother of the Maids, appointed at the same time.

Under questioning later, when the Howards' circumstances had become very precarious, the duchess would be asked to explain what had made her say that 'the King did cast a fantasy toward Katherine Howard the first time he saw her'. This has given rise to the argument that if Katherine was at court several weeks before he met his new wife, an attraction towards her could have coloured Henry's attitude towards the bride he had yet to meet. But which person or persons had told the duchess of the king's fantasy (fancy), if such even existed at that point, and when, is not known.

As the New Year unfolded and Henry VIII could not force himself to be a husband to Anne of Cleves, his attention definitely did turn to Mistress Howard, a lively girl of 19, or possibly younger, in whose company he must have felt like a man who had imbibed of the elixir of youth. In the early summer he was able to spend a few precious hours with his little 'jewel' on her home ground in Lambeth away from the wagging tongues and prying eyes of his court. It seems likely that, as the arrangements to get rid of Anne of Cleves were gaining momentum, Katherine returned to Norfolk House to divert attention from her developing situation with the king – 'lying low' as we would say today – and, like it or not, her family would by then have sensed what the outcome was likely to be.

In the months since his January wedding, Henry's need for the alliance with his wife's brother had diminished, so to rid him of his burden, that good old standby the pre-contract of marriage was dragged out yet again. When not yet in her teens, in 1527 Anne of Cleves had been betrothed to Francis, the son and heir of the Duke of Lorraine, and even though the contract was legally dissolved in 1535 and Henry would not have given it a second thought if Anne had pleased him, it was to become his main vehicle for the annulment. It is interesting to see that from the fairly small pool of suitable candidates in the world of European alliances, in 1541 Francis, by then Duke of Lorraine, married Christina of Denmark.[6]

Again, some early authors seem to have seen accounts or had knowledge of the 1541 machinations, but could not resist taking a few liberties with the story: 'But the King saw her daily, and there were pleasant progresses upon the Thames to Hampton Court or Greenwich, during which Katherine already found herself treated with the respect due to a royal consort'. At first Queen Anne accompanies them, but all too soon three becomes a crowd and she is left behind 'while Katherine queened it in her stead'.[7]

The supposedly clandestine royal visits to Lambeth would have required Duchess Agnes to adhere to rules of breeding and protocol and pander to every whim of Henry and his entourage, whatever she felt about his attraction towards Katherine. However, the old girl knew how to throw a good party, or so we are told:

> From his palace windows at Lambeth my lord of Canterbury saw the lights and heard the nightly music which told of the royal courtship in Norfolk House; and learning that Mistress Katherine was sage as well as seductive, betook himself into retirement at Croydon, there to abide events and prepare himself, if necessary, for the new stretching of his elastic conscience.[8]

Cranmer possibly was at his palace at Croydon, but whether it was as a result of worry where his Lambeth neighbours' loud partying might be leading is not known.

It has hardly ever been suggested, but it must be a possibility, that the Dowager Agnes actually lived in some fear of the king and did not throw her arms in the air with delight when Katherine caught Henry's eye, but rather was filled with foreboding. Life was on a knife edge for everybody during these troubled times, and the Howard family's latest romantic involvement with the already four-times-married monarch must have concentrated the old lady's mind wonderfully, probably sending a shiver down her spine.

If Henry, 'the Royal Bluebeard of English history' as Agnes Strickland called him, should be successful in discarding Anne of Cleves and married Katherine, she would be safe only as long as he continued to find her attractive. When his interest waned, and his past record showed that before too long it surely would, woe betide Katherine, and her relatives, if, like her cousin Anne before her, she had failed in her duty of filling the royal cradles with baby princes.

The first recorded sign of Henry VIII's interest in his wife's maid of honour had come in April, three months after his marriage, when 'Katherine Howard, servant of the Queen Consort Anne' was granted the goods and chattels of a father and son from Sussex, both named William Ledbeter, indicted for the murder of one Richard Bolokherd.[9] The Royal Wardrobe accounts show that soon after, on 18 May, 'Twenty-three quilts of quilted sarcenet...[were] given to Mrs. Haward.' Sarcenet was an expensive lightweight silk, so this gift was of significant value, and it was unusual for a king to be making such to a minor servant, which is what Katherine still was in the great hierarchy of court life. She did well though not to be lumbered with the next item on the royal accounts list, 'Seven pieces of imagery [tapestry] which sometime hung in the tennis play gallery, sore worn and moth-eaten'.[10]

Thomas Cromwell, a major architect of the latest marriage and thankful to have survived the Anne of Cleves fiasco, was granted the earldom of Essex on 18 April, but in reality, and no doubt to the delight of Norfolk and Stephen Gardiner, Bishop of Winchester, his time was up. With Henry VIII it is difficult to tell what his long-term plans for Cromwell had really been. Granting him the earldom implied that all was well and he was in firm favour, but perhaps it was done only to conceal his real purpose until he could make his move, for a mere fifty-three days after the earldom was bestowed upon him, Cromwell was in the Tower. Henry seems readily to have accepted as truth Norfolk and Gardiner's accusations of Cromwell plotting against him and agreed to his arrest.

On 10 June, as the earl arrived for a meeting of the Privy Council a cry of 'traitor' had gone up. The king's guards seized Cromwell and the victorious Norfolk ripped the seal of office from around his neck. Henry, however, still needed his former chief minister's great skills as a lawyer to finalise the annulment from Anne of Cleves, which he was forced to work on from captivity in the Tower. After the annulment of Henry's fourth marriage, Parliament obligingly went through the expected charade of petitioning him to marry again for the sake of the succession.

On 28 July 1540 Thomas Cromwell was most hideously butchered by a bungling headsman on Tower Hill. His expert legal skills meant that should he be brought to trial he just might save himself, so it had been decided to use a bill of attainder against him, as he had done against many others, leaving him no chance to defend himself. It is to this beheading that Norfolk's gloating son, the Earl of Surrey, was later claimed to be referring when he declared, 'Now is the false churl dead, so ambitious of others' blood. These new erected men would, by their wills, leave no noble man a life. Now he is stricken with his own staff!'[11] That afternoon, at one of his lesser-known palaces, Henry VIII took Surrey's cousin, Mistress Katherine Howard, to be his lawful wedded wife.

## Chapter 17

# No Other Wish but His

The girl who had waited on the duchess at Norfolk House and whose future had not looked especially interesting, had risen in the space of eight months from the lower levels of the queen's household staff to becoming queen herself. Now the first lady in the land, with riches, attendants and attention beyond her wildest dreams, she also had the potential to be the mother of a boy who would be second in line to the throne after Jane Seymour's little son. Her every whim and command, within her own immediate circle at least, would be satisfied and obeyed without being challenged, which for her was to prove fatal.

The wedding had been a secret affair at Oatlands Palace near Weybridge and it was not until 8 August that the former Mistress Howard was introduced to the court as the new queen. After that the first months of the marriage were spent travelling around the king's many hunting lodges and smaller palaces on the annual summer progress. The summer of 1540 was unbearably hot and followed by drought, but the royal party managed to make a not too energetic progress through East Anglia taking in Ampthill, where a decade before Katherine of Aragon had been detained for a short time.

It was at this time that Charles de Marillac, the French ambassador travelling with them on the progress and seeing Katherine for the first time, described her as being graceful rather than beautiful, and of short stature, noting the king was so amorous of her that he could not treat her well enough and caressed her more than he had the others. He added that she and all the court ladies dressed in French style and her badge was a rose crowned bearing the motto *Non autre volonté que la sienne*, 'No other wish but his', which was very apt in view of what was to become of her.[1] 'Rose without a thorn' is an epithet long said to refer to Katherine Howard, but is now believed actually to have been a reference to the rose symbol of the Tudor dynasty; some time earlier Henry VIII had had a coin struck with his coat of arms on one side and a Tudor rose on the other. The confusion with Katherine can be traced partly to Agnes Strickland.[2] Another epithet, 'a jewel for womanhood', found in a letter from colleagues in London to the English diplomat William Paget in Paris discussing Katherine more than a year after her wedding, may or may not have been used by the king himself.[3]

The Queen's Council and her chancellor, Sir Thomas Denys, took care of her vast lands and properties, eventually including some previously in the hands of Cromwell, the Countess of Salisbury and various abbeys and monasteries. Whether Katherine would eventually have taken an active interest in the management of her huge estates as her predecessors had done will never be known. Obviously there would be perks for her relatives too, for example her brother, Charles Howard, was promoted to Gentleman of the Privy Chamber, but her Uncle Norfolk, still today frequently accused of pulling her strings for his own gain, was actually away for a large part of her first six months as queen and seems to have gained little.

On 5 December 1540 Chapuys, who had been out of England for the best part of 1539–40, wrote to Mary of Hungary that relations between Princess Mary and her new stepmother were fraught.[4] Mary Tudor was educated, clever and proud of her Spanish and English royal blood, so to her Katherine Howard must have seemed nothing but an upstart nonentity. Princess (still officially 'Lady') Mary had harboured no lasting ill-feeling towards either Jane Seymour or Anne of Cleves, neither of whom had caused harm to her mother; the lowly Katherine Howard, however, was not only her fourth stepmother in seven years, she was also five years younger than Mary, and already starting to complain that her stepdaughter was not showing the respect and deference due to her as the queen consort.

Some of Mary's attendants were to be taken away as a result of Katherine's fit of pique over what she saw as her insolence, but by Christmas the two appeared to have begun to make it up and Henry was pleased with Mary for sending her stepmother a New Year gift and sent his daughter valuable presents on Katherine's behalf. However, the rapprochement, if there was such, was temporary and in February the attendants were removed, much to her, and their, distress.

Having found himself not too inconvenienced by the fearful drought of 1540 that caused crops to fail, cattle to die and left his people facing prolonged hunger, Henry VIII continued enjoying a new lease of life with his fifth wife into the winter months. Up at the crack of dawn, out riding and hunting on one or other of his many lesser estates, his health and temper improved significantly, while life with his little bride seemed like one long holiday. A cloud hanging over him, however, was his less than chivalrous treatment of Anne of Cleves.

Henry was grateful to Anne for the dignified way she had handled her demotion from his queen consort to her new honorary position of 'Lady Anne, the king's sister', not that she had a great deal of choice in the matter. Shortly after their marriage ended he visited her at her new home at Richmond Palace and expressed the hope they would keep in touch, so in what amounted to a Tudor public relations exercise she was invited to stay at Hampton Court in the New Year and gracefully accepted, even though it would coincide with what under normal circumstances would have been her first wedding anniversary. Eustace Chapuys wrote that on the way to Hampton Court with her suite of attendants, either by accident or design, she came across Katherine's uncle, Lord William Howard and his entourage, 'Milord Guillaume, the Duke of Norfolk's brother, who, having met her on the road to this city, could not well, for courtesy's sake, refuse to accompany her to the gates of Antoncourt [sic]'.[5]

The former queen behaved impeccably towards her successor, and young Katherine herself was the model of friendliness and magnanimity. Anne of Cleves made a deep curtsey to her former servant 'who received her most kindly, showing her great favour and courtesy'.[6] Henry appeared only when it was obvious there were to be no fireworks between the two women 'and after making a very low bow to Lady Anne, embraced and kissed her'. When they all sat down to supper Anne occupied a seat near the bottom of the table, which has been taken by some to have been a slight, but would have been within the strict rules of protocol, she being the king's 'honorary' sister, whose annulment could be interpreted as meaning she had never really been a queen and so would not merit one of the most prominent places in the seating arrangements. Afterwards Henry, more than old enough to be their father, retired early and left his fourth and fifth wives dancing together.[7]

This potentially nerve-racking occasion of the former spouse's visit is often quoted as being such a great success due to a pragmatic approach and good-nature on both sides, but Chapuys tells us that, prior to their meeting, the 'king's sister' had to be kept waiting while her former servant was put through her paces by Lord Chancellor Audley and Lord Great Chamberlain the Earl of Sussex as to what would be appropriate behaviour, given such an odd and unprecedented scenario.[8]

Anne of Cleves, who had been mocked exactly a year earlier for her strange dress sense and lack of refinement, looked very well and was beautifully attired in the latest fashion; her English was coming on in leaps and bounds and she, who upon arrival in England had had little or no skill at the dance, was now able to spend two pleasant evenings dancing and taking part in the chatter and entertainments. The great irony of the discarding of Anne of Cleves is that she appears after all to have had the qualities to be a successful and popular queen consort and possibly might have borne Henry the male children he so badly wished for.

The fact she looked so well and that they all appeared to be on good terms would perhaps make Henry's critics think that his appalling behaviour towards her had not done too much damage after all. In truth, in spite of the palaces, lands and wealth heaped upon her, Anne of Cleves had been horribly humiliated by the manner in which she was repudiated. Henry was apparently unable to consummate the marriage because he believed Anne not to be a virgin, citing her 'slack breasts', which, among other very intimate details, he discussed with his advisors, as being a telltale sign.

Before her annulment, Anne, who had done nothing wrong, had to suffer the indignity of being examined by doctors, and of sensitive private conversations with her ladies, who suspected the marriage was not consummated, being made public. She also had to agree to restrictions in travel and having her visitors and correspondence vetted, but wisely she chose to make the best of her situation.[9] Nevertheless, when Henry's marriage to her successor began to unravel it seems that Anne would have come back to him and her brother, the Duke of Cleves, might have concurred, possibly because Henry's appallingly unchivalrous behaviour had weakened her chances of making another marriage and her brother was at a loss what to do with her if Henry sent her home.

For Katherine, who at the beginning of January would have been married just over five months but had only recently taken up residence in any of the large royal palaces, Anne of Cleves's successful visit to Hampton Court was a good result, and must have been a welcome confidence-builder. Like her cousin Anne Boleyn before her, Katherine Howard was not fond of her uncle the Duke of Norfolk, so it would be no great loss for her that in the early stages of 1541 he continued to be heavily involved in the northern counties and the Borders. Her half-uncle, Lord William, however, appointed to replace Sir John Wallop as ambassador to France would be missed, although de Marillac did not rate him highly, 'a good young gentleman, but not suitable for such business'.[10] With Hampton Court being some distance by river from Lambeth it meant that her step-grandmother and aunt, Katherine Bridgewater, were also out of immediate reach.

The celebrations over, Queen Katherine found herself spending the winter days in her own spectacular apartments in great comfort in a massive palace, but among virtual strangers. Apart from Katherine Tilney, her old friend and sometime bedfellow from Horsham and Lambeth, whom she had taken into her service as one of her chamberers, Isabel Baynton one of her half-sisters and the king himself, whom she would not necessarily see every day, there was no one to whom she was particularly close at this point. Even Henry was going to be leaving her soon to go to the south coast to inspect a number of forts and ramparts, which constructed only in the past two years were already starting to disintegrate. However, he went down with an illness before he could set off, which troubled him for some weeks, although de Marillac wrote that the expected associated weight loss would be no bad thing.[11]

Henry was sufficiently recovered by the end of the first week in March to stand beside Katherine on the royal barge as they passed through London on the Thames. The summer drought of the previous year had been followed by plague, so this was her first journey through the city as queen and she was given a good reception. After some days at Westminster she was proclaimed queen at the Tower and from there moved to Greenwich Palace, where she had last stayed as a humble maid of honour.

Henry VIII had in custody Sir Thomas Wyatt, the Earl of Surrey's great friend and fellow poet, and Sir John Wallop, Lord William Howard's predecessor as ambassador to France. Wyatt had been accused by Edmund Bonner, Bishop of London of derogatory comments about the king, of dealing with the exiled Cardinal Reginald Pole and of unfavourable statements about foreign courts while ambassador to the court of Charles V. Sir John Wallop, according to Chapuys, was detained in the house of the Lord Privy Seal upon his return to England, Henry having learned he had said something in favour of Pope Paul III. All of these were tenuous charges and Henry needed a way of releasing the men without appearing weak, so in a piece of public theatre Queen Katherine begged her husband for their lives, and so to please her they were granted pardons.[12]

In 1538 it was sixty years since George, Duke of Clarence had been executed for treason against his brother Edward IV, Henry VIII's maternal grandfather, but he still had the power to cast long and dangerous shadows over his surviving daughter Margaret and her family. Born Margaret Plantagenet, and a first cousin of Henry VIII's mother, with the execution of her brother the Earl of Warwick in 1499 she was the last of the legitimate Plantagenets of high rank. Her husband, Sir Richard Pole, died in 1505 leaving her a widow of little means with five children, but with the accession of Henry VIII she was created Countess of Salisbury in her own right and came to court in the service of Katherine of Aragon.

In the 1530s the Pole family retained strong Roman Catholic sympathies, but in public Margaret distanced herself and family from her errant middle son, Cardinal Reginald Pole. An outspoken critic of Henry VIII living in safety abroad, he had been encouraged by the Pope to get his contacts at home to drum up support for the Pilgrimage of Grace, and in private his brothers remained in touch. One of their servants, possibly a spy planted in the household, denounced them and in November 1538 Margaret's sons Henry Pole and his brother Sir Geoffrey were arrested and charged with treason.

They were committed to the Tower, where on 9 January 1539 Henry Pole, Lord Montagu, was executed. Under questioning Geoffrey had tried to explain that although his family disagreed with the religious changes and had corresponded with his brother the cardinal, they would never have contemplated treason, but he entangled himself enough to condemn his brother Henry and relatives. Although pardoned on 24 September 1540, he was said to have tried to commit suicide over the part he played in his brother's death. The Countess of Salisbury, then in her mid-sixties, had been arrested a few days after her sons and questioned relentlessly for hours at a time, first in her own home, and then at the house of William Fitzwilliam, Earl of Southampton, where she was held until mid-March 1539 before being committed to the Tower. Henry also had a grudge against her for her continued devotion to his daughter the Lady Mary, whose governess she had been.

Margaret Pole enters into the story of Katherine Howard at about the same time as the latter's triumphant entry into London. Confined to the Tower for the past two years and now aged 67, she was complaining of the cold and damp playing havoc with her rheumatism, and tradition has it that Queen Katherine stepped in to help by having her own tailor, John Scutt, make warm garments for her. The lovely young queen taking pity on the poor old woman's suffering has the makings of a heart-warming story, she risking censure, or even imprisonment herself, for relieving the distress of one of the king's elderly and frail incarcerated enemies. Henry William Herbert seems almost smitten by Katherine when writing of her kind gesture as being 'a sweet, beautiful touching memorial [to Katherine]. It shows a feeling heart'.[13]

However, even if she had knowledge of the old lady's circumstances, Katherine Howard would not have had the power, and probably not the inclination, to do such a thing. The idea seems to stem from Agnes Strickland and has proliferated through writers passing it off as fact ever since. Contemporary documents show that items were indeed ordered for the Countess in March and *were* made by Katherine's own tailor, but it was on the orders of the Privy Council and they were paid for by the king, with no mention of the transaction or invoices for such apparel recorded in Katherine Howard's own accounts. Proceedings of the Privy Council record that on 12 April John Scutt received £11 16s 4d from the king's household expenses for delivering two nightgowns, a woollen kirtle, a bonnet, four pairs of hose, four pairs of shoes and a pair of slippers to the Tower for the Countess of Salisbury.[14]

Margaret Pole was not the only Plantagenet in the Tower. Also requiring warm clothes was Lord Lisle, Arthur Plantagenet, an illegitimate son of Edward IV and therefore Henry's uncle; it was his wife who had dosed Katherine's father with medicine for 'the stone' with the unfortunate, if amusing, consequences in Calais. Lisle, accused of knowledge of a plot to betray Calais to the Pope and Cardinal Pole, which he denied, had been imprisoned in the Tower since May 1540. As a prisoner of status and royal blood, like Margaret Pole he would be allowed some degree of comfort, with garments made for him by the king's own tailor at the same time as John Scutt made those for the Countess, and likewise paid for out of Henry's own household expenses.

On Palm Sunday 1541 Ambassador de Marillac wrote that Katherine Howard was thought to be pregnant, and if so there would soon be preparations for her coronation. Either the pregnancy story was wishful thinking, the queen by then having been married eight months, or there was a miscarriage. In May, after ten months of marriage, she arranged her first meetings with her stepchildren, first with 7-year-old Lady Elizabeth, to whom she gave some little presents of jewellery, and then persuaded Henry to accompany her on a visit to Prince Edward, who was living with Lady Mary at Waltham Holy Cross. Mary was subsequently allowed to return to live at court which, according to Chapuys, 'the Queen has countenanced with a good grace'.

So, all appeared to be settling down well. Later in that month, though, there is a sign that possibly something was not quite right. Ambassador Chapuys informed Mary of Hungary he had heard 'from a good source':

> ... that this queen being some days ago rather sad and thoughtful, and the King wishing to know the cause, she declared to him that it was all owing to some rumour or other afloat that he (the King) was about to take back Anne de Cleves as his wife. To which the King replied that she was wrong to believe such things.

According to 'the good source', the king, in a statement hardly designed to alleviate a young woman's insecurities, had assured Katherine that if he did marry again it would never be with Anne. Chapuys was known for his gossiping and for sometimes reporting events before he had the full or corroborated facts, but in this case, even if his information was questionable, his assessment of the character of Henry VIII was spot on. The ambassador wrote he tended to believe that, whatever the circumstances, Anne of Cleves would never make a comeback 'because of the King's natural condition, which is never to feel affection for a person he has once loved and then abandoned'.[15]

The day after Chapuys wrote his letter, Margaret Pole was informed she had only hours to live. Over Easter 1541 there were the beginnings of another rebellion in Yorkshire and unfortunately for the countess some of her relatives were involved. Never having been sure from the beginning of her incarceration of what she was accused, she seemed not to be able to take in what was being said and went to her horrific death at the hands of an inexperienced executioner still having had no proper charges read. It was a private execution with few witnesses and as the word spread there was disbelief among Londoners; she was old, one of her sons was executed already, another was a broken man, a teenage grandson was still in the Tower, her son the Cardinal was banished abroad, and from her prison cell she could have had little influence on the latest northern uprising in the Wakefield area.

The following day, 29 May, the stunned French ambassador wrote that:

> ... the countess of Saalberi, [Salisbury] mother of Cardinal Pol [Pole] and the late lord Montagu, was yesterday morning, about 7 o'clock, beheaded in a corner of the Tower, in presence of so few people that until evening the truth was still doubted. It was the more difficult to believe as she had been long prisoner, was of noble lineage, above 80 years old, and had [already] been punished by the loss of one son and banishment of the other, and the total ruin of her House.[16]

He was mistaken as to her age, but at 67 she was old for the times. The secret nature of the execution with so few witnesses present and the ineptitude of the executioner who had to take more than one blow, led to the now entrenched rumour that, although she was being hacked to pieces, the old lady had enough life left in her to try to run from her killer, which seems not to have been the case. The new clothes had hardly had time to be worn, but since the Tudors were great recyclers would doubtless find their way into that vast store of clothing, jewellery and household goods, much of it confiscated, which came under the aegis of the department of the Royal Wardrobe, to be followed not too far into the future by those recently made for Lord Lisle.

1. Elizabeth (Talbot) Mowbray, the last Mowbray Duchess of Norfolk, with Elizabeth (Tilney) Howard, Countess of Surrey, grandmother of both Anne Boleyn and Katherine Howard. (Courtesy of Long Melford Church, Suffolk. © Marilyn Roberts)

2. Memorial commemorating lives lost on both sides at Flodden, 1513, looking south towards Branxton Hill. (© The Remembering Flodden Project)

3. Old photograph of what survives of Framlingham Castle, Suffolk. The incredible funeral procession of Thomas Howard, the second Howard Duke of Norfolk, departed from here in 1524. (Author's collection, courtesy of Margaret Bell)

4. Thomas Howard, third Howard Duke of Norfolk, uncle of both Anne Boleyn and Katherine Howard. Hans Holbein the Younger, painted in 1539 when the duke was 66. (Royal Collection Trust / © His Majesty King Charles III 2024)

5. The Humber Bridge, linking North Lincolnshire (foreground) and Yorkshire on the north bank, lies approximately where Robert Aske made the 1¼ mile ferry crossing in October 1536. (© Marilyn Roberts)

6. Romsey Abbey, Hampshire, was dissolved in 1539. Henry VIII sold its church to the town for £100 in 1544. (© Marilyn Roberts)

7. Lambeth House [Palace] 1647, by Wenceslaus Holler, detail. The church where Duchess Agnes, her daughter Katherine Bridgewater and her stepdaughter Elizabeth Boleyn were interred can just be seen above the trees to the right of the palace's Morton Gate, while Norfolk House lies to the right of the church, between the trees. The landing stage from where Agnes was rowed into captivity can be seen. (Courtesy of the Metropolitan Museum of Art Harris Brisbane Dick Fund, 1917. Public Domain)

8. 2023, the same location from Lambeth Bridge; the buildings on the right are where Norfolk House stood and the modern landing stage is in much the same place. (© Marilyn Roberts)

9. Gainsborough Old Hall, south façade. Duchess Agnes's house would have been in this style. (© Marilyn Roberts)

10. Foundations of the north façade of Norfolk House now lie beneath the Novotel and part of Palace View Apartments, Lambeth Road, SE1 7LS, formerly The King's Highway. (© Marilyn Roberts)

11. Artist's reconstruction of the detail on Duchess Agnes's tomb brass, Church of St Mary at Lambeth. (© Shaun Clark, Whisker Hills Pottery)

12. *Portrait of a Young Woman*, workshop of Holbein the Younger c.1540, believed by some to be Katherine Howard, but by no means certain. (Courtesy of the Metropolitan Museum of Art, New York, the Julius Bache Collection, 1949)

13. Henry VIII in his mid-forties, after Holbein. (Author's Collection, Public Domain)

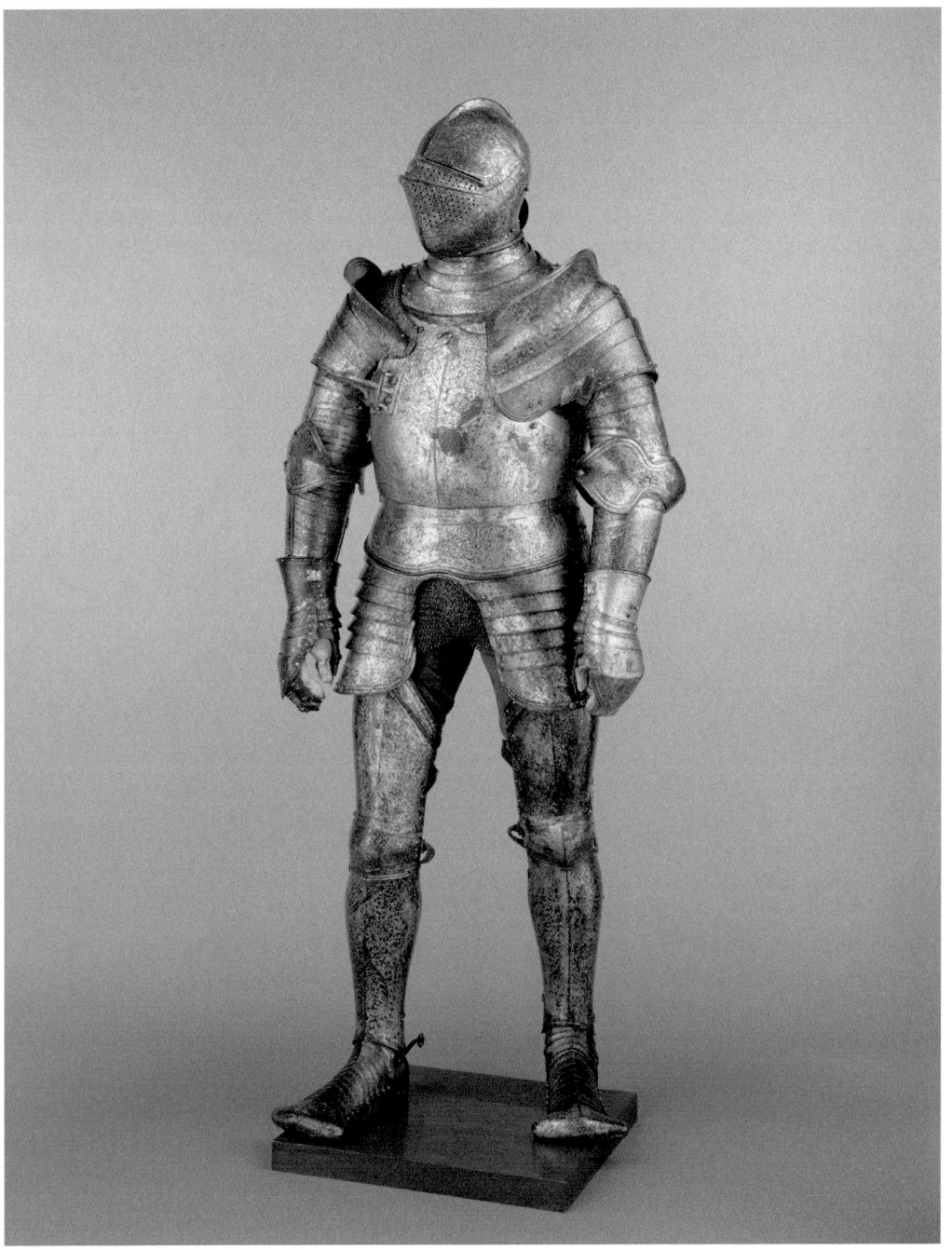

14. Suit of armour of Henry VIII, designed by Holbein the Younger, made at the Royal Workshops in Greenwich in 1527 and comprising steel, gold, copper alloys and leather. The height of 6-foot one inch and the pair of shapely long legs, of which he was justifiably proud, show that in the early years of his passion for Anne Boleyn, the 36-year-old king was a fine figure of a man. (Courtesy Metropolitan Museum of Art, Purchase, William H. Riley Gift and Rogers Fund 1919. Public Domain)

15. Field Armour of Henry VIII worn at the siege of Boulogne in 1544, two years after Katherine Howard's death, reveals the king to have lost his youthful figure. Italian, steel, gold, textile, leather. (Courtesy Metropolitan Museum of Art, Harris Brisbane Dick Fund, 1932. Public Domain)

16. Mannequin of Katherine Howard wearing a recreation of the cloth of silver dress she wore at Lincoln; created by costumier Pauline Loven of Crow's Eye Productions. (http://www.periodcostume.co.uk/a-gown-for-queen-catherine-howard/ Photo © Marilyn Roberts)

17. Lincoln Cathedral where Henry and Katherine knelt at the Great West Door (centre) in August 1541. (© Marilyn Roberts)

18. Lincoln Cathedral Great West Door, detail. Alas Katherine, in her shimmering cloth of silver gown, appears to have paid no attention to the depiction of the perils of fornication and later that day met Culpeper in secret. (© Marilyn Roberts)

19. Ruins of the Bishops' Palace, Lincoln, with the cathedral behind; in Katherine's time the latter still had its spires and was the tallest building in the world. (© Marilyn Roberts)

20. The Alnwick Tower, Bishops' Palace, Lincoln, a possible location for Katherine's trysts with Culpeper. (© Marilyn Roberts)

*Above*: 21. Pontefract Castle in the seventeenth century, it was here Katherine Howard's former lover Francis Dereham turned up in August 1541, adding to her already very complicated domestic situation. (Taken from *The History and Legacy of Old Castles and Abbeys*, J. Dicks, London, 1850. Public Domain)

*Right*: 22. On the left, the retrospective arms of Edward the Confessor; on the right, the arms of Thomas of Brotherton with a difference. (A silver label, showing a 'difference' is a horizontal band with three downward points lying across the shield to distinguish the holder from the head of the family and show position in the hierarchy.) (*A Complete Guide to Heraldry*, Fox-Davies, Arthur George, 1909)

23. Henry Howard, Earl of Surrey, engraving after Holbein; Lodge, 1835. (Public Domain)

24. Sir Thomas Wriothesley, later Lord Chancellor and Earl of Southampton aged 30, 1535, Holbein the Younger. In 1541 he interrogated witnesses to Katherine Howard's behaviour and in 1547 passed the death sentence on her cousin the Earl of Surrey. (Courtesy of the Metropolitan Museum of Art, New York, Rogers Fund 1925. Public Domain)

## Chapter 18

# Faces from the Past

When Katherine Howard became queen some of her old acquaintances reappeared, seeking favours and positions in her household. This was not unusual: the Howards would look after their own kith and kin and retainers, which was no more than any noble family would have done in similar circumstances. Joan Bulmer, formerly Joan Ackworth, who had been the original object of Francis Dereham's attention at Norfolk House, was now married, not too happily it would seem, and living in York, according to Brenan and Statham, 'No doubt ... abundantly tired of Yorkshire, and the sight of endless Catholic corpses rotting from the trees'.[1]

Joan's letter from York, written sixteen days before Katherine's marriage, shows that although plans were supposedly secret, in some quarters it was already anticipated, and writing from a distance of 200 miles away Joan seems confident her old roommate will become queen in the near future. Hoping for a position at court, she wrote she had heard that God had led King Henry to discover Anne of Cleves had already made a pre-contract with someone else before she married him, so he was about to divorce her and grant Katherine the honour of becoming his wife. Joan thought that her husband would have to let her go to London if Katherine sent for her, as he would not dare challenge a request from the future queen, and she hoped her old friend had not forgotten her.[2]

There is no way of knowing whether the letter was a hint to Katherine to take care of her or Joan Bulmer would have plenty to tell, or whether she was just a bored young woman expressing hopes of escaping what was proving to be a disappointing new life. It is usually taken for granted that Katherine did take her into her service, but it is not conclusive. Although Joan appears in documentation as being among those later questioned about Katherine's life while residing with Duchess Agnes, and was committed to the Tower, she has no specific post-Norfolk House job-description at court, whereas their old roommate Katherine Tilney had. Instead, Joan is recorded as 'young Bulmer's wife', does not appear on the list of the queen's household, and was questioned only about Katherine's behaviour before her marriage, whereas Tilney was also questioned several times about what she knew of her life since.[3]

Some historians see the queen's old bedfellows Francis Dereham and Katherine Tilney being taken into her service as a bribe to keep them quiet about what they knew of her dubious past, and it is certain that nobody knew more about that than those two. Both Tilney and Dereham were related to the Howards, but whereas Katherine Tilney would have been a welcome familiar face in the private royal apartments, Dereham certainly had the potential to be a massive problem for the queen, and his reappearance in her life was much more complicated than Tilney's presence. When Katherine Howard left Norfolk House to go to court, she may or may not already at some stage have promised to marry him. He maintained she had.

After a relatively short period of being separated from her in the autumn of 1539, Dereham heard rumours that Mistress Katherine was being pursued by a gentleman of the court, Master Thomas Culpeper, a young man of the king's privy chamber, whom gossips were predicting she would marry. If he had been biding his time at Norfolk House in the expectation that Katherine would eventually come back and officially marry him, or he was merely still harbouring slim hopes, it is not surprising that Dereham made his way to court to confront her about his rival. She told him it was none of his business, 'What should you trouble me therewith, for you know I will not have you; and if you heard such reports, you know more than I do know'.[4] The situation was probably brought to a conclusion when it became obvious that the king was eyeing Katherine, leaving her other suitors with no choice but to back off.[5]

His world turned upside down, the usually arrogant and forthright Dereham found himself lovesick, humiliated and defeated and sought permission to leave the duchess's service, but was refused. Reasons for the refusal suggested by authors include her fondness for him and sense of obligation to him as his kinswoman – the same reasons some writers have given for not having dismissed him for unacceptable behaviour with the women in her care. Dereham then decided to leave of his own accord, after going once more to court to tell Katherine he was going away, but refusing to say where, and asking her to take care of £100 of his savings, which she could keep if he failed to return.

In the months following his departure from Norfolk House, Francis Dereham made his living as a merchant of sorts in Ireland, but in his absence his beloved Katherine had suddenly become so far out of his league that the chances of having even a platonic friendship with her were unlikely. The term 'merchant' covered a multitude of activities and it could have been because the authorities in Ireland were seeking to quiz him about his various businesses that he returned to London.

It was probably late in October 1540, three months after Katherine's marriage, that he reacquainted himself with Duchess Agnes at Norfolk House, hoping she could pull strings to secure him a place at court.[6] For the duchess this request from Francis Dereham could have been quite a blow, even though she appears at this stage still not to have realised the full nature of his former relationship with her step-granddaughter. Should he be warned off or have his wish granted? What were the Howards going to do about Dereham?

The member of the family most likely to strike fear into him should he try blackmail tactics on Agnes would have been the third duke, but he was away in the North and, despite all he has been accused of in the centuries since, appears to have had little to do with either Norfolk House or Chesworth and had no idea of what had gone on there, so it would have seemed wiser to continue keeping him in ignorance. Agnes knew that a hot head like Francis was not a person who could be depended upon to act with caution; she also knew that when he ran away he had left some of his possessions in a trunk at Norfolk House which probably included a set of love ballads he had written about Katherine, and possibly other incriminating papers.

The duchess therefore looked for support to her son Lord William and daughter Lady Bridgewater. Nothing would have appeared suspicious when Lord William turned up at court, probably in November, with Dereham in his retinue, introducing him as the Duchess of Norfolk's former Gentleman Usher. Later Katherine would say 'My lady of Norfolk hath desired me to be good to him, and so I will'.[7]

It has been said that Dereham was appointed the queen's secretary but this seems unlikely, for at least two reasons. Firstly, it is doubtful he possessed either the qualifications or experience required of a secretary to the queen. There are no records of a salary being paid to him at this time nor does he appear to have had *bouche of court*, that is, the board and lodging, stabling and four servants to which a queen's secretary would have been entitled. Secondly, the queen in her short time as consort is known to have had two established courtiers as her secretary, one Thomas Derby and a John Huttoft.[8]

It is difficult to surmise what it was that Dereham really wanted. He was a man who might yet find himself in a difficult situation through his racy past witnessed by others, which in the current circumstances would have been wise to conceal, but seems not to have foreseen the obvious dangers. No doubt Duchess Agnes would have considered taking him back into her household, if only to keep an eye on him, but he was aiming higher. He had no hopes of becoming Katherine's husband, now or ever, and surely was not expecting to become her lover again. However, a position at court could, if he played his cards right, set him on the road to a comfortable and interesting life and a good marriage with someone else, both of which he might have felt he was owed for his personal loss.

With the benefit of hindsight we can see that for Katherine Howard all could never have ended well, for when a secret is known by a number of people it is a secret no more, and it will be but a matter of time before it bursts out into the open, which Katherine's did at the end of October 1541. As she and Henry were making their way south after four months on the Northern Progress, Mary Hall, who as Mary Lascelles had tried to warn off Henry Manox, revealed to her brother the perilous details about the queen's previous love life.

Mary had since married and was living quietly in the country, and when pressed by her brother John to tell him why she was not going to seek a position in the queen's household, said she would rather not be involved with Katherine, who had led a scandalous 'light' life at Chesworth and Lambeth and proceeded to tell him that Henry Manox the music teacher knew of 'private marks' on the queen's body, and worse, she 'had lain with Dereham a hundred nights'.

Not the 'shiftless hanger-on of the Howards' as he has been portrayed,[9] John Lascelles came from a good Nottinghamshire family and was a courtier who had been trained in the Law. Well aware of the terms of the 1534 Treasons Act, his sister's news put him in something of a quandary: if he did not disclose such outrageous information about the queen's past he could thereby become an accessory and if found out face charges of misprision of treason – the failure to report to the appropriate authorities the knowledge of a crime against the king planned, or already committed, by another party. At this stage, though, Katherine's misdemeanour was a sin rather than a crime, but Lascelles decided it was better to err on the side of caution. Questioning the queen's good character was a risky business, so he decided to seek an audience with the Archbishop of Canterbury who was acting together with Lord Chancellor Audley and Edward Seymour, now Earl of Hertford, as regent for Henry during his absence on the progress.

We must pause here to lift the veil of time a little in order to glimpse what might have been a hidden agenda, bearing in mind that John Lascelles was a passionate religious reformer who had been in the service of Thomas Cromwell through 1538–39. Seeking even greater religious reform, he saw the traditionalists Bishop Gardiner and Norfolk as standing in the way, and in September 1540 had advised his impatient comrades to bide their time and let the two men be the instrument of their own downfall, '... [they should] not to be too rash or quick in maintaining the scripture, for if we would let alone and suffer [allow] a little time they would (I doubt not) overthrow them selves'.[10]

Katherine, being a Howard, young, and recently arrived at court as she was, would have had powerful enemies from the outset without ever having struck a verbal blow. Unlike her cousin Anne Boleyn, she was not a particular advocate for either side of the religious divide. True, the Howards were, and still are today, staunch Roman Catholic by persuasion, but the third duke could happily stretch his conscience far enough to keep himself, and his widespread assets, safe, while neither Duchess Agnes nor her daughter Katherine Bridgewater, who were constants in the teenage Katherine Howard's development, were noted religious dissenters, and as queen consort Katherine left little or no impression on either politics or religion. Nevertheless, the downfall of the Howard queen and the stigma that would attach to her family must have been an interesting prospect for Lascelles, who, however, failed to follow his own advice. He did see the ruin of Katherine Howard, but proved to be the impatient and over-zealous reformer and was burned at the stake the year before Henry VIII died.[11]

After advising the other two regents of Mary Hall's revelations, Thomas Cranmer came to the conclusion that the king must be told, but had only a relatively short breathing space in which to summon his courage before the royal party arrived home from the Northern Progress.

## Chapter 19

# The Northern Progress

The Northern Progress which took the king, queen and much of the court away from the Capital for four months had set out on 30 June 1541, eleven months after Katherine Howard's wedding. High-profile companions of political necessity included the dukes of Norfolk and Suffolk with various members of the Council; some foreign ambassadors were invited along and Henry's daughter the Lady (Princess) Mary was also in attendance.

The summer progress was an annual event; apart from enabling the king to show himself to the people, it conveniently took him and his court out of an overheated, smelly and disease-ridden Capital into the fresh country air. Here, he and his vast entourage would live at one or other of his many homes and also accept free board and lodging for weeks on end in the mansions of the nobility and some of the more affluent local worthies. In 1541 the size of the endeavour hinted there was more to this particular excursion than that; de Marillac concluded, correctly, that Henry was nervous after the recent disturbances in the North:

> Everyone here knows that the King today commences his progress, which extends as far as York. He will not return to this town [London] until the end of October; as appears by a memorandum of the places he will pass, the sojourn he will make there, and the provisions necessary: an order rendered necessary by the company, which may number 4,000 or 5,000 horse, whereas ordinarily he takes only 1,000. As the thing is new, nothing else is talked of. More than 200 tents are carried, artillery is sent by sea and river to within ten miles of York, and the great horses are taken as if it were a question of war; all because the King, during his reign, has never visited these places, where, for his first entry and for the danger of the daily rebellions, he wishes to be well accompanied by men of these parts in whom he has more trust.[1]

Ever since the Pilgrimage of Grace, the Duke of Norfolk, whose administrative and military experience in the northern shires was greater than anyone else's, had been trying to persuade Henry to make the effort to visit the area in the hope of healing the savage wounds that still existed between the Crown and the people of the north over the vicious reprisals.[2]

When he finally set out it was a few months short of the fifth anniversary of the outbreak of the uprising in Lincolnshire and only weeks since the new pockets of unrest in the Wakefield area of Yorkshire. Obviously Henry thought it was time to remind these errant northerners, or the 'rude commons' as he had described them, of who was in charge. On the other hand, the royal tour had to be in part a charm offensive as well, for, as Norfolk would have been well aware, the king still held onto his younger self's dream of subjugating France, and if he decided to make one final effort he needed to be sure the northern counties would put up resistance in the event of the Scots swarming over the border as they had in 1513. There were also hopes of a meeting in York with James V of Scotland.

The weather was atrocious at the beginning of the progress, leaving the dirt roads, poor at the best of times, in a perilous state, much to the annoyance of the royal travellers and their retinue more accustomed to the smooth and speedy river journeys along the Thames on their luxurious private barges. As the party comprised hundreds of individuals with their cartloads of baggage as well as their horses and carriages, added to which were the 4000 soldiers travelling with them, an enormous glutinous trail of churned up mud was created for upwards of 200 miles. In the early stages the queen was taken ill, and but for the mind-blowing expense already laid out, the king, already disenchanted with life north of the comforts of Windsor, would have abandoned the venture.

During this royal progress Henry intended to make an unforgettable and spectacular impression of might, power and wealth, so no expense was spared. And where better to do that than at Lincoln, the city he so despised? Nothing had come of his threat to set up a permanent garrison there but the local officials who had known the ill-fated Thomas Moigne and witnessed his poor body being torn apart in public in 1537 while he still lived and breathed would have been under no illusions. This was not merely a goodwill visit, but rather a requirement for them to be intimidated, chastened, grovelling and to hand over expensive presents.[3]

The Lincoln visit began on 9 August. Queen Katherine, we learn, at the main events played her part to perfection. As always, she presented herself well and was the epitome of charm and good manners in public. Attired initially in scarlet velvet then changing into cloth of silver (Henry reserved the cloth of gold for himself) and smothered in precious jewels, she would have cut a splendid, sparkling little figure as the sun beat down outside the great cathedral. It was a day which, had her mind not been preoccupied with other things, should have been one of the greatest experiences of her young life. However, whether her mind was wandering or not, in the eyes of observers and her adoring husband she was the perfect wife and queen consort and even managed to charm the citizens by securing pardons for two convicted felons, one a Helen Page, *alias* Clerk, of Kedby (Keadby) in the north of Lincolnshire.[4]

Lincoln Cathedral is a magnificent edifice standing close to the castle. Begun in 1072, only six years after the Norman Conquest, at the top of a hill continuously occupied from pre-Roman times, it can be seen from miles away across the flat Lincolnshire landscape. When Katherine and Henry visited, all three of its towers still had their spires, the central tower with its spire reputedly reaching a height of 525 feet (160 metres), making it the tallest building in the world at the time, surpassing even the Great Pyramid at Giza until the spire collapsed in 1548.

Even today articles and TV documentaries occasionally claim that in 1541 the royal party stayed at the castle nearby, and that it was there Katherine Howard committed some of the incredibly foolish acts that would cost her her life, but this is not so. Henry VIII visited the castle to inspect it, and Katherine did behave with incredible recklessness while in the city, but that was a few hundred yards away at the Bishops' Palace beside the cathedral, where they were lodged for the duration of the visit.[5]

As the royal party arrived at the cathedral's Great West Door, the king and queen found stools and cushions covered with cloth of gold waiting for them on a rich carpet. They knelt (a challenge for Henry?) and the Bishop of Lincoln took up the crucifixes that were lying on the cushions and presented them to the royal couple to kiss, after which they went into the cathedral to pray, passing the tomb of Henry's ancestor Katherine Swynford and her daughter Joan Beaufort. That done, before retiring to their quarters for the night, the king and queen and leading members of their entourage partook of a great feast, courtesy of their esteemed host.[6]

However, for all its vast size and astonishing beauty, parts of Lincoln Cathedral carry a message that would have been loud and clear in Tudor times: deviate from the laws of God and you shall regret it. As the king and queen knelt on the cushions, did their eyes register the carvings in the stone around the great doorway of the souls in Hell who had committed what were referred to as lewd acts, and two figures, possibly Adam and Eve, being tormented by a serpent biting their private parts? Maybe Henry's thoughts were elsewhere, on the cataclysmic religious changes he had brought about and the blood he continued to shed, or probably they were not, but Queen Katherine ought to have taken note and kept those warning images firmly in her mind before going ahead with her secret assignation already arranged for that night at the Bishops' Palace.

From Lincoln the royal party departed for Gainsborough where they are believed to have stayed at the home of Lord Burgh, Katherine Parr's first father-in-law and former Chamberlain to Anne Boleyn, although by then he had moved to his second wife's home in Suffolk, thence, via appalling roads, to the royal manor and chase of Hatfield in Yorkshire where Henry and his guests had a wonderful time slaughtering thousands of creatures.[7] Their next stop was the great castle at Pontefract, the vast royal stronghold forever associated with the demise of Richard II in 1400 and the 1483 executions without trial of Anthony Woodville, his nephew Richard Grey, respectively uncle and half-brother of the boy king Edward V, together with his elderly tutor Thomas Vaughan on the orders of the future Richard III. A betting man might have said that if an ill-omen was going to appear to Katherine Howard on the Northern Progress it would happen here. And on 25 August it did, when none other than Francis Dereham presented himself at the castle gatehouse.

Whether the queen's former lover had been hanging around the court for several months or so in the hope of being given a proper job is unknown, but at this stage it appears to have been necessary for Katherine to take him officially into her household. This was a dangerous situation, but perhaps all might have been well if only Dereham had not been such an arrogant fool and had fully understood that the Norfolk House days, where he seems to have got away with doing more or less anything he pleased, were long gone. This was the court of the king and, incredibly, Katherine Howard was now the queen, and a former servant of the Duchess of Norfolk needed to know his place. Was he now given a post of responsibility within the queen's household? Or was he, as was claimed later, a general factotum with occasional access to his old love's private apartments?

Sadly, being the man he was, rather than lying low until he had the measure of the situation, Dereham immediately managed to draw attention to himself, leading people to question where on earth he had sprung from. In a very short time eyebrows were raised at his insolence towards his superiors and, what was worse, he boasted of a long-term close friendship with the young queen. 'Go to Mr. Johns, and tell him I was of the Queen's Council before he knew her and shall be when she hath forgotten him', he bragged with a clever play on words when a messenger was sent from a high official to ask just what he thought he was doing taking his supper with the senior members of Katherine's household and deliberately dawdling over it when everyone else had left the table.[8]

Life for Queen Katherine was becoming far too complicated. As well as her husband, she now had a former lover and a former roommate who knew all her secrets living under the same roof. She was also becoming estranged from her staff, including Lady Baynton, her own half-sister, through her secretive behaviour with Jane Rochford, also a member of the queen's household, and widow of her cousin, the late George Boleyn.

In mid-September, after spending time in Hull which must have brought back memories to Norfolk of his satisfaction of seeing Sir Robert Constable hanging in chains there, and a short stay at Cawood, the location of Wolsey's old palace, the king and his vast entourage arrived in York, where, one would hope, the rotting remains of Robert Aske had been removed from Clifford's Tower. The locals were every bit as cowed and humiliated as their counterparts at Lincoln had been, and similarly handed over pots full of gold coins as a peace offering. The royal party and the most important of their retinue stayed at the former Abbot's House of St Mary's Abbey, recently renamed the King's Manor, which had hastily undergone extensive alterations following the dissolution of the monasteries.[9]

De Marillac wrote that throughout the summer months in excess of 1200 men had worked to prepare the premises for the royal visit, and commented on the endless cartloads of valuables, gold plate, furniture, tapestries and fine food and wine arriving from London. When royalty and the nobility travelled between their various residences they took a large part of the contents of their home with them, from the cutlery to the tapestries and beds, religious paraphernalia and, in the monarch's case, a throne would also be necessary.

The ambassador thought the volume of goods being transported on this progress excessive, even for Henry, and concluded that if it was a massive display of wealth being assembled to impress James V of Scotland, it was a waste of time, effort and money, predicting as the September nights began to draw in, and correctly as it turned out, that he had no intention of showing. A meeting with James and his wife would have been very interesting on a personal level for Henry, since the Scottish queen consort was the former Mary of Guise, the princess he had fallen for only weeks after the death of Jane Seymour, but had yet to meet.

The ambassador was more inclined to go along with the rumour it was all being done in preparation for Katherine to be crowned in York Minster in an attempt to acknowledge that the errant and wild North did have a place in the king's scheme of things, and probably a sign she was pregnant. He was both right and wrong in his predictions: King James did fail to turn up, but Katherine failed to be crowned, nor was she pregnant.[10]

The return journey south began on 25 September and was expected to take about a month. After a few further overnight stays in Yorkshire the party crossed the Humber to Barrow Haven, three miles east of where the unfortunate Robert Aske had done in the autumn of 1536. The itinerary through the north of Lincolnshire took in Thornton Abbey, suppressed on 12 December 1539, although none of the buildings can have been despoiled immediately, for Henry and Katherine are believed to have stayed there overnight.[11]

At various stages of the journey nobles began leaving the retinue to return to their own estates. On 12 October de Marillac sent news to Francis I that the Duke of Norfolk left the progress while in Lincolnshire, presumably intending to take some leave from court and head home to sort out his own affairs in Norfolk and Suffolk. He also sent news the duke had told him Lord William Howard, whom the ambassador had predicted was not suitable for an ambassadorial post, was to be recalled from France and would be replaced for the time being with a secretary of the Council named William Paget.[12]

Further stages in the journey south for those remaining in the party included a second stay at Grimsthorpe Castle in Lincolnshire, the home of the king's best friend Charles Brandon, Duke of Suffolk, also honoured with his presence on the outward leg, and Collyweston, the former home of his grandmother Margaret Beaufort. They were welcomed at Chenies Manor in Buckinghamshire, the home of the Lord Admiral, Lord Russell on 24 October, where the Privy Council met the next day, and it was here that Katherine was reunited with yet another face from her past.[13] Whether Alice Wilkes now lived nearby and had requested the meeting or Katherine had expressed the wish to see her again is not certain, but Katherine Tilney and Francis Dereham were sent to bring her to the queen. Since the Norfolk House days she had married, and was now Alice Restwold.[14] Apparently pleased to see her old bedfellow, the queen gave her valuable gifts of jewellery and clothes and made a fuss of her.[15]

It was now more than two years since Alice had confided to Mary Lascelles her embarrassment at Katherine and Dereham's efforts between the sheets in the maidens' chamber and had requested to be allocated a different bed. Meanwhile, at about the same time Mary Hall was well and truly letting the cat out of the bag in her conversation with her brother, and back at Hampton Court Archbishop Cranmer was racking his brains as to how he might break the awful news to the king when he came home.

On a short stopover at Windsor Castle Henry learned that his sister Margaret, the dowager queen of Scotland, had died following a stroke. By the time the royal party was almost back at Hampton Court news came that Prince Edward was suffering from a quartan fever, an attack of malaria where the symptoms recurred every fourth day, so serious he might die. The child survived, but it was a timely reminder for Henry, now turned 50, that after 15 months of marriage to Katherine Howard there was no sign of a baby. However, upon his return to Hampton Court the king was, apparently, a very happy man counting his blessings by giving thanks to God on All Saints' Day, 1 November, for his good life with his wife, which he trusted would continue. This was the final time they would ever see one another. On All Souls' Day, 2 November, he would again attend Mass, but without his wife, and this is when Cranmer grasped the nettle and informed him of what John Lascelles had revealed.

Unable to gather enough courage to stand in front of the king and utter the words in person, the archbishop did what Manox had done in Lambeth: he left a letter on his pew and Henry appeared to laugh off the accusations. Nevertheless, the two men Mary (Lascelles) Hall had named as Katherine Howard's former paramours were to be picked up for questioning, if only to clear the queen's good name. Alas for all concerned, it would turn out to be nowhere near that simple.

If Henry VIII, who did almost anything he liked, had told Cranmer to ignore the accusations, treat them as malicious rumour and arrange for the intimidation of anybody who spoke out of turn, it would have been done. That Katherine Howard, if left in ignorance of the gossip about her old life, would have continued to become inextricably enmeshed in her increasingly intense relationship with one of her husband's favourite servants, seems highly likely.

# Chapter 20

# A Time of Reckoning

Having read the letter Cranmer had left him and appearing to brush it off as mere gossip, the king met the archbishop, Audley, Hertford and a small group of his closest councillors in secret. William Fitzwilliam, Earl of Southampton, Sir Thomas Wriothesley, Sir Anthony Browne and the Lord Admiral John Russell were tasked with seeking out and interviewing potential witnesses; once they had reported to him, Henry would decide if and how to proceed.

On Saturday 5 November, possibly earlier, interviewed by Southampton, John Lascelles stood by what he claimed to have heard from his sister Mary Hall. The earl then went into the county of Sussex to interview Mary. All was to be kept as low key as possible, so when he and a companion arrived at the house they told her husband they were on a hunting trip and seeking a short rest. Once Mary had been put in the picture she confirmed her brother's story, divulging that when she tried to warn off Henry Manox at Horsham he had coarsely retaliated, leaving nothing to the imagination, by bragging about his erotic fumblings with Katherine Howard. She then went on to detail the goings on in the maidens' chamber at Lambeth and how it used to be locked for the night and the keys brought to the duchess in her own chamber. Mary, as a chamberer to the duchess, also sometimes slept in the old lady's private rooms and Mistress Katherine asked her to steal the keys for her – which she admitted she did – or sometimes Katherine would steal them herself.

Mary said she had never told 'my lady of Norfolk', Lord William or his wife or anyone except her own brother. She did believe, though, that the old porter [John] Walsheman, Grooms of the Chamber John Baynet and Richard Faver, 'and Margery, my lady's chamberer, can tell much', adding the golden nugget that Alice Wilkes, who was Katherine's bedfellow, was so embarrassed when Dereham got into the bed with them that she was desperate to get a different bed share with someone else. Mary had told Alice to 'Let her alone, for [if] she hold on as she begins we shall hear she will be nought within a while'.[1]

In Lambeth, also on November 5, Henry Manox, questioned by Wriothesley and Cranmer, quickly confirmed what Southampton had heard already from John Lascelles. Yes, he had entered the Duchess's service 'five years past' (1536) at Horsham when he and one Barnes were appointed to teach the queen, then Mistress Katherine Howard, to play the virginals. He and Katherine fell in love, he claimed, and the old lady of Norfolk had lashed out when she found them embracing and told them never to be alone together again.

He admitted he had been jealous of Dereham after the household moved to Lambeth, and with the help of his fellow musician had written the anonymous letter to Duchess Agnes which was left on her pew in St Mary's Church. Manox claimed that Katherine, suspecting he was the letter's author, stole it from the duchess's chamber as she slept, Dereham copied it, Katherine returned the original, and a slanging-match ensued between her lovers, when Dereham, accompanied by Lord William, went to the house of Manox and his wife and challenged him.[2]

He named others who would corroborate his evidence: Joan Bulmer, then Ackworth, who was sometimes Katherine's bedfellow and had also entertained Dereham before he turned his attention to her; Dorothy Dawby, then a chamberer with the duchess, who carried messages and tokens for him and brought Katherine's to him in return; Katherine Tilney, 'now chamberer with the Queen'; Edward Waldegrave, now 'servant to my lord Prince'; Mary (Lascelles) Hall and Malyn Tylney, the widow of Duchess Agnes's brother Sir Philip Tilney, 'can speak of the misrule between Deram and Mrs. Katherine'.[3] The fact that Manox recommended that Mary Hall might be helpful suggests he did not realise she was one of the sources of the information that had led to his interrogation.

Manox, seen as not being a suitable candidate for these dormitory frolics, seems to have known a lot about them, or could refer Wriothesley to people who did. Was it guesswork on his part, or insider information, possibly from Dereham's so-called friend Edward Waldegrave, another regular visitor to the maidens' chamber? Or had there actually been more informed gossip in the neighbourhood about the goings-on in the duchess's house than is generally thought? And to what extent could Barnes the musician have been relied upon to keep what he knew to himself?

Manox went on to enlighten his interrogators as to how he had loved Katherine before Dereham ever came on the scene, but she had made no bones about telling him they could never marry. In desperation he had asked her for certain very intimate favours, and Katherine had obliged but always refused sexual intercourse. He agreed he had arranged a secret meeting in the duchess's chapel, 'my lady's chapel chamber', at the Horsham house. According to the musician, not only did the young lady turn up as arranged but also allowed him to go a lot further than he had anticipated, allowing him to feel 'the secret parts' of her body.

If Henry Manox was interrogated again the documentation has been lost. His behaviour towards and lack of respect for the girl he had once thought he loved was distasteful but he would prove to be the small fry in this unfolding tale, always denying having had 'full carnal knowledge' of her, and kept his life, despite Katherine having allowed him to 'feel more than was convenient'.[4]

November 5 was a busy day for Sir Thomas Wriothesley, for he then went to the Tower to examine Francis Dereham. Being in the queen's service he would have been easy to find and had possibly been picked up two days earlier on the pretext of having been involved in piracy when in Ireland. Whether or not he was sent to the Tower immediately, he must have had an idea there was more to it than that, which doubtless terrified him. Like Manox, once Dereham started talking there was no stopping him and he readily confessed to 'lying in bed by her in doublet and hosen divers [many] times and six or seven times in naked bed with her' at Norfolk House. He agreed that Katherine had taken him into her service since her marriage and he had on occasion been in her private rooms where she had given him £3 for hose, while on another occasion had told him 'take heed what words you speak', and once had given him £10.[5]

Dereham seems to have confessed very readily, considering it was the honour of the future queen of England he stood accused of having compromised. Perhaps he reasoned that he had committed no crime, since Katherine had been a single woman at the time of their lovemaking, even pre-contracted to him, if he is to be believed, and that co-operation with his interrogators would bring leniency. How can a man be so dreadfully mistaken?

So, within only three days of opening Cranmer's letter, what Katherine's apparently adoring husband had initially hoped was fabricated and malicious gossip was fast appearing to be the awful truth, corroborated by four of the story's main characters, who could readily provide names of witnesses. Now Cranmer, Southampton and Wriothesley had the daunting task of returning to Hampton Court to face Henry with evidence of his young wife's sordid past.

Later that day Cranmer and his team of investigators set out for the king what was known. News later leaked that he listened intently, seeming calm, but then suddenly burst into floods of tears.[6] The Dereham connection dealt a double blow: Henry, who had probably never heard of him, on learning he was now employed by Katherine immediately surmised, as did others, that she had taken him into her service to take up where they had left off at Norfolk House, although there is no evidence that was the case. Late at night messengers were sent to the dukes of Norfolk and Suffolk instructing them to come to Hampton Court.

Duchess Agnes had realised early on that with all the extra activity at Lambeth Palace there was something serious afoot and had soon sent a messenger named Andrew Pewson to Hampton Court, ostensibly to buy wood, where he learnt from a servant of Queen Katherine's Master of the Horse that Francis Dereham was thought to be under arrest. Like other members of Katherine's household, the servant might have believed the piracy story rumours, although there must have been others who would have had an idea of what was really unfolding.

Later her employee Robert Damport would reveal that when Pewson brought back the news, Agnes had Dereham's trunk broken into and removed several items, which she took to her private rooms. Rather naïvely, she did so in front of witnesses. Not only were Robert Damport and Dunn, who broke the lock on the trunk, present, but also her chaplain, Father Borough, and her elderly servant, William Ashby, who a few days later was sent to the Duke of Norfolk with some of the papers. Questioned later whether Agnes had destroyed any items, nobody knew for sure.

There had been meetings at different locations in an attempt to throw the curious off the scent, but the duchess learned her stepson Norfolk was at Lambeth Palace and sent Damport to seek him out on Saturday night and invite him to sleep at Norfolk House because it was too late to go home. She hoped a full stomach and a warm bed might loosen his tongue but he was much too cunning to fall for that and politely refused, saying he had to go to the king, which was true. It is noteworthy that although the survival of a noble family sometimes depended on members advising and protecting each other, the duke, who by then probably had been made aware his niece was in desperate trouble and what that could mean for Agnes, did nothing to warn her, although in fairness to him he was in a very awkward position.

On the morning of Sunday 6 November King Henry quietly removed himself to a meeting with advisors in fields surrounding Hampton Court on the pretext of a hunting trip. Norfolk having been summoned was confirmation that something was gravely wrong, as one of his servants had recently died of plague and he had been ordered to stay away from court for two weeks.[7] At dusk, late afternoon, Henry was ferried to London in an anonymous vessel for a meeting with various advisors lasting until four or five in the morning.[8]

For those who guessed that the king was the passenger in the barge, speculation must have been intense. If Henry himself was secretly on the move late in the day something very serious was afoot. Upon hearing rumours Chapuys thought negotiations with France over a marriage between Lady Mary and the Duke of Orléans might have reached a crucial stage, while Ambassador de Marillac speculated there might be urgent trouble in Ireland, a Scottish invasion was imminent or even that there could have been a discovery of embezzlement on a massive scale.[9]

Katherine last saw Henry at the service on All Saints Day; the clean break, giving the accused woman no opportunity to explain herself, was ever Henry's style. She had been told to keep to her rooms, but had not yet been informed of his departure, so the story that she ran screaming hysterically down the corridors at Hampton Court in an attempt to speak with her husband is a myth. Agnes Strickland's colourful account of Katherine's crazed attempts to plead with him is not backed up by references other than that the information is 'according to the historical traditions of Hampton Court'. She has the wretched queen realising Henry might be at prayer in the chapel, so escapes from her room only to be dragged back struggling violently, her pitiful screams heard by all. Her next attempt is quite ingenious: she does escape from her chamber 'through the low door in the alcove at the bed's head, into the back stairs lobby and, though instantly pursued, reached the foot of the private stair, called the maid of honour's stair', but, once again, is foiled.[10]

Monarchs and their wives lived under the same roof but kept different households; this, coupled with huge demands on Henry's time meant there would be some days when Katherine did not see him at all. In fact later under questioning she recalled that at six o'clock in the evening the king would send Sir Thomas Heneage to tell her what he had been doing all day, so not seeing him for a couple of days would not have unduly disturbed her at first.[11] But this time it was different, with five days gone since she last saw him, and no updates from Heneage, Katherine Howard was already as good as under arrest and the countdown to the end of her life had begun.

After the king had left Hampton Court, Lord Chancellor Audley, the Bishop of Winchester, Cranmer and Norfolk remained to interrogate Katherine about her past, confronting her with the claim she might have been pre-contracted to Dereham, and thus a bigamist, but in the familiarity of her own apartments she was able to keep reasonably calm and denied everything. Cranmer thought he had a better chance of persuading her to talk on a one-to-one basis.

In an undated letter to the king, but written on 6 or 7 November, Cranmer revealed that his plan at first had been to 'exaggerate her demerits', that is, unnerve the queen by lecturing her on how wicked she had been and what serious trouble she was in, then to explain where she stood regarding the law and justice, and finally to tell her her husband intended to be merciful. By the time he saw her, however, she was sobbing and in such a hysterical state he had to leave her to calm down. On his return her servants warned him she was much the same and he wrote to her husband that her state would have 'pitied any man's heart to see'.[12] He had therefore reversed tactics and began by assuring her that Henry intended to be merciful which, after another outburst, calmed her enough for her to begin to talk to him.

There were three known confessions of Katherine Howard: the first is now lost; the original draft of the second was lost in a fire in the eighteenth century but had been recorded in 1679 in Lord Herbert of Cherbury's, *Life and Raigne of King Henry the Eighth*; a third, dated 7 November, which takes the form of a letter to Henry, goes some way to contradicting the second.

The second confession of Queen Katherine Howard is a rather sad piece of work, giving a few glimpses of what her easy but mundane life at Lambeth was like, with Katherine herself coming across in some ways as a naïve and rather ordinary sort of girl. This had not been a studious, multilingual teenager with her nose stuck in a book for much of the day as Lady Jane Grey and Princess Elizabeth would be at her age. Like Manox and Dereham she too poured out everything she remembered, made a good few denials, but also gave a lot away.

Parts of this second confession are often quoted piecemeal, so it is not always obvious they came from the accused, and consequently should be read as a whole, as it shows her memory of events was good and helps to put the major points into context. Apart from a few anomalies such as saying she gave Dereham money at the beginning of the Northern Progress, when actually it was already several weeks underway before he turned up at Pontefract, it seems to be a fairly honest account recalling events from her past.

It is long. If the questions put to the queen were based on evidence already taken from others, more people than are now known about could have been questioned already and had contributed to the accumulating evidence in some detail. It is known for example that a Roger Cotes who worked for the duchess was interviewed by Wriothesley as early as 4 November, and there could have been others whose testimonies taken towards the beginning of the investigation are now lost.[13]

Katherine agreed that at Norfolk House Dereham had many times asked her to marry him, but insisted that had never been her intention, nor had she said 'I love you with all my heart'. She confessed to 'carnal knowledge, *as I did before*' that is in the previous confession to Cranmer, now lost:

> As for carnal knowledge, I confess as I did before, that diverse times he hath lain with me, sometime in his doublet and hose, and two or three times naked: but not so naked that he had nothing upon him,

> for he had always at least his doublet, and as I do think, his hose also, but I mean naked where his hose were put down. And diverse times he would bring wine, strawberries, apples, and other things to make good cheer, after my lady was gone to bed.[14]

Shortly after Cranmer had concluded his questioning and left, Sir Edward Baynton, her brother-in-law, sent word Katherine had fallen into in a fresh state of panic. Having realised how much she had compromised herself, she began to deny what she had said and wanted to see the archbishop again immediately.

The third confession, made some hours later, is quite different from the second. Katherine throws all the blame for her misdemeanours on others and goes so far as to claim Dereham 'procured me to his vicious purpose', although she does not elaborate on the 'many persuasions' he had used to achieve that, and whether or not they had been menacing and she had actually been raped.

In her previous confession she had admitted to 'carnal knowledge' but, crucially, at no point had suggested she was forced to have sex with Dereham against her wishes. Cranmer had written down her previous confession himself, but, apart from the preamble, the words seem to be Katherine's own, whereas the language and structure of the third confession are more formal, perhaps indicating that he helped her organise it into the form of a letter to Henry. Frequently this version of events is quoted as the only version of what she claimed had happened and the other is not quoted in detail, but both need to be seriously considered, and in the right order.

This third confession, which survives, consists of three parts. In the first Katherine confesses her faults without going into any great detail, beginning with:

> I, your Grace's most sorrowful subject and most vile wretch in the world, not worthy to make any recommendation unto your most excellent Majesty, do only make my most humble submission and confession of my faults.

In the third part, begging the king's forgiveness, she claims to have kept her past a secret because she was so anxious to come to court and had been 'blinded by the desire of worldly glory' and asks him to take into account the 'subtle persuasions' of young men and the ignorance and frailness of young women, and to understand that she intended 'to be faithful and true unto your Majesty ever after'.

It is in the middle section that she accuses both Manox and Dereham of abusing her, although admits she should not have allowed it:

> First, at the flattering and fair persuasions of Manox, being but a young girl, I suffered [allowed] him a sundry times to handle and touch the secret parts of my body which neither became me with honesty to permit, nor him to require. Also, Francis Dereham by many persuasions procured me to his vicious purpose, and obtained first to lie upon my bed with his doublet and hose, and after within

the bed, and finally he lay with me naked, and used me in such sort as a man doth his wife, many and sundry times, and our company ended almost a year before the King's Majesty was married to my Lady Anne of Cleves and continued not past one quarter of a year, or a little above.[15]

Although she had been young and in a very difficult situation when Manox pursued her, Katherine Howard had been chastised by her guardian, and so had he, leaving her in no doubt that such behaviour was frowned upon. She was past her mid-teens when Dereham used to turn up 'to make good cheer' in the maidens' chamber and in her previous, more spontaneous, confession she had not expressed any fear of him. Naturally Cranmer was not convinced she was being entirely truthful and the messenger carrying the letter of confession to Henry was also furnished with a separate report that said the archbishop had more to tell him about the confession when they next met in private, in which he tells him that Katherine revealed she had not sought Dereham's affections, but instead what 'he dyd unto her was of his importure forcement and in a maner violente rather than of her free consent and wil'.[16]

As early as 8 November Hampton Court was placed under guard, and on the king's orders the Privy Council was already making plans for Katherine's household to be broken up and for her to be moved to the dissolved Syon Abbey. Cranmer was not officially informed of those arrangements until Friday 11 November:

> The King, having considered their letters, wills them to persevere in attaining knowledge of the truth and to execute his pleasure before signified to them; foreseeing that they take not from the Queen her privy keys till they have done all the rest. She is to be removed to Syon House, and there lodged moderately, as her life has deserved, without any cloth of estate, with a chamber for Mr. Baynton and the rest to dine in, and two for her own use, and with a mean number of servants, as in a book herewith. She shall have four gentlewomen and two chamberers at her choice, save that my lady Baynton [her half-sister Isabel] shall be one, whose husband shall have the government of the whole house.[17]

The Lady Mary, with some of Katherine's servants, was to move temporarily to the home of her brother Prince Edward. Two of the queen's 'Great Ladies', Lady Margaret Douglas and Norfolk's daughter the Duchess of Richmond, would be sent to the duke's house at Kenninghall in Norfolk, while the maids of honour, with the exception of Anne Basset, were to go home to their friends or families. Anne's stepfather, Lord Lisle, was still in the Tower and her mother Honor Lisle was going through a nervous breakdown, so Henry decided he would provide for the young lady himself.

Cranmer was also informed that the next day, Saturday the 12th, the Lord Chancellor would assemble the full Council and declare to them 'the abominable demeanour of the Queen without mentioning any pre-contract which might serve for her defence, but only to show the King's just cause of indignation'. On Sunday those who knew the full story so far were to inform the ladies, gentlewomen, and gentlemen of Katherine's household and declare to them the whole matter, omitting all mention of pre-contract and emphasising Katherine's awful behaviour and how shamefully poor Henry had been deceived by her.[18]

The ambassadors Chapuys and de Marillac have to be admired for being so good at their job, part of which involved infiltrating the court for information. Not only did they have good networks of contacts, they were remarkably quick off the mark. Chapuys was writing to the Queen of Hungary as early as Thursday, 10 November about all that had happened thus far, and already had the extra details, not released to Cranmer until the following day, of the Privy Council intending to dismiss the queen's staff, seal coffers at Hampton Court and guard the doors. According to him the queen's brother, Charles Howard, was now forbidden access to the king's privy chamber.

The king, he relates, pretends Katherine was betrothed to Dereham which would invalidate his own marriage to her. Chapuys thought this might be rather convenient for Henry, as ongoing circumstances indicated he perhaps needed to reconnect politically with the Duke of Cleves and would be prepared to remarry Anne. This was absolutely the last thing the Queen of Hungary and her nephew Charles V needed to hear and the ambassador vowed to do all in his power to prevent it.[19] Then the final nail was hammered into Katherine Howard's coffin when the unbelievable news broke of yet another liaison, this time with 'a young Gentleman of the King's Privy Chamber named Colpepre'.[20]

# Chapter 21

# Master Thomas Culpeper

As far as is known, Thomas Culpeper had no connection with Norfolk House or Duchess Agnes, and only came into Katherine Howard's life after she left home. He was reasonably well-born and, judging from one of his conversations he claimed having had with Katherine at the Bishops' Palace in Lincoln about his other women friends, was an attractive, affable and popular ladies' man.[1]

When 18-year-old Katherine Howard arrived at court as a trainee maid of honour in 1539 Culpeper was probably in his mid-to-late twenties, trying to work his way up towards a title, and as such would not have been a bad catch for a girl with impressive genealogy but few material assets. In November 1541 Francis Dereham, incarcerated in the Tower and accused of rekindling his previous relationship with Katherine, claimed it definitely was not so: she was involved with Culpeper, not him. The French ambassador, de Marillac, writing one of his long 'the story so far' letters to Francis I ten days later said Thomas had replaced a Mr Nourriz as a gentleman of the king's privy chamber, meaning the Henry Norris executed in 1536 for supposed inappropriate behaviour with Anne Boleyn.[2]

As his unusual surname suggests Thomas and Katherine were related, her mother having been Joyce Culpeper, but it was at some distance and they do not appear to have been acquainted before Katherine came to court, although Agnes Strickland wrote she had been reared by Thomas's father 'at Holingbourne, in the nursery'.[3] As his brother was also called Thomas, we should be cautious when told Culpeper was involved in a brutal rape of a park keeper's wife and the murder of the villager who tried to come to his victim's rescue, as it is unclear against which of the Thomas Culpepers the allegations were directed. However, gossip following the revelation of his association with Katherine concluded the rapist was her lover, who had been pardoned of the crimes because of his then closeness to the king. The rumour Katherine would marry Culpeper had caused Dereham such great anxiety he challenged her about it, but later Katherine would not confess to having promised herself in marriage to Thomas saying that those, like Dereham, who thought it was so 'know more than I do know'.[4]

The vivacious, tiny young woman and the irritable, limping, elderly giant with the leaking and foul-smelling leg ulcers that Henry VIII had become must have made an odd couple. Not at all the 'big wife' he had been searching for before he married Anne of Cleves, Katherine Howard was described as being very young and very small.[5] She would have been brought up to think of him almost as being not of this world, and more than likely could have been fond of him after a fashion owing to his kindness and outstanding generosity towards her.

Alas, Queen Katherine seems to have been neither mature nor bright enough to understand that, as long as Henry lived, the excitement of finding love's young dreams elsewhere must elude her. Nor must she be seen to be over-flirtatious, or to be paying any particular gentleman of the court more attention than was thought decent – a difficult scenario in an environment where 'courtly love' was an art form, as her cousin Anne Boleyn had found to her cost.

And so it could have been that for Katherine Howard, the novice courtier suddenly promoted to queen consort, who in many respects would have had little idea at the outset of what her position really involved, and was at least thirty years her unattractive lumbering husband's junior, the novelty of court life, and her remarkably exalted, but sometimes lonely, position therein, soon began to lose some of its sparkle.

In February 1541, before he was able to make his planned inspection of the south coast forts, Henry had fallen ill with a tertian fever, a type of malaria. The wounds doctors deliberately and continually kept open on one of his legs to allow the pus from his ulcers to drain closed up, which could prove deadly if it could not escape, as had almost happened five years earlier. It was during the latest bout that de Marillac thought the inevitable weight loss 'should rather have profited than hurt him, for he is very stout, but one of his legs, formerly opened and kept open to maintain his health, suddenly closed, to his great alarm, for, five or six years ago, in like case, he thought to have died'.[6]

Terrified and in great pain, Henry VIII did what he did best: blamed everybody else for his misfortunes. His advisers and ministers had let him down and were out to feather their own nests, he cried, and had persuaded him to execute Cromwell, the best servant he ever had (conveniently choosing to overlook that one word from him could have saved the man's life any time he chose). And as far as his ungrateful, whingeing subjects were concerned he was going to make them so poor and afraid that they would never again be able to make any sort of move against him.[7] For several days during the latest crisis the king was feeling so ill and was in such a black mood that he did not even want to be bothered with his wife, or perhaps did not want her to see him for the vulnerable and ailing man he really was.

Eventually the blockages were opened and the stinking pus released itself before it could kill him, but Henry's illness had knocked a great deal of his lately newfound stamina and enthusiasm for life out of him. Traditionally Shrove Tuesday was a feast day of merrymaking before Lent, but at Hampton Court all was strangely quiet – a miserable place with few friends around for a fun-loving young woman easily bored and being kept in the dark about what was really happening in the king's privy chamber.

However, it was not until Maundy Thursday, 14 April, well after her husband recovered and about a month after her triumphant entry into London, that the queen arranged to meet up with an old flame. Perhaps initially just simply needing attention and seeking congenial male company nearer her own age and of her own choosing, Katherine ordered one of the ladies of her privy chamber, Jane Boleyn, Viscountess Rochford, to send one Henry Webb, a messenger, to fetch Thomas Culpeper to her apartments where, away from prying eyes, she met him in a corridor.

If suitably chaperoned, the gentlemen of the king's privy chamber were allowed to socialise with the queen's ladies in her apartments, but this does not mean Katherine herself would have seen him on his own since her wedding. Their reunion did not go as well as she had hoped, however, for when she gifted Thomas a fine velvet cap and told him to hide it in his jacket, he quipped it was a pity she had not done it before she was married. The ill-mannered and flippant nature of his response indicates he was a confident individual who still saw her as a girl he once knew rather than as his sovereign's wife.

Katherine, who had always been the one chased by admirers, was offended to find Thomas not overwhelmed or falling over himself to be near her; it was a rare experience and she did not, for the time being, try to see him again. She seems to have been very attracted to Culpeper from the start though, and this was the second time he had hurt her. A few months later she would confess to him she had regretted playing hard to get when they first met in 1539, for when he seemed not to care and quickly moved on to someone else, she had cried in front of the other maids of honour who shared rooms with her.[8] Perhaps they did not meet again for two or three months after the disappointing reunion at Greenwich, although she must have been watching him, for when Thomas was taken ill she sent a servant named Morris with meals prepared in her own kitchens.

Queen Katherine needed to start thinking clearly about her position. Unusual as it was for a consort to be sending food to her husband's staff, this in itself could be seen as simply being an act of kindness, but people would not have forgotten there was once talk, and not so very long ago, that these two young and attractive people would marry.

At 20-years-old or thereabouts in 1541, even if life with the duchess had left her largely ignorant of the evils and cruelties of the world beyond Norfolk House, Katherine Howard must surely have had some idea of the fate of her predecessors Katherine of Aragon and Anne Boleyn, both of whom Henry had once loved so much. His almost sleight-of-hand dealings with her own former mistress, Anne of Cleves, had demonstrated wonderfully to Katherine and the world at large just how quickly, with what ease and for what little genuine reason Henry was willing and able to divest himself of a wife. Perhaps Katherine was over-confident, believing her husband to be so besotted by her youth and beauty she would be able to talk herself out of anything. If this was the case she was sadly mistaken. The fun and games of a young, single girl of little importance at Norfolk House was one thing, but when the wife of a man as dangerous as Henry VIII began stepping out of line, with one of his favourite minions no less, it was in a different league altogether.

As a Gentleman of the Privy Chamber, Culpeper was *au fait* with the state of the king's declining health. He was sometimes his bedfellow or 'son compagnion de lit', as Chapuys would later describe him, and would know better than most that Henry had potentially serious health issues.[9] Attracted to Katherine as Thomas undoubtedly was, there has been speculation over the ensuing centuries that essentially he was a self-serving schemer, thinking ahead to when the ailing monarch died and his wife became a very important and wealthy widow, perhaps even regent for her stepson. Apart from his duties of making sure that everything in the private apartments was running smoothly, as a close servant and companion when the king was off duty his was a position of the utmost trust, and Master Culpeper was definitely going to be included in the huge retinue due shortly to depart in June 1541 on the Northern Progress.

Where the romance between Queen Katherine and Thomas Culpeper was rekindled on that long journey is not certain, although under questioning later the chamberer, Katherine Tilney, admitted to feeling uneasy at Grimsthorpe Castle, the Lincolnshire house of Henry's friend Charles Brandon, when on the outward leg she was told to carry a message from the queen to Lady Rochford to see if she 'had the thing she had promised her'.[10] The Duke of Norfolk had been away inspecting the Borders when the progress first set out and eventually joined it at Grimsthorpe but seems not to have been in any great favour with his niece or spent any private time with her. At the city of Lincoln Mistress Tilney would find herself being drawn ever deeper into the subterfuge with Culpeper, which for someone in her position had the potential to be extremely dangerous.

After the successful presentation to the cowed citizens of Lincoln and the celebration of Mass at the Cathedral where the queen had impressed in her beautiful shimmering cloth of silver gown, there had followed a massive feast at their lodgings at the Bishops' Palace a few hundred yards away.[11] After such a busy and exciting day Queen Katherine's attendants were expecting her to retire relatively early, but instead, after dismissing most of them for the night, she took the small flight of private stairs to Lady Rochford's room on the floor above hers, in the full knowledge that the viscountess had been busy arranging for her to meet a friend that would lead to a different sort of excitement to round off a very successful day.

No matter where a queen consort was, day or night there would always be someone at her beck and call; if she wished to speak with a member of her household someone would go and fetch that person to her. It was unheard of for a queen to be going upstairs to the room of an attendant, even if she was a viscountess, and the bewildered chamberers Katherine Tilney and Margaret Morton, accompanied her to Jane Rochford's door but were then quickly dismissed without instructions about whether they were supposed to wait or retire.[12]

Lady Rochford had discovered that through a second door to her room she could reach the lower floors via the backstairs. The configuration of the Alnwick Tower, which still exists, suggests this could have been the location, although much of the bishop's other prestigious accommodation that has not survived cannot be ruled out. Somehow she got a message to Thomas Culpeper that Katherine wanted to see him that night. Just inside the door at the foot of the 'secret' stairs they waited for him in the dark. Even the best laid plans, however, have the potential to unravel, and the approach of a watchman who immediately noticed the door ajar surely frightened them. The man closed the door, locked it and fortunately was off the scene before Culpeper arrived, accompanied by a friend of many talents who immediately set about picking the lock to the lodgings of Henry VIII's wife.

Henry had a fixation about his security and travelled with his own locksmith, so it is likely the locks on his own rooms at Lincoln had been changed; whether he afforded the same security to his wife in this case is unknown. Likewise, no information survives as to whether the watchman reported the open door or whether the lock had been damaged and had to be replaced. An article written in 1910 points out that the lock would have been substantial and taken some time to pick, suggesting that the stairs could have led to a small concealed inner courtyard.[13]

Culpeper was a mature man who knew he had replaced the executed and innocent Henry Norris as one of the king's right-hand men, so his actions, in front of a witness, beggar belief. Likewise, those of the queen, one of whose predecessors, her own cousin no less, had been executed on fake and ludicrous 'evidence' of having committed adultery with five men, and of Jane Rochford, whose husband, one of the five falsely accused, had suffered the same fate. Even if Katherine was totally besotted with Culpeper, for all three of them, and Culpeper's mysterious friend, to have been so irresponsible in the light of what had gone before, is incredible.

The locations of some of Katherine Howard's secret liaisons with her various lovers were hardly the stuff of romantic fairy tales either. Under questioning both Margaret Benet and Joan Bulmer later deposed that at Norfolk House they had seen Dereham follow Katherine to the jakes, that is the lavatory, where they spent some time together.[14] In the Lincoln Bishops' Palace with Culpeper it was no different, for they went into Katherine's stool room, her private lavatory, which seems to have been at a lower level than the rest of her rooms, where Lady Rochford fell asleep as the other two talked of old times, with the queen speaking of her former admirers Manox and Dereham, while Thomas, not very gallantly, entertained her with the details of his latest conquest, Bess Harvey. Then, according to Culpeper when under questioning later, Katherine started flirting, claiming, 'If I listed [wanted to] I could bring you into as good a trade as Bray hath my Lord Parr in'.

Dorothy Bray, one of Katherine's maids of honour, was known to be having an affair with the unhappily married Thomas Parr, a younger brother of Katherine Parr, the then Lady Latimer. As queen, Katherine Howard was responsible for her women's welfare and behaviour and ought to have been discouraging that relationship instead of joking about it. When Culpeper replied that he thought Katherine was not that sort of girl she replied, according to him, 'Well, if I had tarried in the maidens' chamber I would have tried you.'[15]

Meanwhile, the two chamberers left hanging around outside Lady Rochford's room, unsure of what they were supposed to be doing, had retired to their beds, but in the early hours Margaret Morton was still awake wondering whether Katherine had left the upstairs room yet, so decided to take a look. Once back in bed she was able to confirm to Tilney that the queen had returned to her own room 'even now'; it was possibly as late as three in the morning.[16]

The next day, late in the evening, having performed her queen consort duties to perfection throughout the day with dignity, while at the same time adding a touch of glamour and youthful beauty to the proceedings, Katherine was eagerly anticipating another meeting with Thomas, again arranged through Lady Rochford. As before, Katherine Tilney was required to accompany her up the stairs and this time was ordered to sit outside the room with Jane Rochford's maid, putting her in a position that a few weeks later would cause huge trouble for her. Beyond the viscountess's 'secret' door there was a replay of the previous night, again in the insalubrious surroundings of the stool room, but this time, while Lady Rochford dozed in the shadows, the talk was of love, Katherine confessing she loved Thomas and he promising he loved her 'again above all other creatures'. When they finally parted Thomas kissed Katherine's hand.[17]

From Lincoln the party travelled to Gainsborough where they are believed to have stayed at Gainsborough Old Hall and from there took ferries across the River Trent en route to Scrooby in Nottinghamshire for a short stay, all of which in such a rural area must have been a great challenge for the locals, most of whom were living hand-to-mouth, when food was requisitioned for the visitors at a knock-down price. The roads were appalling at the best of times and after further heavy rain would be so bad after the baggage wagons that went ahead had used them that advanced parties were sent out to reconnoitre an alternative route for the immediate royal party.

On 18 August the progress arrived at the King's Manor and Chase at Hatfield, eight miles from Doncaster, where they stayed three days and were joined by prominent local guests in what was really a two-way exchange: Henry needing to win them over, they anxious to please him and put the horrors of the Pilgrimage of Grace behind them, although the Duke of Norfolk would not have forgotten his 1536 encounters with rebels nearby.

Ambassador de Marillac, who had been invited and had recently joined the progress, was pleasantly surprised by the level of luxury in 'the barbarous and mutinous provinces'.[18] The sojourn at Hatfield was a huge success, with tremendous slaughter of beasts, fish and water fowl, the hunters congratulating themselves on their skills although, as with royal hunting trips in exotic parts of the British Empire in later centuries, the creatures were driven so close the hunters could hardly miss, but Henry had enjoyed a thoroughly good time and shared some of the spoils with the local gentry.

The queen, it seems, had little taste for the hunt on this occasion and gave it a miss, but when the dashing Culpeper passed her window Katherine's longing, dreamy glances in the direction of handsome Thomas did not go unnoticed by Margaret Morton, who realised there might 'be love between them'.[19] Maybe it was at that point that the queen's secrecy, the late night meetings with Lady Rochford who was now her preferred companion, and Katherine's increasingly short temper with her other women she was keeping at a distance began to make sense.

Jane Rochford, née Parker, then in her mid-thirties, had weathered the Boleyn storm of 1536, and after her husband and sister-in-law's executions might have lived out her days quietly in comfort and financial security at Blickling Hall in Norfolk had she not opted for a return to court, the only life she had known since she first went there in about 1522. In 1526 she married George Boleyn, whose fortunes, like those of his family as a whole, were about to become bound-up with Henry VIII's infatuation with his sister, and in 1529 he was created Viscount Rochford. After his execution his widow was subsequently a Lady of the Privy Chamber to both Jane Seymour and Anne of Cleves, and was one of the ladies who explained to the innocent Anne that Henry saying 'Goodnight sweetheart' at bedtime and kissing her in the morning, was not sufficient to bring about a pregnancy.[20]

The distance from Hatfield in South Yorkshire to Pontefract is about twenty miles. Katherine Howard arrived inside the town's castle precincts on 23 August; Francis Dereham turned up two days later. Clearly by this stage of the Northern Progress Katherine would have been very stressed. She was a fairly recently married woman now lovesick for a young servant of her elderly husband, increasingly at loggerheads with her attendants and probably half-aware it could not be too long before people began to suspect something was awry, so the arrival of Dereham with his swagger and loose tongue was the last thing she needed. Nevertheless, once she had agreed to take him onto her staff he seems to have been left largely to his own devices while she continued in the pursuit of Culpeper.

Poor Katherine Tilney was again being sent backward and forward between the queen and Lady Rochford, with such peculiar verbal messages that she did not know how to pass them on, and Margaret Morton and her colleague, a Mistress Luffkyn, got the sharp end of the queen's tongue for following her to the viscountess's room, chastised to such an extent they feared they would be dismissed and replaced with Lady Rochford's maids.[21]

Thanks to Lady Rochford having surveyed their latest accommodation, Katherine is believed to have seen Thomas Culpeper at Pontefract when he had finished his duties in the privy chamber and the king had gone to bed. On one occasion Henry sent his messenger, Mr Dane, to Katherine's room but the door was bolted on the inside and, receiving no reply, he left; what he told the king, who probably had sent for her to spend the night with him, is not known.[22]

It seems that when Henry left Pontefract Castle to inspect the defences at Hull, Thomas Culpeper was in attendance but Katherine remained; they were back by the 15th and the king and his vast retinue arrived in York on 18 September. It was at the King's Manor in York the queen confessed to Thomas she had cried when he abandoned her for someone else in her early days at court.

# Chapter 22

# As Long as Life Endures

On 3 November 1541 a proclamation was made regarding the expansion of Hatfield Chase in Yorkshire. Henry had had such a good time there in August, and judging by his plans for its future might have been hoping one day to return, despite the distance from London. The first item on the agenda for further development of the royal hunting ground was to continue replenishing the red deer which had been slaughtered in such great numbers and then incorporate more local land, including some previously held by religious orders.[1]

However, at the time the proclamation was made Henry would still have been mulling over the contents of Cranmer's letter left on his pew the previous day, while those charged with investigating its veracity were already hard at work and getting remarkable results. Suddenly the king's world had been turned upside down when the allegations of his wife's pre-marital behaviour proved to be true, and nine days later, on November 12, she was about to be questioned again, on Dereham's revelation about her behaviour with a third man, this time after her marriage.

A large and intimidating delegation comprising Norfolk, Cranmer, Russell, Southampton, Sussex, Wriothesley, Hertford, Anthony Browne and other members of the Privy Council arrived at Hampton Court. In the earlier interrogations Katherine had been confronted with questions framed from information her inquisitors had already gleaned from others; in this latest case it would appear at first glance to have been solely from information extracted from Dereham, but that can hardly be so.

Katherine was questioned on the 12th, the same day he revealed the Culpeper connection by insisting he had not rekindled his relationship with her as she was involved with Thomas, but the questions put to her were very detailed, including events that happened before Francis had joined the royal party at Pontefract. There he had been the new boy, a swaggering and bad-mannered new boy at that, and it is hard to think anyone would readily have rushed to befriend him or share scurrilous gossip about the queen.

Nor had the details come from Culpeper himself, who was still a free man when the queen's inquisitors arrived, probably armed with testimonies, now lost, from person or persons who had been witness to Katherine's illicit assignations, who would include Katherine Tilney, Margaret Morton and Lady Rochford. If under questioning Dereham had been able to reveal Katherine and Culpeper's secret in any detail he must have learned of it from someone on the Northern Progress. With Lady Rochford he more than likely would have had little or no contact, Morton possibly, but he definitely knew Tilney from the days in the dormitory at Norfolk

House, but she, apparently, was not interviewed until the 13th. Another possibility is that the Council had already tracked down and questioned Tilney and others who had been on the progress but the documentation is now lost.

Queen Katherine now insisted under further questioning that she had started seeing Culpeper to stop Lady Rochford pestering her to do so, and admitted meeting him secretly at Lincoln, Pontefract and York. Later in the day Sir Ralph Sadler wrote to Cranmer and the other inquisitors that the king, having read their report, believed Katherine had more to tell, 'He desires them to essay again to get more from her, if her wits are such that they may do so without danger to her'.[2]

Culpeper is thought to have been out hawking when the queen was being questioned; how much he, as one of Henry's closest attendants, knew of the reason for the comings and goings at Hampton Court is uncertain. Arrested on the 12th, or possibly early on the 13th, he was a godsend for Katherine's accusers, completely blowing apart her heartfelt insistence in her confession letter to the king that she had mended her ways before her marriage and had always intended to be a good and faithful wife to him. Culpeper's fate was decided more or less immediately, more than two weeks before he was brought before a court. Under interrogation on Sunday 13th he said Katherine had made all the running, and although he came to her willingly it had been Lady Rochford who had 'provoked him much to love the queen'.[3]

Many questions remain unanswered as to just how Jane Rochford fits into the story of Katherine Howard. Was she in some way a poisonous and sinister force who led her young mistress astray for some peculiar self-gratification, or merely a go-between who had no option but to obey orders? Whichever, she was sucked into this most dangerous of liaisons as a facilitator and a third party who, should their secret meetings be discovered, could vouch for their innocence, and who, now that they had been found out, might even make a convenient scapegoat.

In the hands of his interrogators, Culpeper confessed to he and his companion picking the lock at Lincoln and to the meetings in the stool room, where he and the queen had talked about old times and his various love interests since he had stopped seeing her. It was now he revealed that Katherine had said that if she still lived at Norfolk House she would have 'tried him'. What is astonishing in the light of the 1534 Treasons Act, with which he must have been familiar, is he confessing that he had hoped, and expected, he and the king's wife would eventually become lovers. Even if Lady Rochford had been roped in as a witness to corroborate their claimed innocent behaviour, now it was all in vain: Thomas's declaration of intent was sufficient to condemn himself, and the queen, of treason under the provisions of the 1534 Act.

Katherine Tilney's first recorded interrogation was by Wriothesley on the 13th, although, as already said, she could have been questioned earlier. She related the meetings at Lincoln and how she had been sent to Lady Rochford with obscure messages and did not know 'how to utter them', similarly at Grimsthorpe Castle on the outward journey and again 'at Hampton Court lately', the last revelation indicating that the affair looked set to continue once the queen was back home.[4]

Meanwhile, Margaret Morton was confessing to Sir Anthony Browne of having noticed the loving glances at Hatfield, how she expected to be dismissed in favour of Lady Rochford's maids and how at Loddington [sic] she was going to and fro with messages and thought Lady Rochford was 'the principal occasion of her [the queen's] folly' and when the two were together at night the queen locked and bolted the door.[5]

The same day Jane Rochford, confronted with information received from the others, insisted she heard and saw nothing of what passed, for the queen was always at the other end of the room and Culpeper on the stairs, ready to slip away should anyone arrive. She confirmed that one night at Lincoln she and Katherine were at the back door at 11 o'clock waiting for Culpeper, when a watchman came with a light and closed and locked it. She thought Culpeper 'has known the Queen carnally', but did add later this was only her opinion based on the loving looks they exchanged.

Lady Jane, Viscountess Rochford was committed to the Tower, and three days later was 'seized with a fit of madness by which her brain is affected' so was put into the care of Lord Russell's wife at their house on the Strand, with the king's own doctors attending.[6] This was no munificent gesture on his part – according to the law as it stood at the time, in order to execute her she first had to be cured of her madness. No time had been wasted in confiscating the first of Lady Rochford's possessions – on 13th were taken seven items of plate, eleven items of apparel, a purse with £40 in it and some items of jewellery.[7]

Thomas Culpeper's goods were inventoried on 14th prior to confiscation, usually a sign that either the death penalty or life imprisonment was imminent. Having rooms at court, he appeared to have spent little time at his own properties and there was little of material interest among his goods and chattels there.[8] What was of enormous value, however, but not of a monetary kind, was a letter purportedly written to him by Katherine Howard, *after* her marriage to Henry VIII:

Master Culpeper,

I heartily recommend me unto you, praying you to send me word how that you do. It was showed me that you was sick, the which thing troubled me very much till such time that I hear from you praying you to send me word how that you do, for I never longed so much for a thing as I do to see you and to speak with you, the which I trust shall be shortly now. That which doth comfort me very much when I think of it, and when I think again that you shall depart from me again it makes my heart die to think what fortune I have that I cannot be always in your company. My trust is always in you that you will be as you have promised me, and in that hope I trust upon still, praying you that you will come when my Lady Rochford is here for then I shall be best at leisure to be at your commandment, thanking you for that you have promised me to be so good unto that poor fellow my man which is one of the griefs that I do feel to depart from him for then I do know no one that I dare trust to send to you, and therefore I pray you take him to be with you that I may sometime hear from you one thing. I pray you to give me a horse for my man for I had much ado to get one and therefore I pray send me one by him and in so doing I am as I said afor, and thus I take my leave of you, trusting to see you shortly again and I would you was with me now that you might see what pain I take in writing to you.

         Yours as long as life endures,

            Katheryn[9]

The actual date it was written is unknown, but the mention that he was ill could point either to the time before the Northern Progress when Katherine sent him meals, or when they were staying at York. It could be that they did make up after she was displeased with him at Greenwich, and he might have suffered a further bout of illness before the progress, but the reminiscing at Lincoln over old times suggests the first assignation in the stool room had been their first meeting of any duration since the spring. York seems a more probable place of writing as she is sorrowful he will be leaving her, which more than likely he did for a few days to accompany the king on his second visit to Hull.

 There seems to be little doubt Katherine was desperate to see Thomas, and other evidence indicates that, even if hers was not destined to be a forever love, she was definitely infatuated with him. In recent years, however, it has been suggested this is not necessarily a love letter, but was referring rather to some problem playing on her mind that she needed urgently to discuss with him. According to historian Retha Warnicke, Queen Katherine was afraid of what Culpeper knew of her relationship with Dereham and, far from being in love with him, was trying to appease an aggressive suitor who knew of her past.[10] Surely, though, this interpretation seems unlikely, for Culpeper, in threatening Henry VIII's young wife, would have been dicing with his own death.

 Culpeper's possible motive for keeping the letter that amounted to the queen's death warrant, and his own, is thought-provoking too: is it possible it had been kept as a treasured love letter, or, as Warnicke suggests, an investment for some future rainy day? Had he ever even seen the letter, or was it planted when his house was searched? The actual letter itself throws up some questions as well, for although it is still extant, in the absence of another signature, apart from that on her confessions, it is difficult to say whether Katherine wrote it or not. The presence of what appear to be two different styles and different colour inks would suggest that a personal assistant, an amanuensis, began the letter and then after the first sentence the queen continued it and signed 'yours as long as life endures', which might have been a declaration of devotion, or merely a flowery equivalent of today's 'yours sincerely', although perhaps it was unusual for a queen consort to be signing off thus.[11]

 Looking at Thomas Culpeper's testimony, his involvement with the queen had been more wishing and hoping, it would seem, than actually doing, but in the eyes of her husband, whose confidant and close companion he had been, it was bound to be interpreted as wishing his master would die and leave the way to Katherine clear for him – more than enough for a charge of treason to be brought. Also, his admission he had hoped, and believed, they would in the near future embark on a sexual relationship could be seen as putting the succession in jeopardy should the queen become pregnant by him, again an act of treason. Culpeper had successfully condemned himself to death, and probably Katherine too.

The story of Katherine Howard standing beside the executioner's block saying she would have wished to die Culpeper's wife rather than as a queen is no more than romantic fiction; none of the participants went to their deaths proclaiming their undying love. Instead, at some stage in the inquiry they all blamed each other, which added a rather sordid and pointless dimension to the so-called love story, although in his defence we have to say that no amount of persuasion would make Culpeper confess that his liaisons with Katherine after she became queen had, as yet, involved any physical contact other than touching her hand.[12]

As had previously been arranged, on November 14 Katherine was moved to two rooms at Syon with a skeleton staff under the supervision of her brother-in-law Sir Edward Baynton, now technically her jailor, who was to observe her closely and report all to the king. She was to be allowed six plain, dark velvet gowns and no trappings of queenship, although she still retained the title, but was not to be treated like a prisoner. Cranmer was instructed that before the queen's ladies were dispersed Lady Margaret Douglas was to be taken aside and given a good talking to, 'and afterwards you are to call Lady Margaret Douglas apart and show her how indiscreetly she has acted, first with Lord Thomas [Howard] and then with Charles Howard, and bid her beware the third time'.[13]

There must have been some sort of mutual magnetic attraction between Margaret Douglas and the younger men in the Howard clan, for in spite of being incarcerated in the Tower over her connections with Duchess Agnes's son Lord Thomas and he having died there, she was at the time of Katherine's arrest involved with Charles Howard, one of the queen's brothers. Charles and Katherine's father, Lord Edmund, and the late Lord Thomas were half-brothers, making Charles Howard Lord Thomas's half-nephew although the two were close in age. Henry returned to Hampton Court with some of his Council shortly after Katherine's departure for Syon, while others of his advisors remained in London to continue the interrogations. The king instructed Sir Ralph Sadler to take an inventory of the queen's jewels, which was a very bad sign. The list is phenomenal, considering how little time they had been married, and the descriptions reveal jewellery, clocks and books not only of outstanding value but also of exquisite workmanship.[14]

Aware that the nature of many of the charges against Anne Boleyn had been widely recognised as works of fiction, and that poor Margaret Pole was purported to have gone to the block still begging to be told what her crime had been, the king and his closest advisors, including Katherine's uncle, began to follow a path of greater openness as her case unfolded. On 14 November de Marillac wrote to Francis I that Norfolk had confirmed to him the queen was at the root of the current uproar, having had sexual encounters before her marriage and, as she had taken into her service a 'former lover called Durand [*sic*], probably since as well'. Katherine's uncle had spoken to the ambassador of her going out of her mind with fear, but de Marillac noted that the tears in Norfolk's eyes were for the king 'who loved her much', and for the trouble she and Anne Boleyn had brought to the House of Howard. De Marillac had begun his letter on the 13th but the next day saw Norfolk again, who told him the additional news that intensive questioning had revealed the behaviour with Culpeper when in the North. He added that the king was so grieved that he proposed never to take another wife.[15]

Questioning of witnesses continued on 15 November with one Andrew Maunsey, a servant of Duchess Agnes, revealing that about a year before she went to court he had three times seen Mistress Katherine in bed with Francis Dereham at Norfolk House. Katherine Tilney was also in the bed at the time and could confirm it, and he thought a laundrywoman named Besse might also be helpful. At first sight it is so very difficult to understand why he and the others did not report this sort of behaviour to a higher authority, unless, of course, Dereham *was* his immediate higher authority, and in any case how would a humble servant set about informing on the private life of the granddaughter of a duke?

Once again it was confirmed that the Dowager Agnes had been seen to strike Katherine for her loose behaviour, but now a new and very dangerous dimension was added, for according to Maunsey she had once said to someone looking for Dereham that he would more likely than not be found in Katherine Howard's chamber. Right from the start those questioned had been consistent in saying that the duchess would get very angry with Katherine and had indeed struck her on more than one occasion for her antics with Manox and Dereham, but what Maunsey now claimed she had said, about finding Dereham where he knew he should not have been, probably said in weary exasperation, would soon be repeated by others and turned into a vital piece of evidence against the old lady. The implication was that she had knowingly long been turning a blind eye to the indiscretions taking place under her roof and should have let the king know her step-granddaughter was damaged goods before he became too involved with her.[16]

At some stage the whole embarrassing story would have to be brought out into the open and local juries would need to deliver their verdicts, so on the 16th the Privy Council called up the Lord President of the Council of York and the Earl of Shrewsbury to appear at Doncaster on 24 November, and the earl of Rutland to preside at Lincoln the day before for the same purpose.[17] Chapuys appears to have been coming in second to de Marillac in the dash to send out news of the scandal, as it was not until the 19th he sent his 'compagnon de lit' letter about Culpeper to the Emperor Charles V. He had asked the Lord Privy Seal what the king meant to do in this case and was told that he would show more patience and mercy than many might think – more even than the queen's own relations wished, meaning Norfolk, 'who said, God knows why, that he wished the Queen was burned'.[18]

On 22 November de Marillac again related the whole story of Katherine's case, with added titbits such as Culpeper having from childhood been brought up in the king's chamber, and ordinarily shared his bed, 'and apparently wished to share the Queen's too', who from now on was 'to be named no longer queen, but only Katherine de Auvart [Howard]'. The ambassador also informed his master Francis I that, 'They have sent to Lincoln and other places where she was found with Culpeper, to have her solemnly judged, and Norfolk says she shall die, and especially because the king could not marry again while she lives'. Culpeper's estates had already been distributed, according to de Marillac, and he imprisoned in the Tower awaiting execution, even though he had not yet had his trial.[19] Writs of summons to the new Parliament due to sit on January 16 1542 were sent out on 23 November.

Katherine Tilney, examined as to whether the Dowager Duchess of Norfolk was privy to the familiarity between the queen and Dereham, thought the duchess knew only that 'there was love' between them, and the old lady had once found Dereham 'embracing Mrs. Katherine Howard in his arms and kissing her, and thereat was much offended and gave Dereham a blow, and also beat the Queen', and Joan Bulmer (then Ackworth) received a blow merely for being present and not having stopped them. But also according to Tilney, when someone was looking for Dereham the duchess had said, 'I warrant you if you seek him in Katherine Howard's chamber ye shall find him there'. She also revealed the duchess seemed not to have known Dereham had gone to Ireland, for one time when Katherine Howard came from court to visit her, the duchess asked whether she knew where he was, but she replied she did not.[20]

# Chapter 23

# The Fate of Dereham and Culpeper

December 1541 was a nightmare for Duchess Agnes. On the first day of the month the Privy Council requested Wriothesley to send those questions 'devised for the lady Dowager of Norfolk' for the king's approval.[1] Henry's persecution of the Howards for having kept him in ignorance of Katherine's behaviour before her marriage, and their encouraging her to take Dereham into her royal service since, was about to begin. But first he wanted to dispose of Dereham and Culpeper, who were brought to trial at London's Guildhall accused of treason the same day he requested to see what questions were to be put to the duchess.

Although a policy of openness was later adopted, it had been decreed when the news of the queen's misdemeanours first broke that the investigations would be carried out with the utmost secrecy, not only to contain the emerging scandal as long as possible but also to avoid potential witnesses getting together to fabricate or sanitise stories about her. Therefore, it was often the interrogators themselves, not secretaries, who wrote down the statements, at times in almost illegible handwriting.

The signatures of some of those interrogating and taking evidence strike fear into the reader of the documents, for among them were Sir Thomas Wriothesley and the newly involved Sir Richard Rich, neither man renowned for his gentle methods. Five years later religious martyr Anne Askew would be racked so badly under examination by these two, even though the racking of a woman was illegal, that she had to be carried on a chair to the stake to be burned to death at the same time as the reformer John Lascelles.[2]

Francis Dereham had been subjected to several bouts of torture but there is no record of his state of health as he stood before the Commissioners who included the Duke of Norfolk. The Lord Chancellor Audley put before Norfolk and the rest the findings from juries, all males of course in those days, from the counties where the unsavoury behaviour was claimed to have taken place, namely Yorkshire, Middlesex, Surrey, Kent, Lincolnshire and the cities of Lincoln and York.

The indictment from of the Doncaster jury, which had met on 24 November, delivered a long statement incorporating details of the sad story from start to finish, compiled after studying information given them that they had no opportunity and, given their recent past history with Henry VIII, probably no inclination, to question. They came to the conclusion:

> That Katherine, queen of England, formerly called Katherine Howard, late of Lambeth, Surrey, one of the daughters of Lord Edmund Howard, before the marriage between the King and her,

led an abominable, base, carnal, voluptuous, and vicious life, like a common harlot, with divers persons, as with Francis Derham of Lambeth and Henry Manok of Stretham... Also the said Queen, not satisfied with her vicious life aforesaid... at Pomfret [Pontefract], and at other times and places before and after, with Thomas Culpeper, late of London, one of the gentlemen of the King's privy chamber, falsely and traitorously held illicit meeting and conference to incite the said Culpeper to have carnal intercourse with her; and insinuated to him that she loved him above the King and all others.[3]

The rest of the juries returned similar verdicts but with some variations that show some lack of co-ordination of information – Middlesex for example alleging the offences to have been committed at Hampton Court and Westminster; Surrey jurors thought Oatlands Palace had been a secret meeting place; while the Kent jury alleged the offences to have been committed at Greenwich 'and elsewhere in Kent'.

The County of Lincoln jurors sitting at the castle in Lincoln included a John Candysshe (Candish), who had received the lands and buildings of the Carthusian monastery at Low Melwood near Epworth after the butchering and martyrdom of its prior Augustine Webster, and a Henry Portington of Sawcliffe, whose family had connections with the ill-fated Robert Aske. Here it was stated that alleged offences were committed at Gainsborough and 'elsewhere in Lincolnshire', which is possible since Katherine had been behaving strangely as early as the initial stay at Grimsthorpe Castle and is believed later to have stayed at Gainsborough Old Hall.[4]

The tradition the king and queen had separate bedrooms there because the room originally intended for them in the tower was too difficult for him to access via the spiral staircase is probably inaccurate, as protocol dictated that they would be given separate rooms. If Culpeper, on duty as a Gentlemen of the Privy Chamber, had a secret meeting with the queen at Gainsborough, and the lack of testimonies suggests he did not, he would have needed to be very resourceful to get past Henry and his attendants, as the only access to the tower appears to be through the ground floor room in which they were sleeping.[5]

The hearing at London's Guildhall was cut and dried in less than a day. The judgement on Culpeper and Dereham was that they were, '... to be taken back to the Tower and thence drawn through London to the gallows at Tyburn, and there hanged, cut down alive, disembowelled and (they still living) their bowels burnt, beheaded and quartered'.[6] However, after the trial they were to be kept alive a few more days for further 'questioning' pertaining to the role the Howards played. It is likely that the last few days of Francis Dereham's life would have been truly horrendous. As ever, Henry VIII's marital difficulties were music to the ears of his traditional enemies of course, with Francis I, despite his apparent sorrow, surely stifling a laugh as he wrote to de Marillac that he felt the grief of the king, his 'brother', as his own. Still, his 'good brother' should 'consider that the lightness of women cannot bind the honour of men, and that the shame is confined to those who commit the crime'.[7]

Writing back to his master a few days later, de Marillac said many people in London thought the publication of the 'foul details' of the case very strange, but that the intention was to prevent it being said afterwards that the accused were unjustly condemned. Another disturbing thing that Londoners were talking about was that during the proceedings Katherine's Uncle Norfolk, 'even in examining the prisoners, laughed as if he had cause to rejoice' at the defendants' impending doom, while the brothers of the queen and Culpeper rode about the town to show that they did not share the crimes of their relatives. However, the ambassador noted that since then Norfolk had gone back to his house, 'fifty leagues hence, which makes people think ill, and at least that his influence is much diminished'.[8]

It was under what was probably rather 'serious' questioning in the presence of Richard Rich on 2 and 3 December, Dereham's friend Robert Damport revealed that when the Duchess found out Dereham and Katherine 'were taken' (arrested) she thought it might be for something that had happened at Norfolk House but did not think the two would die for their behaviour as it had all happened before the girl had met her future husband, but said, 'I am sorry for the King, for he taketh the matter very heavily'. This was very damning as it confirmed, yet again, that Agnes knew her step-granddaughter was nowhere near as innocent as she was supposed to have been at the time of her marriage, but had chosen not to reveal it. She also feared, Damport claimed, that Katherine would be sent back home to her.

Agnes had told him of the letter left on her pew in St Mary's Church, saying, 'but I took it to be a warning for me to take heed between Hastings and .... [name missing]', which further confirmed she knew there were others involved in romantic liaisons at Norfolk House. It had been 'on Sunday after All Saints' Day last' that the duchess sent Damport 'to my lord of Norfolk, being at my lord of Canterbury's at Lambeth, to invite him to sleep at her house as it was too late to go home'.[9]

On 4 December Wriothesley and Southampton wrote requiring Sir Ralph Sadler to inform the king that they and Mr (Richard) Pollard 'went this day to my lady of Norfolk, as if [pretending] only to visit and comfort her'. They found she was not as sick as she had previously made out and was fit enough to go to the Lord Chancellor Audley's house, to which she was advised to agree, because he had some questions to ask her. 'At that she began to be very sick again, "even at the heart", as she said.'[10]

When they came for Agnes, 'my lady of Norfolk', where was she in that great house of hers with its imposing mullioned windows with their very expensive leaded-lights and its fashionable glossy diaper-patterning set into the red brickwork? What part of the Novotel on Lambeth Road now lies where her tapestry-hung walls and fine belongings were displayed? When had she last been for her stroll with her attendants in the grounds of what amounted to her private kingdom that was Norfolk House and its environs, or busied herself in the vast kitchens inspecting preparations for a feast?

Had she had sufficient stamina to check on the activities of the laundrywomen, including the mysterious Besse who apparently had knowledge of the younger Katherine's antics? How long was it since she had last overseen the making of preserves with fruit from her own extensive gardens and orchards, or brewed and distilled her famous concoctions for curing her ailing neighbours? Had she prayed in the Howard Chapel at the church across the way on this dreadful day Henry VIII's inquisitors took her away? Or was she, after a month of hearing of the persecution of others and fearfully awaiting her own turn, by now a mere shadow of her once-great self, and suddenly a frail and feeble old woman who truly was 'sick at heart'?

My Lady boarded her barge at Lambeth for the last time, well aware of the similar circumstances of her fellow elderly noblewoman Margaret Pole's detention, which had led to a long imprisonment in the Tower and ultimately to her execution. As soon as she passed Wriothesley's house, Crown official Richard Pollard left to put her Lambeth house in order; the same evening a Mr Peter set out to take charge of Chesworth House near Horsham. Wriothesley ominously added to his missive 'tomorrow morning they will examine her'.[11]

Based around statements already extracted from other witnesses, thirty-seven questions had been compiled to be put to the duchess. In what sort of way she did educate and bring up Mistress Katherine? What change of apparel did she give her yearly and what apparel and advice had she given the girl once she realised Henry was so besotted? Who had told her that 'the King's highness did cast a fantasy' to Katherine Howard the first time that ever his Grace saw her? What had she taken from Dereham's coffer (trunk) apart from the ballads to which she had confessed? Had she ever struck Mistress Katherine for her behaviour with Manox and Dereham? Had she rebuked Dereham? Had she asked her step-granddaughter to find him a position at court? Had she ever said he could be found in the future queen's chamber? Had she caught Dereham and Katherine kissing? Did she know anything about a pre-contract between them?[12]

On December 5 they began the questioning of the duchess, starting with what her steward William Ashby had revealed at his second interrogation by Richard Rich, in whose custody he was being held. Agnes was quizzed about breaking into Dereham's coffers and taking away all writings in them, and whether she had been afraid Alice Wilkes would tell Lord William of the familiarity between the queen and Dereham? Was it true she had she intended to send to Calais to warn her son Lord William of the developing situation? Agnes was then reminded that although she had said the queen ought not to die for offences committed before her marriage, she had nevertheless sent one of her grandsons, 'young Rhys', to Borough, her comptroller, for the book of statutes kept in the house in order to ascertain the possibility of a general pardon for those having inadvertently broken the law.[13] At the end of the day, after having intensively questioned Agnes at the Lord Chancellor's house, the Earl of Southampton sent word to the king, 'All things here proceed well; and surely for my lady of Norfolk such matter there groweth continually against her, whereby she hath so meshed and tangled herself that I think it will be hard for her to wind out again'.[14]

During other business of the day, word arrived for the Council that Damport had more to tell and requested to speak to someone, so Sir Richard Rich and Sir John Gage, the Constable of the Tower, were sent to him. He had suddenly remembered

Francis Dereham telling him that when Henry took a fancy to Katherine he, Dereham, finally accepted he had to let her go, but had added 'but an [if] he were dead, I am sure I might marry her'. The Council members were not altogether convinced Damport was telling the truth, as up to that point he 'would not do it for any torture he could be put to', that is, tell that his friend Dereham appeared to be wishing the king's death, so they intended to examine him, and Dereham, again later in the day.[15]

Robert Damport, like Dereham employed by Duchess Agnes, was not, as far as is known, connected with aiding or abetting Katherine Howard's association with either Manox or Culpeper and was undergoing torture because as Dereham's friend he knew about him and Katherine and might yet add to the accumulating evidence against the Howards in general. Like Dereham's, his torture was 'serious' with later rumours that his teeth were pulled.[16] When Damport requested to see a member of the Council, he had already been subjected to questioning on and off for nearly a month, part of that time in the Tower. It was four days since Dereham had been sentenced to death and for him there would be no reprieve; Damport might have been informed of his friend's fate in order to frighten him, and so decided to save his own skin and try for leniency by making up the story.

The duchess underwent questioning again all day on 6 December, but was still denying having 'any suspicion of evil' between her step-granddaughter and any gentlemen employed at Norfolk House, whereas Edward Waldegrave, also questioned, had apparently heard the old lady say several times that his friend Dereham would be found in the girls' dormitory, 'Where is Dereham? I am sure he is sleeping in the gentlewomen's chamber'. And she often 'sent to prove it and he was often found on one bed or another'. This seems very contrived, and is wonderful hypocrisy, coming as it does from Waldegrave, who was just as seedy as his friend, but, happily for him, his own dalliances in the dormitory had not been with a future queen.[17]

Unfortunately for Duchess Agnes, several members of her household continued to tell the same story: she had been aware of inappropriate behaviour and had shown her displeasure, but had failed to act forcefully enough or, better still, to dismiss Katherine's lover. The king was informed by the Council in London on 7th that, 'All yesterday, they examined the lady of Norfolk, who denied all knowledge of the abomination between the Queen and Dereham and pretended that she opened the coffers in order to send anything material to the King'.

They were not too concerned though, as by now they had 'sufficient testimony otherwise', and during the day had conferred with leading lawyers who thought, as did the Lord Chancellor (Audley) and Chancellor of Augmentations (Richard Rich), that misprision of treason was proved against the lady of Norfolk and her son Lord William, 'and that Lady Howard, Lady Bridgewater, Alice Wylkes, Katherine Tylney, Damport, Walgrave, Malyn Tylney, Mary Lasselles, [Joan] Bulmer, [William] Ashby, Anne Howard [a sister-in-law of Katherine] and Margaret Benet are in the same case'.[18] Margaret Benet was one of those who were especially helpful when questioned, for not only had she seen Manox follow Katherine to the jakes at Chesworth House, she also, 'through a hole in the door' at Lambeth, saw

Dereham lift Katherine's skirts and claimed also to have overheard them comparing methods of contraception.

The gentlemen in London were not yet done with their questioning though, and were planning to examine Lady Bridgewater, and also Bulmer and Wilkes at the Lord Privy Seal's house. The letter to the Council, in Wriothesley's hand, includes the signature of the Archbishop of Canterbury and ends with the chilling statement that Dereham 'cannot be brought to any piece of Damport's last confession' which would indicate he would not confess to having said he might marry Katherine if Henry died, therefore they 'would [wish to] know the King's pleasure touching the execution of him and Culpeper'.[19] On 6 December, Dereham had made an appeal for remission of some part of the extremity of his judgment, pleading for simple beheading rather than being hanged, drawn and quartered.[20]

The servant William Ashby, interrogated for the third time on 7 December, wearily related yet again how Agnes held a candle as she took from Dereham's trunk a notebook on how to play the lute, papers, which she told him were ballads, and a copy of the letter Manox had left on her church pew. She had told Ashby that she and Dereham had fallen out over it 'about the beginning of the King's progress' and she had 'commanded him out of her gates'. If true, this could help explain why Dereham suddenly turned up at Pontefract Castle a few weeks later. Ashby ended his confession, written in his own hand, by begging his inquisitors to leave him alone, 'I have opened to your Lordships as much as I know as to my ghostly father [confessor], and beg you to pity me, thus troubled in my old age through a wilful woman'.[21]

After reading the reports from Sir Anthony Browne and Sir Ralph Sadler, the king decided the duchess's actions in rifling through Dereham's belongings and not admitting to it for four days until her stepson Norfolk had been sent to search her house, had been an attempt to cover up treason and that she had known all along 'of the former naughty life between the Queen and Dereham'. She, Dereham and Damport should be 'seriously examined' again and her ladies questioned as to whether they saw her burning any letters. The duchess was not tortured, although that is what the euphemism 'seriously examined' usually meant. This same day, 7 December, Henry refused Francis Dereham's plea for his sentence to be commuted to simple beheading.[22] He had deflowered the future queen, which alone was bad enough, but he having been taken into her royal service suggested the sexual relationship continued, so he must face the full horror of the punishment, although there was no evidence it had.

Henry VIII, initially at Hampton Court with part of his Council and then at Oatlands Palace, was kept informed of all developments and personally issued orders throughout the investigations. Occasionally there were leaks, however: for example on 7th de Marillac, perhaps with a little artistic licence, wrote to Francis I of the king calling for a sword to slay Katherine, 'And finally he took to tears regretting his ill-luck in meeting with such ill-conditioned wives, and blaming his Council for this last mischief. The ministers have done their best to make him forget his grief'.[23] It was true that, according to protocol, after the break from Anne of Cleves the ministers had urged Henry to remarry, but he had already made his decision, so any blame for his poor choice of wife must lie entirely with him.

# Chapter 24

# The Sorrow of the Women

December 8 saw the king ordering Duchess Agnes, Lord William and the rest to be committed to the Tower for misprision of treason and their houses and goods put in safe keeping. Mary Hall, who had not sought to go into the queen's service and appeared genuinely sorry Henry had married her, was to be freed 'as an encouragement to others to reveal their cases'. 'As for Culpeper and Dereham, if the latter can tell no more, they are (with convenient warning to prepare their souls) to be executed.'[1]

Replying the next day, the Council members in London related the gist of their own mixed bag of events of 8 December. As to be expected, most of the details are bleak, but there is a small ray of humour, although the gentleman whose problem it was would have been far from amused. The Lieutenant of the Tower was in a quandary because he did not have enough suitable lodgings for so many high-class prisoners about to be delivered into his care, 'Mr Lieutenant says there are not rooms to lodge them all unless the King's and Queen's lodgings be taken'. He requested the king either to send his duplicate keys for the royal apartments or give permission to change the locks, 'or else signify whether the great personages may be committed to the Tower and the rest to other custodies until rooms may be prepared for them'. It is good to know that like many of we lesser mortals, Henry VIII was also guilty of having no idea of the whereabouts of his keys – he could not remember having had any and 'Mr. Lieutenant' was given permission to change the locks.[2]

In a significant new development, the duchess, still detained at the Lord Chancellor's house until the accommodation at the Tower was sorted, and probably only able to guess at what was happening on the outside, was to be examined as to where her money and treasure were. At that point she must surely have understood all too clearly the extreme gravity of her situation and what the charges against her were going to be. Afraid about her age and state of health and determined not to let her goods slip through their fingers, the Council in London wrote to the Council members with the king:

> As she is old and testy, and might take her committal to heart so as to endanger her life, [we are] ask[ing] whether to indict her and the others, which may be done in four or five days, whereby Parliament shall have better ground to confiscate their goods if any of them should chance to die before their attainder.[3]

In the case of attainder, if the accused died before being convicted their property could still be passed on to their families, whereas an already attainted person's possessions would automatically go to the Crown.

The inquisitors had been all day with Joan Bulmer and Alice Wilkes (now Restwold) but Lady Bridgewater had been hard going: 'Bridgewater shows herself [to be] her mother's daughter and will confess nothing'.[4] The Privy Council in London appointed a John Skinner to take an inventory of goods at Lord William's Reigate house; Wriothesley and Pollard to do the same at his Lambeth property and also at Norfolk House. Lady Bridgewater's houses in Kent and Southwark were also to be gone over. Lord William, now returned from France, was to be committed to the Tower. They determined that Culpeper and Dereham should be executed the next day, 10 December.[5]

Remembering the response to the shocking treatment of Margaret Pole, the king wrote to the Council in London that rather than rush through her attainder as they had suggested, he wanted the duchess to be seriously examined again, 'thinking it better to have her own confession, and that through her more may come to light'. He had received news at Oatlands that Lord William had had news that all his belongings were lost in the Channel crossing, but the king and the members of Council with him were not convinced and ordered an investigation. Henry gave instructions for the staff of the households of the accused to be discharged, with the servants receiving three months' wages, and the houses and goods left in safe custody.[6]

Writing from London the same day to Sir Ralph Sadler who was with the king, Wriothesley expressed his dislike for Lord William:

> Yesterday we committed Lord William and his wife and Anne Howard. Lord William stood as stiff as his mother. I did not much like his fashion. This day [I] go to my guests and the Duchess herself.
> I am now going to Lambeth, with Mr. Attorney and Mr. Pollard, to take the inventory.[7]

Meanwhile, Thomas Culpeper and Francis Dereham were being dragged on hurdles to their deaths at Tyburn. Unlike Culpeper, a onetime trusted servant of the king who was allowed a simple beheading, the more humble Dereham suffered the full horrors of hanging, drawing and quartering. Both men's severed heads were placed on spikes on London Bridge to act as a deterrent to potential wrong doers.

The following day, with the case against the Howards still gathering momentum, the Council in London wrote to Henry needing advice as to who should have the custody of their various houses, and what to do with Lord William's children. His sister, Lady Bridgewater, had a daughter and two sons in the Duchess of Norfolk's house, so arrangements also needed immediately to be made for them. The Council were able to confirm that except for the horses and mules that had been lost at sea, Lord William's goods are 'come safe'.[8]

As for Duchess Agnes, they would do their best to get her to confess to the things testified against her and make her 'cough out' more. 'The money yet found in the duchess's house is 2,000 marks more than will defray these households, but the plate is not worth past 600 or 700 marks, and the jewels are very base. Most of the money and plate is conveyed, for safety, to the King's palace at Westminster.' How much money in total had been found thus far we do not see, but if after deducting the estimated expenses for winding up the household there was already an excess of 2000 marks, or almost £1300, that alone, according to the Bank of England Inflation Calculator, would today have an equivalent of about £990,000.[9] It is interesting that the plate and jewels are described as 'base', as the large amount of jewellery left to Agnes by the second duke would more than likely have been of significant value.

On 11 December 1541 the 'old lady of Norfolk' was committed to the Tower by the Council, who, to avoid trouble in her conveyance, promised her spending money and women to wait upon her. She then showed that she had at home £1000 in money more than she had yet declared. Even allowing for inflation, £1000 was still a considerable sum for the duchess to have in her house in 1541: the Bank of England Inflation Calculator gives an equivalent of £762,000 in November 2023.[10] Wriothesley and Pollard were expecting to be another three or four days at the duchess's house, for she had, 'besides good stuff, much trash, baggage and many odd ends'. Wriothesley soon found the hidden £1000 and more plate. As for Lord William's and Lady Bridgewater's children, the king decided that, 'those that are too young to help themselves are to be nourished' and those old enough put to service.[11]

The following day it was declared that Agnes Rice (Rhys), Lady Bridgewater's daughter by her late first husband, was to be sent to Lady Oxford, while her brothers, Griffith and Thomas Rice, were to go the Archbishop of Canterbury and Bishop of Durham respectively. Wriothesley would be made responsible for Norfolk House, while the keeping of Chesworth House at Horsham was committed to a Mr Carrell, Lady Bridgewater's to Sir Richard Long, and Lord William's at Reigate to John Skinner.[12] The French ambassador reported to the English court that his master, Francis I, was so sorry to hear of his good brother's trouble, 'caused by the naughty demeanour of her lately reputed for Queen, but would remind him that his honour did not rest in the lightness of a woman, and that he should comfort himself in God's goodness'.[13]

The Duke of Norfolk had been lying low at his huge mansion at Kenninghall for at least a week. On 15 December he finally plucked up the courage to send Henry a grovelling apology for his family's 'false proceedings', having learnt, 'That mine ungracious mother-in-law [stepmother], mine unhappy brother and his wife, with my lewd sister of Bridgewater, were committed to the Tower, and [I] am sure it is not done but for some false proceedings against your Majesty'. He was at great pains to remind His Majesty that much of this unfortunate business had come to light through his own reporting of his 'mother-in-law's' words to him when he was sent to Lambeth to search Dereham's coffers and found that she had already rifled through them. His 'own truth and the small love' his stepmother and nieces (Anne Boleyn and Katherine Howard) bore him, made him hope that Henry would not desert him, and he begged for some assurance of the king's favour, without which he would never desire to live.[14]

Questioned on 19 December, Malyn Tilney, the duchess's recently widowed sister-in-law, revealed that when she was released after being questioned the first time, Agnes had sent a servant to find her at another house in Lambeth and promised to help her because her husband, Sir Philip Tilney, had left her in debt. Malyn probably had had little knowledge of past events at Norfolk House, but now deposed that when the duchess tried to find out from her what she did know, and whether she thought the queen would die, she told her she was sworn to secrecy and refused to be led. The old lady had also asked whether she thought Lord William knew anything.[15]

Just how much Lord William did know of the escapades at Norfolk House is ambiguous – it would appear he knew some the girls under his mother's guardianship were a lively bunch, but was perhaps unaware of the extent of the dormitory adventures. Biographer Lacey Baldwin Smith, however, takes Lord William's lighthearted approach as being due to, 'himself having an affair with one of Katherine's dormitory mates' whom he does not name and gives no other reference than 'Malyn Tilney questioned on 19 December'. Letters and Papers of Henry VIII for this date reads:

> ... and asked whether she thought Lord William knew [about Katherine with Dereham][Malyn Tilney] said she could not tell, but the Duchess then said, 'Alas! my daughter Haward [Lord William's wife] told me that if Alys Wekes [Alice Wilkes] knew anything thereof that then she hath told it unto him'.

Certainly Alice had firsthand experience of Dereham and Katherine Howard's behaviour and it is believed Lord William gave her a job after she left Norfolk House, but it hardly indicates an affair with her employer, and while in his service she had met and subsequently married Anthony Restwold.[16]

In actual fact, on 22 December both Katherine Tilney and Alice Wilkes deposed that Lord William had been told of the unseemly behaviour of the future queen and Dereham, but he had made light of it, saying, 'What mad wenches! Can you not be merry amongst yourselves but you must thus fall out?' He agreed under questioning he had said it but, 'denying nevertheless suspect of evil. It appears by the deposition of his own wife that he knew it, and has been a great maintainer of Dereham since the Queen's marriage'.[17] Of the involvement of his sister Lady Bridgewater, Bulmer and Wilkes deposed that she knew of the banqueting late at night, to which she confessed after her former maid named Philip also revealed it under interrogation; the countess said she had warned Katherine that 'if she used that sort [behaved in that way, that is the midnight feasts in the dormitory] it would hurt her beauty'.[18]

On 20 December Wriothesley and the Earl of Southampton had found the duchess ill on her bed in the Tower 'and apparently very sickly'. Agnes begged the king's forgiveness for not having disclosed what she knew of her step-granddaughter's affairs before the marriage and confessed to having a further £800 hidden at Norfolk House. She was sobbing and presumably so completely terrorised that she was trying to trade all her worldly goods for her life. They described her 'sorrowful protestation' that she did not know the full extent of what was happening between Katherine and Dereham. She implored them to ask the king not to give away her house at Lambeth.

The other ladies too were very much changed, and Lord William's wife appeared not to have a clue as to what was going on: even Wriothesley said she 'seems a very simple woman, and neither thought she had offended nor lamented her imprisonment'. However, when her 'crimes' were pointed out to her she was very repentant, and the men reported having tried to comfort her in her confusion and terror, as they had the others.

Writing to Henry of the meeting with the distraught old matriarch the previous day, Wriothesley and the others explained they planned to go back again shortly to speak with the rest, and to see Lord William's state, 'who is said to be wonderfully troubled'. Wriothesley had already found the Duchess's hidden £800 at Norfolk House. By now 5000 marks in coin (£3,333) and £1000 worth of plate were being stored at Westminster Palace, with a value today of £3,303,000 (Bank of England Inflation Calculator); he was extremely anxious and 'would sleep better' if someone else could be assigned responsibility for its safekeeping, or if the king would have it taken to Greenwich Palace where he was now staying, to which he agreed the following day.[19]

On the morning of 22 December, Lord William's wife and ladies formerly of the dowager's household were arraigned for misprision of treason, that is, for not having revealed Katherine Howard's behaviour with Manox and Dereham, and all submitted to the king's mercy. In the afternoon Lord William Howard and Robert Damport were arraigned for the same crime. As customary, Lord William changed his plea to guilty, and abjectly apologised for his 'light demeanour' when committed, in words 'much to the King's honour'.

The verdicts were as expected: loss of goods and perpetual imprisonment. Some members of the Council, thought the King should know that:

> They [the women] are so sorrowful and changed that some cannot live long unless they have some liberty within the Tower. [We] Desire to know the King's pleasure in this, for the lord Privy Seal and Wriothesley are to go tomorrow morning to the Tower to give them some further hope and cause Mr. Lieutenant to give them some liberty and let honest friends visit them.[20]

They must have been in a very bad way for a hard man like Wriothesley to be moved by their plight. However, the reply the Council received shows there would be no mercy yet, for late that night Sir Ralph Sadler wrote back to the Council in London that:

> The King thanks them for their proceedings this day, [but] as to the sorrow of the women, His Majesty, though he seems to intend to show them mercy, thinks they should not be so soon restored to liberty

within the Tower, and desires the lord Privy Seal and Wriothesley to forbear going thither tomorrow for that purpose.[21]

The aged duchess was left to sweat it out in the Tower over Christmas and it looked as though her fate would be decided along with that of Katherine Howard, Lady Bridgewater and Lady Rochford when the new Parliament convened in mid-January. The king, meanwhile, appeared to have been coming out of his shell a little and was getting himself comfortably settled in at Greenwich Palace in time for the yuletide festivities.

# Chapter 25

# That Vicious Life Before

On the first day of January 1542 de Marillac wrote to Francis I that Norfolk was expected back for the new Parliament and, even though he was not accused of any complicity in the treason of his niece and other Howard family members, there was speculation as to what his future standing would be. Of the accused of higher status, Lord William was already sentenced, but his mother and sister, together with Lady Rochford and the former queen were to be judged by Parliament through a Bill of Attainder, leaving no chance of self-defence for them.[1] The country's general administrative and legal business carried on, as it had of course since the start of the current scandal, but there would be a lull in the saga of Katherine Howard, as she now was, until Parliament reconvened on 16 January.

New parliamentary business at the beginning of the first session included, 'For due process to be had in high treason in cases of lunacy or madness', presumably to enable Henry to go ahead and execute Lady Rochford whether or not she had made a recovery while in the care of Lady Russell.[2] All told there was a wide variety of items on the agenda, such as 'buying of fish upon the sea', 'against conjurations and witchcrafts and sorcery and enchantments' and 'the abolition of the sanctuary of Manchester'; but then, tucked in among all the rest, came 'Attainder of Katherine Howard and others'. Seen in full, it is immediately apparent from the actual Bill of Attainder to be debated by the House of Lords, that the defendants had no chance:

> Katherine Howard whom the King took to wife is proved to have been not of pure and honest living before her marriage, and the fact that she has since taken to her service one Francis Dereham, the person with whom she used that vicious life before, and has taken as chamberer a woman who was privy to her naughty life before, is proof of her will to return to her old abominable life. Also she has confederated with lady Jane Rocheford, widow, late wife of Sir Geo. Boleyn, late lord Rocheford, to bring her vicious and abominable purpose to pass with Thos. Culpeper, late one of the King's Privy Chamber, and has met Culpeper in a secret and vile place, at 11 o'clock at night, and remained there with him until 3 [in the morning], with only that bawd, the lady Jane Rocheford. For these treasons, Culpeper and Dereham have been convicted and executed, and the Queen and lady Rochford stand indicted. The indictments of such as have lately suffered are hereby approved, and the said Queen and lady Rochford are, by authority of this Parliament, convicted

and attainted of high treason, and shall suffer accordingly; and the said Queen, lady Rocheford, Culpeper, and Dereham shall forfeit to the Crown all possessions which they held on 25 Aug. 33 Hen. VIII [1541]. The Royal assent to this Act shall be given by commission.

And where Agnes duchess of Norfolk, widow, and Katherine countess of Bridgewater, wife of Henry earl of Bridgewater, are indicted of misprision of treason for concealing the first treasons, and Lord William Howard, Lady Margaret Howard his wife, Edw. Walgrave, Kath. Tylney, Alice Restwold, Joan Bulmer, Anne Howard, Robt. Damporte, Malyn Tylney, Marg. Benet, and Wm. Assheby have been convicted of the said misprision, all of them shall forfeit their goods to the King, and be imprisoned for life, and the King shall take the revenues of their lands from 1 Oct. 33 Hen. VIII. for term of their lives.

To avoid doubts in future, it is declared that the Royal assent given by commission shall be valid in all cases hereafter, that any lightness of the queen for the time being may be revealed to the King or his Council, and that an unchaste woman marrying the King shall be guilty of high treason.[3]

Obviously part of the purpose was to give retrospective parliamentary sanction to executions, imprisonments and seizure of goods and property which had already taken place. The declaration 'an unchaste woman marrying the King shall be guilty of high treason', suggested that next time, it would perhaps be a good idea for Henry to opt for a respectable widow – which is exactly what he did.

Some good news, but not affecting Katherine, was mentioned by de Marillac in a letter to Francis I the following day: her father's old friend and colleague from his Calais days, Arthur Plantagenet, Lord Lisle, for whom clothes had been made only a few months earlier 'who was made prisoner in the Tower two years ago, is going to have his pardon. The Order of the Garter is said to have been sent back to him, and indeed he has liberty within the Tower, where he used to have but one narrow chamber'. Although not actually released yet, some freedom of movement within the Tower grounds would have been a great relief for him, but it looked as though his 'narrow chamber' would be getting another high-class occupant when he was finally released. In the same letter the ambassador writes of Norfolk having returned to court and appeared to have been well received, considering his circumstances.[4]

The Bill of Attainder had its first reading in the Lords on January 21. Up to this point Katherine Howard's fate had been entirely in the hands of her husband, a man who could bring about anything he wanted, but made no effort to save her life. It is true that even if he could have found it in his heart to forgive the Chesworth and Norfolk House behaviour, the possibility that after her marriage Katherine had carried on with her relationship with Dereham and committed adultery with Culpeper, or was planning to, meant he could not have kept her as his wife. A king could father as many illegitimate children as he wished, whereas a queen, as the prospective mother of the heir to the throne and the leading model of behaviour for married women, had to lead a life beyond reproach.

On the other hand, being a man whose every word was feared and who had resorted to every sort of legal manipulation to rid himself of three wives already, it has to be wondered why Henry did not make use of the pre-contract, which Dereham insisted took place, to avail himself of a quick annulment and let her live, especially in the light of Katherine's young age and his once all-consuming love for her, and send her to some country backwater for the rest of her life. Then again, would banishment to the back of beyond have been a fate worse than death for a lively girl who seems to have loved attention and exciting, young male company? In fact, even if it had crossed Henry's mind to resort to the pre-contract, Katherine always denied having such an arrangement with Dereham.

This way of thinking that expects Henry VIII to show understanding and compassion is to be looking at him through twenty-first century eyes and seeing him as a flesh-and-blood human being, which is not at all how he would have seen himself. In his own mind he was God's anointed, whom no one must question, challenge or belittle. What today may seem like vindictive and pointless killings and outrageous sentences for an old woman and her servants, to him would have seemed the right and proper punishment for people who had let him down and made him look a fool.

Then there is another possibility: was there more to it? When he was ill in the springtime of 1541 he had not wanted to see Katherine, so was he growing tired of this girl with whom he had little in common, and who so far, despite her youth, showed no sign of being able to produce more sons for him? Had he already begun to wonder how he might move on? Eustace Chapuys, who the previous May had written of Katherine's rumoured feelings of insecurity and fretting Henry might set her aside and take back Anne of Cleves, wrote another gossipy letter to the Queen of Hungary on 10 November, as the news of Katherine's fall from grace began to leak out, 'Wrote [to you] last Lent that this King, feigning indisposition, was ten or twelve days without seeing his Queen, or allowing her to come in his room, during which time there was much talk of a divorce; but owing to some surmise that she was with child, or else because the means for a divorce were not arranged, the affair slept till the 5 inst [i.e. 5 November 1541]'.[5]

However, on this occasion we have to take what Chapuys said with a pinch of salt – his master was Katherine of Aragon's nephew and the ambassador had done his best to fight the original Queen Katherine's corner. Also, Henry's illness that spring had been real enough. Chapuys detested Anne Boleyn, whom he branded 'a whore' and 'a concubine', and perhaps was more than happy to view her young cousin in the same light. But does the fact that he mentions other people gossiping about Katherine's insecurities and the very mention of a divorce indicate those closest to the king had sensed that the marriage made in heaven was, after less than twelve months, perhaps no longer looking quite so heavenly?

At some stage in the days following the recall of Parliament in January, some in the House of Lords, including Lord Chancellor Audley, felt uneasy that Katherine was not to be given any opportunity to defend herself in public; the outcome was a foregone conclusion, but it would look better in the eyes of the world if they appeared to have given her a chance to state her case. When the delegation comprising Cranmer, her uncle Norfolk, Suffolk and the Bishop of Westminster approached her at Syon and offered the chance of a trial, Katherine declined the offer saying she had no more to add, except that she hoped her family would not be made to suffer for her wrongdoings.[6]

Chapuys wrote on 29 January summarising the outcome of Parliament's deliberations in the House of Lords where, despite his former concerns for Katherine to be seen to have fair treatment, Audley's speech:

> ... aggravated the Queen's misdeeds to the utmost, whereupon the Lords, four days ago, found the Queen and lady Rochford guilty of high treason. The Dowager Duchess of Norfolk and her daughter are sentenced to perpetual imprisonment, with confiscation of property, on the same grounds as Lord William and his wife, and the rest of the accomplices.

Chapuys informed his master that having had its third reading the Bill would then go to the Commons, and indeed, even as he wrote, heard that the first reading there supported the decision of the Lords. He felt that although two more Commons readings would have to follow, the outcome was a foregone conclusion and that Katherine Howard would soon be conveyed to the Tower.[7]

After the House of Lords had given its verdict, Henry, 'who had never been merry since first hearing of the Queen's misconduct' had suddenly sprung to life by organising a supper and banquet. At his table there were twenty-six ladies and some gentlemen and thirty-five more guests at another. He was paying particular attention to the wife of Sir Thomas Wyatt, who had repudiated her for adultery but had been forced by the king to take her back, which, given Henry's own circumstances with his own wife awaiting a possible death sentence for the same offence, was particularly hypocritical.

Wyatt's wife was not alone, for as the old Duchess of Norfolk would have put it, Henry 'did cast a fantasy' towards the daughter of Sir Anthony Browne, and Chapuys speculated that the sudden recent kindness towards Lord Lisle might have something to do with the king's liking for his stepdaughter Anne Basset, one of Katherine's former maids, in whom he appeared to be especially interested that evening.[8] (Sadly Lord Lisle's story does not end well, for when he finally had his freedom from his 'narrow chamber' he was so overcome he suffered a heart attack and died shortly afterwards, on 3 March 1542.)

The Bill of Attainder was to have its second and third readings in the Commons and pass into law before mid-February. It was, of course, a foregone conclusion that the Act would be passed and Katherine Howard would die. She had been under house arrest, in reduced circumstances but in no real physical discomfort, since the middle of November, so how much did she know of what is going on in the outside world? Did she, for instance, know Culpeper and Dereham were already butchered, that her old step-grandmother was consigned to the Tower, probably for the rest of her days, and might yet be sentenced to death, or that Lady Rochford had become a mental wreck, and that she herself had but a few days left?

The Bill's second reading was on 8 February so, assuming it got through a third reading and became an Act of Parliament, in a matter of days Henry would be able to free himself of his burdensome prisoners. Chapuys ended his letter begun on 9 February with the news that Katherine's household at Syon had been broken up and her few staff dismissed, which he surmised, correctly, indicated she was about to be moved to the Tower.[9]

Syon House, built on the site of the ancient abbey, is today a magnificent mansion belonging to the Dukes of Northumberland. Whether or not the present duke ever makes use of craft on the Thames at the bottom of his extensive garden, in Tudor times the river would have been the main route for travelling, and on 10 February the Duke of Suffolk and Lord Privy Seal the Earl of Southampton arrived by water to escort Katherine Howard on her penultimate journey. Suffolk, Charles Brandon, had been Henry's great friend since their youth and was his late sister Mary's second husband. Their granddaughter, Lady Jane Grey, aged 4 or 5 in 1542, would, almost twelve years to the day, take the same path to the river and thence to the Tower to end her life on the same block now being prepared for her grandfather's terrified prisoner.[10]

In no doubt as to where she was going and what was to happen to her, Katherine Howard struggled and had to be taken forcibly down to the river to the small boat waiting, and then escorted along the Thames with the Earl of Southampton ahead in a large barge and Suffolk behind with a barge loaded with armed men, a very different sight from just eight short months before when she had travelled on her own magnificent gilded vessel with its twenty-six oarsmen to meet the little Lady Elizabeth. It has been written on many occasions that Katherine Howard recognised the heads of Culpeper and Dereham as she approached London Bridge, but this is doubtful. The bridge was a very substantial and tall structure crowded to capacity with buildings of several storeys; specific impaled heads would have had to be pointed out to her from amongst the others, and in any case, the boat conveying her to the Tower is believed to have been covered.

The Bill of Attainder sentencing her to death passed into law after its third reading on 11 February. The following day the former queen was told to 'prepare her soul', as was Lady Rochford; as far as the latter was concerned it now mattered little whether or not she had regained her senses, as the new law allowing for the execution of a mentally unwell person had been passed the same time as the Act of Attainder. Ever anxious to conduct herself well in public, that evening Katherine requested that the block be brought to her room so she could practise placing her neck upon it.

On February 13 or possibly earlier, de Marillac began composing another report to Francis I. Rumour had it, he said, that Katherine's death was to be deferred for a few days as she was in such a hysterical state, although he gave no particular source for that information and the fact she had been clear headed enough to send for the block might contradict that. The Dowager Duchess of Norfolk and her daughter the Countess of Bridgewater had been found guilty, he reported, with the latter condemned to loss of goods and perpetual imprisonment, like her brother Lord William. Their mother's future, however, had yet to be determined:

> As to the old duchess of Norfolk, some say she shall die, others that she shall keep perpetual prison, like her son lord William and daughter the countess of Bridgwater. A few days will show. All her goods are already confiscated, and are of marvellous value, 400,000 or 500,000 cr [crowns], for ladies in this country succeed for life to the movables of their deceased husbands. Norfolk is greatly interested, since the greater part came to her through his late father; yet the times are such that he dare not show that the affair touches him, but approves all that is done.[11]

The third Duke of Norfolk might well have been left the greater part of his late father's estates, but we can understand why he would be salivating at the prospect of his stepmother's attainder and what he might stand to gain from it, provided, of course, it pleased the king to be generous towards him. By the terms of his late father's will the properties at Horsham and Lambeth should revert to him at the duchess's death, but her attainder and possible execution had the potential to complicate the legal side of that.

The Bank of England Inflation Calculator gives de Marillac's lower estimate of 400,000 crowns (£100,000) in 1542 a value of £72,537,873 and 57 pence in September 2023.[12] Even allowing for the ambassador's inevitable exaggerations and the fact that comparisons are not very reliable, we can see that the duchess was an exceptionally wealthy woman, a multi-millionairess by today's standards, who had held a surprisingly large amount of ready cash in her Lambeth house.

Then, in a postscript to his letter, de Marillac wrote he had just heard news that the former Queen Katherine had been beheaded earlier in the day, 13 February, only eighteen months after her marriage, and was followed immediately on the scaffold by Jane Rochford. He had been told that both women made a suitably dignified exit, and were to be buried under the floor of the Tower church.

Contrary to tradition still quoted even today, the former queen appears not to have made the touching and defiant declaration on the scaffold often attributed to her that she would rather have died the wife of Culpeper than as a queen of Henry VIII. This has stemmed from the anonymous *Spanish Chronicle,* the writer of which was not present at the execution but whose work of some years later is worth reading as a piece of light entertainment. In it he has Thomas Cromwell proceeding against Katherine, 'we are surprised indeed that the example of Anne Boleyn was lost upon you and that you should have let the devil come upon you so soon'. Cromwell would have been nowhere near as surprised at her behaviour as Katherine would have been to find herself face to face with him, considering he had already been dead eighteen months, suffering a horrifically botched beheading the same day as her marriage.

The anonymous writer describes her as 'a mere child' at her wedding and as the best-looking and 'the most giddy' of all the wives, a description of her still in use, even in a few scholarly works. According to him, the Culpeper letter written by Katherine was a reply to one Thomas himself had passed to her while they danced together the previous day. He fails to mention either Manox or Dereham, which is quite an achievement when chronicling the life of Katherine Howard, and thought Anne of Cleves had followed rather than preceded her.[13]

Katherine had hoped for a private execution, which was denied her, although there were nowhere near the numbers of observers there had been at the death of her cousin, Anne Boleyn. Fortunately, there survives a letter from Ottwell Johnson, a merchant, present at the scaffold, who wrote to his brother John Johnson that the Queen and Jane Rochford had made a good end:

> I saw the Queen and the Lady Rochford suffer within the Tower ... whose souls (I doubt not) be with God, for they made the most godly and Christians' end that ever was heard tell of (I think) since the world's creation ... being justly condemned (as they said) by the laws of the realm and Parliament, to die, they required the people to take example at them for amendment of their ungodly lives, and gladly obey the King in all things, for whose preservation they did heartily pray.[14]

Katherine Howard, always anxious to conduct herself well in public and at the end concerned in case of reprisals against her family, would never have done any other than go to her death with dignity. Her Uncle Norfolk had been conveniently ill and was absent from the execution, but his son, the Earl of Surrey, was present. The late queen was interred beneath the floor of the Church of St Peter ad Vincula, where extensive repairs in 1876–77 revealed the remains of several prominent offenders, including Anne Boleyn, but nothing remained of Katherine, which led the examining doctor, Professor Frederick Mouat, to conclude her young bones would have disintegrated more rapidly; also there were traces of lime where she was thought to have been interred.[15]

# Chapter 26

# All Has Changed

Then suddenly all began to clear. The wicked young queen was dead and Henry's twisted magnanimity began shining through with the release before the end of February of Lord William's wife Lady Margaret and most of, but not all, the other ladies implicated. By the end of March he had been so perfectly charming towards Lady Margaret there was speculation that her husband, and even the Duchess of Norfolk herself, could soon be freed. The old dowager was pardoned on 5 May, after nearly five months in the Tower, and her daughter shortly afterwards.[1] Free Agnes might be, but her life would never be the same again, not least for having been almost frightened to death, losing her home, and, even though she was pardoned, her goods were still to be forfeit and added to the king's inventory of his money, jewels, plate, apparel, tapestries, furniture and other valuables then in the process of being recorded, until he decided what should be done with them.

To all intents and purposes this inventory looks like yet other list of goods and chattels of an unbelievably rich man, but what a sad story it conceals. Folio 94 is the list of the belongings of the late Queen Jane Seymour; 99b those of Queen Katherine Howard; 104 of Lady Rochford; 101b of the old Duchess of Norfolk: 'a list of stuff received by Nic. Bristowe at the house of the old Duchess of Norfolk'. One was dead following childbirth not five years since and already succeeded by two further wives; a young woman and her demented lady-in-waiting were beheaded after the latter had been nursed back to health after a nervous breakdown only to face the axe; an old woman who had been scared out of her wits and deprived of her home and possessions.[2] On May 20 Duchess Agnes had some of her former manors in East Anglia restored, but none in the Capital or the south of England except for Reigate. Her beloved Norfolk House was granted to her stepson, the third Duke, the following January, although he had to give over some of his other lands in exchange.[3]

Agnes Tilney, Dowager Duchess of Norfolk, appears to have lived her remaining thousand or so days in relative obscurity in East Anglia, dying in Norfolk in 1545 aged at least 68, a very good age for those times. She was buried on 31 May at Thetford, but on 13 October her remains were removed to the tomb she had prepared in the Church of St Mary at Lambeth, Surrey, as directed in her will. Dated 12 March 1542, it should be remembered that, contrary to what has sometimes been claimed, this will was not written while she was in the Tower, which would not make sense, for as an attainted person she had no assets, and it was only after her release in May 1542 and the restoration of some lands and valuables she would have been in a position to make bequests. In her time the New Year began on

25 March, so Agnes actually put pen to paper on what, on the calendar in use in our times, would be 12 March 1543, ten months after her release.[4]

Today nothing remains in the Church of St Mary at Lambeth to indicate the splendour that was once her tomb and those memorials of other members of the Howard family, except for the ledger stone of her stepdaughter Elizabeth (Howard) Boleyn discovered in 2018 and now located in the Bookshop. However, in 1779 Somerset Herald, J. C. Brook, wrote to a colleague:

> After I left you on Saturday I went to lord de Ferrars and was shown by him one of the most magnificent works that I imagine was ever executed in this kingdom, a history & pedigree of the Howard family containing almost 600 folios of vellum done for the earl of Northampton [sic] ... . It contains all their family monuments too numerous to recite to you ... there is a representation of the tomb of the second Duke of Norfolk.... There are also two other brasses for duchesses of Norfolk at Lambeth, now destroyed, so rich and sumptuous that your Joyce Tiptoft at Enfield will appear an orange wench [orange seller] to them [the Tiptoft brass is still extant in the twenty-first century and is one of the finest surviving examples of a medieval brass]. The brasses are done with gold lackered [sic] over in such a manner that they appear exactly like the real metal, and then the lines in black are traced upon it. The book was done by Henry Lilly, Rouge Dragon Pursuivant, who died in 1638 ... and seems never to have been in possession of the Howard family.[5]

The provenance was not quite correct: the book was done for the second duke's great-great grandson Thomas Howard, Earl of Arundel and Surrey (the 'Collector' Earl) in 1638, bought by the Earl of Northampton in 1684 for £100 and given to the fifteenth Duke of Norfolk by the fifth Marquess of Northampton in 1907. Agnes will be one of the Duchesses of Norfolk mentioned, the other being Elizabeth Stafford, her step-daughter-in-law, whose brother provided the memorial brass to her.

The present writer has had the privilege of being shown this marvellous book, now in the Archives of the Duke of Norfolk at Arundel Castle and the images really are beautiful to behold. It was a dismal rainy day and I was with the duke's assistant librarian in a tower room with locked cupboards of valuable documents all around. For one brief moment the clouds must have parted allowing rays of sun to illuminate Agnes's likeness for me. Of course we today can have no idea how lifelike any effigy really is, but this is enormously pleasing and the 'lackered gold' gleamed from the page.[6]

Agnes is depicted as a mature rather than an old woman, wearing a traditional gable hood surmounted by an oversized ducal coronet. Her face is heart-shaped, lips full, eyes large and wide open, but overall the expression might be interpreted as one of weariness. Her neck, which mercifully was spared the axe, is long, and is the neck of a woman younger than Agnes's 68 or so years at time of death. Her long fingers are touching in prayer, and the heraldry surrounding her and etched into her golden robe is a testament to the noble connections within the Howard family; Mowbray heraldry is present but not prominent.[7]

Brook wrote in his letter of 1779 that the fine brasses had been destroyed, but as early as 1633, when the book was being prepared, vandals had already struck, for in the perfect and very legible script that accompanies the illustration in the book we are told that in the Howard Chapel at Lambeth 'is a faire tomb in the middle of the said chappell erected to the memorie of Agnes Duchesse of Norffolke second wife of Thomas the victorious Duke the inscription stolen away the armes on the sides and endes defaced'.

It is not known when Agnes began construction of her tomb at Lambeth or if she deliberately went against her husband's directions that they be buried together in his tomb at Thetford with 'pictures of us and Agnes our wife to be set together thereupon'. If she began construction after the dissolution of the larger monasteries in 1539 it would have made sense to have her tomb constructed in the Howard Chapel in St Mary's Church across the road from Norfolk House and have her husband's remains carried there from Thetford. If that is so, it would appear that as the widow she had had a stronger claim over his remains than his son the third duke, who had other Howards moved to Framlingham. Perhaps her initial burial in Thetford meant her Lambeth tomb was not completed, or possibly in view of her recent disgrace special permission had to be sought for a Lambeth burial.

# Chapter 27

# Those Katherine Left Behind

Duchess Agnes's daughter Katherine Howard, Countess of Bridgewater, was released from the Tower in the spring of 1542, died in 1554 and was buried on 11 May in the Howard Chapel, Lambeth. Having requested to rest close to her mother, it is possible she could have been interred in the tiny chapel rather than in the tomb itself and her resting place marked only with a ledger stone, which was not uncommon. This chapel is now used as the Bookshop for the Garden Museum.

Lady Bridgewater's daughter Agnes Rice (Rhys), who as a young child had been sent to live with the Countess of Oxford, eventually returned to Lambeth and lived with her mother for a time, later achieving social notoriety as the mistress of Lord Stourton. Her brother Griffith Rice, he who was sent by Agnes to find the Book of Pardons in 1541, became a Member of Parliament, but Thomas, their younger brother, placed in the care of the Bishop of Durham when their mother was sent to the Tower, was so unhappy he ran away and in a desperate attempt not to be sent back crossed the border into Scotland, where he was killed during a local insurrection in 1544, before he had reached the age of 20.

Although 'the least charged', Duchess Agnes's son, Lord William, was not released from the Tower until August 1542. Gradually rehabilitated at court, he is referred to in 1545 documents as 'vice-admiral'. His career suffered a temporary setback in 1547 following the disgrace of his half-brother, the third Duke of Norfolk, and Norfolk's son, the Earl of Surrey, but he recovered his reputation in the reign of Edward VI and in 1551 became Governor of Calais. King Edward's half-sister and successor, Queen Mary, made him Baron Howard of Effingham, and Lord Admiral in 1554. Four years later he became Chamberlain to his kinswoman Queen Elizabeth I, and died in 1573. Charles Howard, his eldest son and heir, is associated with the defeat of the Spanish Armada, while one of Charles's daughters, Lady Douglas Howard, born in the year of Katherine Howard's execution, fell foul of her kinswoman Elizabeth I when she bore a son to the queen's favourite, Robert Dudley, Earl of Leicester.

The majority of the accused of lesser status appear to have led quiet lives after their ordeal. Of the girls from the maidens' chamber Katherine Tilney, Margaret Benet and Alice Restwold disappear, while the widowed Joan Bulmer married Edward Waldegrave, who had been restored to his position in the household of Prince Edward, and with him had several children. Waldegrave died in the 1580s and Joan lived until 1590, dying on 10 December, forty-nine years to the day since the execution of Thomas Culpeper and her old flame Francis Dereham. She was buried alongside her husband in the Church of St Mary the Virgin in Lawford, Essex, where their tomb remains.

Dereham's friend, Robert Damport, was released from the Tower. Although tortured he had been sufficiently mobile to be brought to trial, so presumably survived the brutality meted out to him and was released. William Ashby and Andrew Maunsey, both formerly in the service of Duchess Agnes, disappear after their release.

Malyn Tilney, née Chambre or Chambers, the widow of the duchess's brother Sir Philip who had died in 1541 and left her in debt, kept a low profile for the rest of her life. Little is known about the upbringing or education of her son, the Elizabethan courtier Edmund Tilney who in 1579 became Master of the Revels to Queen Elizabeth I, perhaps with a little help from Lord William's son Charles, the second Lord Howard of Effingham. The J. D. Wetherspoon pub 'The Edmund Tylney' in Leatherhead is named after him; apparently he had a mansion in the Surrey town on a site now occupied by the public library.

Henry Manox the music teacher was questioned but released early on in the enquiries and as far as is known was neither interrogated again nor incarcerated at all, and to some extent his subsequent story is generally overlooked. There is a possibility there was actually much more to him than meets the eye and he could have married Lord Edmund Howard's widow, Margaret Jennings, née Mundy.[1]

The diplomat Eustace Chapuys, a Savoyard, apart from a short absence for part of 1539–40 had served as Imperial ambassador to the court of King Henry VIII continuously from 1529 to 1545. By 1545, when he was finally permitted to retire, he was in poor health, but lived until 1556 when he was about 66; his master Charles V died two years later aged 58. Students of Henry VIII are indebted to Chapuys for his detailed and often gossipy correspondence, especially concerning the downfall of Anne Boleyn and Katherine Howard.

Similarly, the correspondence between the ambassador Charles de Marillac and his master Francis I of France is invaluable, as well as being chatty and sometimes showing his puzzlement with the peculiarities of the English. He was ambassador to the court of Henry VIII from 1538 to 1543 and thereafter stayed in the service of the kings of France, becoming Bishop of Vannes in 1550 and Archbishop of Vienne in 1557. He died aged about 50 in 1560, thirteen years after Francis I, who had died on 31 March 1547, only two months after Henry VIII.[2]

# Chapter 28

## Scotland and France

Although well into his old age at the time of his niece Katherine's execution, Norfolk was still the king's most experienced general and in the early autumn of 1542 was appointed Lieutenant and Captain General of the North 'to perform some notable exploit', namely the conquest of Scotland, thus finding himself back in favour of sorts after the recent scandal.

As he must have been half-expecting, his very reasonable pleas for adequate supplies fell on deaf ears, and soon the preparations were in absolute mayhem. On 28 October he wrote to Wriothesley and Gardiner begging them to lobby for his return; apart from his other troubles his old problem with the lax (diarrhoea) is 'marvellous sore' upon him, presumably exacerbated by stress, and he is also complaining of missing out on obtaining a share of the goods and property of the lately deceased Lord Privy Seal that the king was in the process of redistributing. The letter in Norfolk's own hand reminds them his 'cost and pain in this journey has been treble any other man's'.

There was virtually no food or beer left, already nineteen men had died from lack of food and drinking dirty water from puddles, and he expected many more to follow. He commends the army as being 'the goodliest army' he had ever seen, that two months earlier in the year and with proper provisions would have done well. Little more than a week into the venture a combination of shortage of food and weapons and the increasingly bad weather caused Norfolk to abandon any further progress into Scotland, and on the long march back south, having already received letters of Henry's displeasure, prepared himself for the usual snubs, or worse.[1]

Less than a month later there came a massive blow to the duke's ego when news arrived at court that Sir Thomas Wharton, the Warden of the Western Marches, had achieved a decisive victory on 24 November over the invading Scots at Solway Moss on the Carlisle side of the border. Suffering from fever, 30-year-old King James V had not been at the battle, but died on 14 December, six days after the birth of his daughter, his only surviving child, who immediately succeeded him as Mary, Queen of Scots.

Norfolk was surely annoyed by events of the last few months, but for his haughty and restless son, humiliation, anger and aggression were coming to the boil. He had also been devastated by the death of his great friend and fellow poet Sir Thomas Wyatt, who had died in October. It was less than three months after his return from the Borders that Surrey's notorious late-night rampage through London took place. Like Shakespeare's young Prince Hal, the Earl of Surrey with a group of friends, including Wyatt's son, sought temporary refuge from his powerful family and opulent surroundings by frequenting taverns and lodgings in the city, in his case renting rooms at Miss Millicent Arundel's premises on Lawrence Lane between Milk Street and Ironmonger Lane which, although reasonably comfortable and respectable enough, were hardly what he was used to.[2]

It was on the night of 21 January 1543, after curfew, that Surrey and friends decided it was fun time. On affluent Milk Street lived wealthy merchant Sir Richard Gresham, Member of Parliament and one time Lord Mayor of London; Surrey and his pals with their little stone-shooting bows soon made short work of his very expensive stained glass windows. Eventually becoming bored with this mindless vandalism, around midnight the rowdy mates left the jurisdiction of the City of London with its curfew, took a rowing boat south across the Thames to Southwark and had a good laugh taking pot shots at people from the river, again with the little bows.

Their main victims were the colourfully attired 'ladies of the night' plying their trade outside the houses of ill repute on Bankside, the whitewashed properties rented out to brothel keepers by the Bishop of Winchester, although it seems that the Jolly Boys declined, on this occasion at least, to sample the working girls' hospitality and returned to their lodgings at about two in the morning. Surrey was soon arrested and sent to the Fleet Prison where he spent his time writing poetry, but his father's Privy Council colleagues rallied round and he was found guilty only of eating meat on a fast day and of breaking the windows.[3]

On a happier note, in mid-July 1543, seventeen months after Katherine Howard's death, Henry VIII married again. This time the lucky bride was the very respectable twice-widowed Lady Latimer, Katherine Parr, dashing her hopes of marrying the late Queen Jane's brother, Thomas Seymour. Henry, meanwhile, although increasingly ill and irrational still had a dream of restoring England's lost territories in France, so when in the summer of 1544 he entered into an alliance with his old nemesis Charles V against Francis I, the burden of military leadership again fell on the Duke of Norfolk's almost 70-year-old shoulders.

With his son Surrey he set sail for Calais in June, tasked with taking the town and fortress of Montreuil, about twenty miles south of Boulogne; their role in the campaign was hellish from the start and, needless to say, adequate supplies were not forthcoming. With the coming of autumn the campaign ended for the year, leaving the newly taken town and fortifications at Boulogne in English hands, while Norfolk, Suffolk and Surrey returned home with disease-ridden troops who brought their deadly illnesses back with them.

# Chapter 29

# Lieutenant General of the King on Sea and Land

The spring of 1545 found the Duke of Norfolk, unsure of his standing with the king, as ever, and treading very carefully. At Kenninghall, his preferred residence, his mistress Bess Holland, remained the chatelaine. His daughter Mary, by then widowed for nine years, was also living there, as were the Earl of Surrey's family, currently in the early stages of building a palatial home of their own situated on land formerly belonging to St Leonard's Priory near Norwich; with typical arrogance the earl renamed the hill on which it would stand 'Mount Surrey'.[1]

By the summer of 1545 the French had amassed a large fleet with which they hoped to blockade the Channel, and it was while watching the two fleets face each other in the Solent that Henry VIII witnessed the loss of his old faithful warship the *Mary Rose*, which keeled over in the wind and capsized killing 400 men when water entered gun ports which had been left open, ending her thirty-four years of service. The French fared little better, and overwhelmed by disease, soon sailed for home.

By mid-August Surrey was preparing to leave for France with an army of 5000, where he was to be in charge of the vanguard, while Charles Brandon, Duke of Suffolk, the king's great friend and former brother-in-law, would be in overall charge of the operations, but on 22 August, before he had set sail, Brandon died of causes unknown and the substantial army he was due to take with him remained in England. Four days earlier the Captain of the Boulogne garrison had died of dysentery. At first Henry appointed Lord Grey of Wilton as Captain of Boulogne; a week later he changed his mind and the appointment went to Surrey, who was given responsibility for all Henry's operations across the Channel.

Appointed 'Lieutenant General of the King on Sea and Land', and without the steadying presence of his father, Surrey vowed to retain the fort for Henry at all costs and set about a programme of rebuilding and modernising, but at home it was the financial outlay for the king's latest French exploits so far that were causing ever increasing alarm, as the campaign was threatening to bankrupt the country. Unfortunately, Henry had found in Norfolk's son an enthusiastic on-the-spot supporter for his self-indulgent dreams.

Gaining knowledge of his son's out of control spending on Surrey House, where the interior was planned to be contemporary lavish in the Italian Renaissance style, gave the duke some leverage: Surrey must rein-in Henry VIII over Boulogne, and do it soon, or his father would stop paying his bills at home.[2] Even the duke's own treasurer, Thomas Hussey, was discovered to be borrowing money in his own name to lend to the earl and warned him he could not hope to pay off his debts and keep spending at such a rate. When they were discovered in late October Hussey wrote to him warning that his father was apoplectic at the extent of his extravagances[3] and on 6 November spelt it out for Surrey, saying that six days' work by his father and the Privy Council trying to persuade the king to sue for peace with the French could be wiped out in six hours by a letter from him, 'As to Boulogne every councillor says "away with it" and your lordship says "we will keep it"'.[4]

Thomas Wriothesley, now Lord Chancellor, was in deep despair, writing to William Paget, the king's secretary, that he did not know where the money for the next three months was coming from, an incredible situation considering the massive wealth that had been taken from the monasteries less than a decade before. Surrey, blinded by royal attention, ignored them, continuing to lay out huge sums of Howard family money which, given the precarious state of the national treasury, was unlikely ever to be replaced. At this point Norfolk warned his son that if it all turned out badly, even if done with Henry's blessing, the king himself, as always, would take no blame and the hunt would be on to find a scapegoat.

Surrey's successful risk taking had so far given the now visibly failing Henry VIII a brief thrill or two, but it is a wise man who knows when not to overstep the mark, and on 7 January 1546 he took one of those very risks his father had warned him about, when he intercepted a supply convoy of 100 wagons heading for the French fort of Outreau just over a mile from Boulogne. It was a damned if you do and damned if you don't situation. If he had decided he might be outnumbered and so allowed it through he would have been criticised; conversely, he could now be accused of setting himself up to take an unnecessary risk. He wrote to the king immediately, claiming 205 men lost, whereas Venetian sources suggested the total was nearer 1500.[5] The captains on the front line, the least expendable of his men, had been almost wiped out.

On 17 January Secretary Paget wrote a clever letter from Hampton Court, in part supportive but also accusatory in a gentle sort of way, 'His majesty knowing like a Prince of wisdom and experience that whosoever playeth at any game of chance must sometime look to lose'. Paget then assured him, 'I am your poor friend that will honestly stick to you'.[6] But changes were afoot, and whether Paget would keep his promise remained to be seen. In February, Surrey retained his position as Captain of Boulogne, but was replaced as Lieutenant of the Army by Edward Seymour, Earl of Hertford, brother of the late Queen Jane, while the Lord Admiral, John Dudley, assumed responsibility for naval matters; both were men of the 'new erected' nobility Surrey so thoroughly despised. Paget advised him not to stamp off in a huff but instead apply for a position in the new army, thus demonstrating his continuing loyalty, which might even present an opportunity to reinstate his military reputation.

The earl took the advice and endeavoured to keep up correspondence with the king, but it was clear that Henry no longer had much interest in him; the fortifications in Boulogne were to be put in the charge of surveyor John Rogers and Surrey's self-professed new forever friend Paget seemed to be losing enthusiasm as well. A few days after Seymour's arrival in France Surrey was recalled to England on the pretext that the king would better understand the state of the fortifications in Boulogne if they could discuss it face to face. On March 27 Henry Howard arrived at court; three days later he was relieved of the captaincy of Boulogne, but was expecting to return to put his affairs in order there and take up his new post in the army. However, it never happened, and instead he fell into the very pit of anger, resentment and self-pity Paget had warned against, exacerbated by stress over his burgeoning debts.

Henry VIII, 55 in June 1546, was paranoid, unpredictable and seriously in decline, while the country was facing bankruptcy and religion was still divided and confused. The views of conservatives like the Howards were in favour in the earlier months of the year, but chances were, that should the reformers be able get close enough to Henry and subtly yet quickly take control, there would be monumental changes before the year's end. At court a strong sense of self-preservation was about to kick in, when a wise man would see all and say little; as William Paget put it 'then was it dangerous to do or speak [even] though the meaning were not evil'.[7]

Political and religious allegiances were visibly shifting towards the Seymours, whose nephew, the future Edward VI, would be 9 in the autumn; and there, in the midst of all this uncertainty, was the fiery Earl of Surrey, swallowed up by his own sense of importance and angry with the world. Soon tiring of life in rural East Anglia, by 14 July he was back at court, only to be accused by Lord Grey of Wilton of financial corruption in Boulogne. The earl was aghast at the accusation, insisting he would never stoop so low over mere money, and although when examined his accounts were described as 'raw', they were found to be in order and no charges were made against him, although he earned a rebuke from the Privy Council for his pompous attitude and his father made a grovelling apology on his behalf.

Less than a year before, Surrey had revelled in being the king's main military man in France and had, against his own father's sage advice, encouraged him to keep control of Boulogne, but now a peace treaty was in the offing. To add insult to Surrey's injury, negotiations were led by Edward Seymour and John Dudley, mere upstarts in his opinion. Dudley's father, Edmund Dudley, had been half of the powerful Empson and Dudley partnership that had vigorously carried out the less popular financial policies of Henry VII; both were executed in the early days of his son's reign, to some extent scapegoats to boost his popularity. John Dudley, aged 7 in 1510 when his father died on Tower Hill, went on to have a glittering career under Henry VIII and was a leading religious reformer, who knew how to toe the line when Henry's changes of mind dictated it was the safest option.

Meanwhile, changing positions and alliances at court were by now obvious. The four Privy Councillors who had given Surrey an easy time over the noisy fracas in 1543 were no longer to be counted upon, although the earl seems not yet to have realised this. Surrey's father Norfolk and Bishop Gardiner were yesterday's men, fast fading from the scene. The latest Imperial ambassador, Francis Van der Delft, who sadly lacked some of the chatty enthusiasm of his predecessor Chapuys, would be reporting before the year's end that 'affairs change almost daily'.[8]

In 1546 Norfolk was 73 and not in the best of health. Those in the process of shaping the future might therefore have included him, at least for the short term, if only to give an initial appearance of stability and balance – after all, at his age and with his chronic problems with his bowels and fear of cold winters, the old duke might not be with them much longer. But what was to be done with his hot-headed and painfully arrogant nuisance of a son, who was already on record as declaring that when the king died his father should take charge in his successor's minority, and those who thought otherwise 'should smart for it'.

The 'new erected men' had had enough of Henry Howard's disparaging comments, his overbearing snobbery, the cloth of gold robes, the large intimidating band of expensively liveried mounted retainers and the showy semi-royal lifestyle with the building of Surrey House, none of which he could afford, and were all signs that his attitude would not stand him in good stead either as politician at home or a diplomat abroad.

By October Surrey was again back at Kenninghall trying to sort out his debts. A letter to Paget bears a striking resemblance to his late Uncle Edmund's grovelling missives to Wolsey and Cromwell. If Paget could put in a good word for him with the king regarding a property deal in Norwich, he will never ask for anything else and, it goes without saying, will serve the king as zealously as he had always done.[9] In November the earl thought he would have a better chance of sealing the deal if he could see his sovereign in person, so returned to London.

## Chapter 30

# The 'poure prisoner'

A man of his times, Thomas Howard, third Duke of Norfolk had participated in the downfall of many from the higher echelons of Henry VIII's advisors, not least Wolsey and Cromwell, and when dealing with the aftermath of the Lincolnshire Rising and the Pilgrimage of Grace had conducted the purge of the northern rebels, both nobility and common folk, with great gusto, making an example of the guilty and innocent alike. He had treated the diabolically cruel executions of the Carthusian monks almost as entertainment, and was accused of laughing as the courts were about to pass the death sentence on some of his niece Katherine Howard's co-accused. It is not easy, therefore, to feel sympathy for such a man in his own hour of need, but it is fair to say he had been unerringly loyal to king and country all his life, which makes the nature of his downfall in the winter of his years and the destruction of his son all the more shocking.

Technically, Norfolk's eldest son and heir was not entitled to use the style Earl of Surrey. When the father, then Earl of Surrey, became third Duke of Norfolk in 1524 no official machinery was put in place to transfer the title to his 7-year-old son. Therefore, for all his swagger and disdain of others, Henry Howard, whom here we shall continue to call Surrey, actually was using a courtesy title. On 2 December, still hopeful in securing a meeting with the king, at the Palace of Westminster he came upon the captain of the guard, Sir Anthony Wingfield, who asked if he may have a quiet word in private because he needed his help to ask a favour of his father the duke. It was a trap. As he stepped into a corridor Surrey was surrounded by armed men and arrested, with the king's full knowledge.

Not apprised of the charges against him, he was held for the next ten days at Ely Place on Holborn, the palace of the bishops of Ely, at the time rented by Wriothesley. What he was told, however, was that a courtier and Member of Parliament for the county of Norfolk had told the Privy Council he knew things about Surrey 'that touched his fidelity to the King'. This was Sir Richard Southwell, whose family originally hailed from East Anglia and had had connections with the dukes of Norfolk since the Mowbray days.

On 12 December Surrey, the earl-who-never-was, was forced to go on foot like a common man from Ely Place to the Tower, escorted by armed guards through busy streets taking him close to old haunts, including the Fleet Prison. There could hardly have been a greater humiliation bestowed upon such a proud man by those he had always despised and had never been afraid to show it. Meanwhile, tipped off that Surrey was detained, the duke had journeyed to London, arriving at about the same time his son was being marched through the city.

Arrested immediately, Norfolk's high status allowed his transfer to the Tower to be by barge, but like his son he was offered no explanation of his crime and throughout the journey vehemently proclaimed his innocence of any misdemeanour. Ironically, it was five years to the day that, helped along by his testimony, his stepmother Duchess Agnes had spent her first full day in the Tower and his half-sister, Katherine Bridgewater's children had been taken from her.[1] In dangerous times he had always managed to lie low; this time, as Van der Delft wrote two days later, whatever the charges were, the Howards would be lucky to survive, as the absolutely staggered father was already deprived of his Order of the Garter insignia, and his Lord Treasurer's white staff had been taken from him.[2]

Try as they might, even though they dragged in anybody and everybody who might have dirt to dish, Surrey's interrogators could find nothing serious enough to put him away for good. In desperation to get results against him, Seymour and Paget interviewed his father in the Tower, digging up old rumours, including accusing the duke of having been in secret correspondence with the Pope years before; he denied that and everything else thrown at him. Later that day, having had a few hours to digest what had transpired, the old man wrote a letter to the Privy Council to set down his understanding of what had been said at his earlier meeting, 'My Lord Great Master [Wriothesley, now Lord Chancellor] and Mr. Secretary [Paget] examined me here, as far as I can remember, as follows'. He went on to refute all accusations against him and presented a lengthy reminder of all he had done for king and country and requested to see Henry VIII.

In cases such as his, the prisoner did not know for sure of what he was accused until the day of the trial, nor would he have any equivalent of a solicitor of our own times with him while undergoing questioning. Norfolk's mind would have been in overdrive trying to make sense of a dreadful jumble of possibilities so, still pleading to be told what his crime was, he laid out every possibility he could think of, running through an impressive list of those, including his own family, who hated him, which was hardly presenting himself to his interrogators as an erstwhile good sort of chap who for some unfathomable reason was now being shamefully maligned.

To reinforce his loyalty to the Crown he raised the question, 'who was it who showed His Majesty of the words of my mother-in-law [sic], for which she was attainted of misprision of treason but only I!' He did have a point, although some men would have shrunk from bragging that in 1541 they had shopped old Duchess Agnes, who by the time of the duke's arrest had been dead eighteen months. He continued:

> I have always shown myself a true man to my sovereign ... who can think that I should now be false? I humbly beseech you to show this scribble letter to His Majesty, and beg him to grant its petitions and remit out of his noble gentle heart the displeasure conceived against me. By his Highness' poure prisoner, T. Norffolk.[3]

Whether or not the duke realised the full implications of his current predicament, his troubles had barely begun.

On Sunday 13 December at about three in the afternoon, Richard Southwell left London accompanied by John Gate, or Gates, and Wymond Carew, brothers-in-law of Sir Anthony Denny. Gate, like Denny, was one of the custodians of the 'dry stamp', the king's facsimile signature. Before dawn on Tuesday they were at the gates of Kenninghall to break news of the arrests and take charge of the Duke of Norfolk's affairs.[4] Hardly having risen from their beds, it was the first his mistress and daughter had heard of his arrest; the latter was said to have trembled so much they thought she would faint.

Norfolk's great mansion and his son's unfinished palace were to be seized, as was the fine house Norfolk was in the process of building at Mendham in Suffolk for Bess Holland, and inventories made of all their goods and chattels. It was just under five years since, on 20 December 1541, Wriothesley and the Earl of Southampton had found the old Duchess Agnes ill on her bed in the Tower 'apparently very sickly' and she had pleaded with them to ask the king not to give away Norfolk House.

No time was lost in sequestrating Norfolk and Surrey's lands, properties and possessions, but the agents were puzzled over what to do about Surrey's wife Frances and her children, still living at Kenninghall, and she now in the advanced stages of pregnancy. They did not linger long over the problem, however, and on the bitter January day sent her away in a chariot (carriage) with one of Norfolk's 'old and worn' nightgowns trimmed with coney and lamb fur across her lap for warmth.[5] As had been the case with Norfolk's half-sister, her children were taken from her, the younger ones to be placed in the care of Sir Thomas Wentworth, while the son and heir, Thomas, was sent to Sir John Williams, the Treasurer of the Court of Augmentations.[6]

Meanwhile, Norfolk's daughter Mary, Duchess of Richmond, professed herself to be aware of the loyalty she owed her father and brother but knew her duty and would conceal nothing from the king. Her father she 'ever thought to be true to the King', while her brother she believed on occasion could be 'a rash man'. The mistress and daughter were told to prepare to leave for London in the next twenty-four hours; the commissioners were amazed that while Bess Holland possessed many fine jewels and clothes, Mary had next to nothing of value.[7]

On 16 December Wriothesley told Van der Delft that the Howards had planned the seizure of the government of the king by sinister means and intended to kill all the Council, whilst they alone obtained complete control over the prince.[8] The ambassador did not fall for it, but a smear campaign was well underway, and as one of his French counterpart's predecessors had once said, 'When a man is imprisoned in the Tower there is no one living that dare meddle with his affairs or open his mouth, unless to speak ill of him, for fear of being suspected of the same crime'.[9]

Daughter and mistress added nothing of any great significance to the evidence against Norfolk. What did come to light, however, was a difference of opinion in the family over the use of certain arms on Surrey's fine new escutcheon. Bess knew little of the detail except that Norfolk did not approve of his latest effort and had told her not to incorporate certain elements of the heraldic design on the shield into her needlework.[10]

Meanwhile, in the Tower and now several days into his captivity, the duke asked for books from his Lambeth home, which must have been Norfolk House, as for 'this dozen years' he had fallen into the habit of reading prior to going to sleep. He also requested to be able to walk outside, possibly meaning in the lighter and larger of his two rooms, as he had been allowed to do when he was first incarcerated, and not to be locked in the other until night time. Also, he would appreciate some clean sheets.[11]

In his long letter of Christmas Eve to Charles V summarising the events so far, Van der Delft noted Henry had apologised for not seeing him earlier, explaining he 'had suffered from a sharp attack of fever, which had lasted in its burning stage for thirty hours, but that he was now quite restored; his colour does not bear out the latter statement, and he looks to me greatly fallen away'. Then came a most telling paragraph wherein the ambassador noted that Seymour and Dudley:

> have obtained such influence over the King as to lead him according to their fancy… It is even asserted here that the custody of the Prince and the government of the realm will be entrusted to them; and the misfortunes that have befallen the house of Norfolk may well have come from the same quarter… nothing is now done at court without their intervention, and the meetings of the Council are mostly held in the Earl of Hertford's house.[12]

Finally, still having made little headway in their endeavours, it was time for Wriothesley and the others to start scraping the very bottom of the barrel. The vehicle chosen to bring about the Howards' downfall was an accusation that they had traitorously flouted the rules of heraldry.

## Chapter 31

# A Question of Heraldry

Coats of arms were of enormous importance to the Tudors, visibly reinforcing a family's connections and status by displaying images from its ancestral roots. The Howards were entitled to their own symbol of a white band on crosslets, augmented since Flodden by the head of a lion with an arrow piercing its mouth, and others connected with their ancestry, including the white lion rampant on a red background of their Mowbray ancestors and the blue and gold checks of the Warennes.

With the Mowbrays being descended from Thomas of Brotherton, a son of Edward I's second marriage, they could also display three golden lions on a red background with a device known as a 'difference' to signify they were not the main holders. (A silver label, showing a 'difference' is a horizontal band with three downward points lying across the shield to distinguish the holder from the head of the family and show position in the hierarchy.) Henry VIII would have had extensive knowledge of heraldic symbolism – he was surrounded by it every day of his life. However, the niceties might need to be explained to him, and if a questionable use of a heraldic symbol could be put across to him as having been a deliberate sign of ambition, or even as a hint of incipient treason, in his state of mind he would have made an eager listener.[1]

The instrument on which the charges against Surrey were based was the Second Succession Act of 1536. By the terms of Section XII, treason could be committed in speech or writing deemed to be depriving the royal persons of their dignity and position.[2] The accusations about to be made against Surrey were not very convincing, and there was no specific reference in the 1536 Act to breaking the laws of heraldry, but needs must and it would have to do. It also lent a helping hand to those working to ensnare his father, who could be declared guilty by association.

A report submitted to Henry VIII explaining the events regarding the supposed breach of heraldic rules shows that although the senior herald, Christopher Barker, denied Surrey's request to use the arms of the House of Anjou, the first Plantagenets, on his fine new shield, his ruling on the application to use those of Edward the Confessor was less clear. The report reads that Surrey had sought advice from Richmond Herald, and when advised he should not use those of Anjou he readily accepted the ruling, but maintained that legally he could use Edward the Confessor's arms – which was true. However, nobody in authority spelt it out to Surrey that, given the king's current insecurities, it would be wise to steer clear.[3] This information was conveniently absent from his later indictment.

Thinking he was within his rights, which he was, Surrey had designs drawn up in the autumn of 1545 and showed them to his family at Kenninghall, which alarmed his father, who understood that in the current climate of royal paranoia, being descended from Edward I through the Mowbray connections and from Edward III through his mother Elizabeth Stafford, Surrey already faced more than enough potential pitfalls without setting himself up for more.[4] Edward the Confessor, the king whose death as long ago as January 1066 had precipitated events culminating in the Norman Conquest, was in the sixteenth century still held in great esteem. His arms, however, had been retrospectively invented in the age of chivalry, based on a design on his coinage – there were no such things in the Confessor's own times. Nor, as the Howards, and the senior heralds, well knew, were those later attributed to him exclusive to the reigning king. Richard II had incorporated them into his own coat of arms in 1397 and also granted Thomas Mowbray and his descendants right of use.

Surrey, therefore, *was* within his rights, as Thomas Mowbray, first Duke of Norfolk in the first creation, was his great-great-great grandfather. The Mowbrays and the Howards retained the right to display the arms but had rarely used it, and not at all in recent times. But, with what proved to be excruciatingly poor judgement, Surrey had set his heart on the Confessor's 'azure, a cross flory between five martlets or' (that is, a blue background, a cross with finials and five birds in gold) as part of his proposed new coat of arms, and senior herald, Christopher Barker, had not forbidden it outright.[5]

Thomas, Lord Burgh, formerly chamberlain to Anne Boleyn and one-time father-in-law to Katherine Parr, now his queen, was, on 31 December 1546, one of those commissioned 'to inquire touching the treasons in the county of Norfolk'. They in turn required the Sheriff of Norfolk to summon a grand jury to assemble at Norwich Castle on 7 January. This was duly done and the jury found the accusations to be valid and the resulting indictment against the Howards to be 'a true bill'.

The Bill of Indictment was convoluted, the heart of the charges claimed Surrey was considering all sorts of treasonable activities and was therefore a threat to the succession, but the part concerning the Confessor's arms set forth that they were appropriate only for the reigning king and silver labels only for his heir:

> ... nevertheless, one Henry Howard, late of Kennynggale, K.G.[Knight of the Garter] otherwise called Henry Earl of Surrey, on 7 Oct. 38 Hen. VIII, at Kennynggale, in the house of Thomas Duke of Norfolk, his father, openly used, and traitorously caused to be depicted, mixed and conjoined with his own arms and ensigns, the said arms and ensigns of the King, with thre labelles sylver.

Presented to them in such a way, with no mention of the grant by Richard II to his ancestor, or that the silver label, although associated with the reigning king and his heir, was not exclusive, what else was the jury going to do but find the indictment to be 'a true bill'?[6] Thus at Norwich Castle on 7 January 1547 were the Howard father and son indicted for treason and instructions sent to Sir John Gage, the Constable of the Tower, to bring Surrey to London Guildhall, on 13 January next at eight in the morning.[7]

The day before his son was to be tried, Thomas Howard, Duke of Norfolk, in the presence of Wriothesley, Dudley, Edward Seymour and Paget, several Privy Councillors and two judges, signed a confession in the Tower 'without compulsion, without force, without advice or counsel'. More than likely it would have been a pre-prepared document ready for his signature and was probably the first time he was fully cognisant of what the exact charges against him would be. He confessed to passing on state secrets 'to the great peril of His Highness', to displaying the arms of Edward I's son Thomas of Brotherton (the three lions of England) 'borne only by Prince Edward and borne for the realm of England only' and to incorporating a label in silver, borne also exclusively by the king's son. He also confessed to concealing Surrey's treason in using the arms of Edward the Confessor, which he had revealed at Kenninghall.[8]

Norfolk confessing to having passed on state secrets is astonishing; in the light of his long years of service and loyalty to the Crown his guilt seems most unlikely. Equally bewildering is his acceptance of having broken the rules of heraldry himself, which he, of all people, a direct descendant of Brotherton through the Mowbrays, knew he had not done. The College of Arms came under the aegis of the Duke of Norfolk as Earl Marshal, and while the main business of policing the display of heraldic devices was the province of the heralds and various commissions, Norfolk was a proud and well-informed man who would have been absolutely sure of what he was and was not permitted to display. So what possessed him to admit to charges that were blatant nonsense? It seems to have been a last-ditch attempt at self-preservation by an exhausted and frightened old man who had seen so many perish in the past and hoped his great age and grovelling contrition might save him.

Surrey was due to face a trial the next day and his father would have been fed enough information to know his son's was a lost cause and nothing he could say or do could save him. Whether the surviving document is a true and full report of what passed verbally between the duke and those who took his confession, who can tell? Did Norfolk try to put forward any argument that his son had acted in good faith and without malicious intent, or, as his confession suggests, deposed, untruthfully, that he himself had no rights to use the arms in question, so his son could not have had permission from him to do so, 'the said earl by no means or way could make any claim or title, by me, or any of mine, or his, ancestors.'[9] Maybe he hoped that by co-operating he would escape being attainted and it was his way of attempting to salvage something he could pass on to Surrey's children, but as it stands, such a confession, that would further undermine and put the final nail in the coffin of his own son, a father of four young children with another on the way, leaves a nasty taste in the mouth.

On 13 January 1547 Surrey, wearing the black satin coat furred with coney the Lieutenant of the Tower had bought him for his walk through the streets to his trial, was marched out of the fortress through crowds of onlookers, some sympathetic and dismayed that he of all people was in such a terrible situation, for despite his window smashing and whore-baiting antics four years before, he was not unpopular with the people as a whole.[10] With the Constable of the Tower and an armed escort he arrived at Guildhall, another reminder of his non-existent earldom, for a 'proper' earl would have ridden and been tried at Westminster Hall before his peers. Guildhall stood, and still does, close to Milk Street where, thanks to Surrey and his pals, Sir Richard Gresham's lovely and very expensive stained glass windows had come to grief. Inside, among the jurors standing by waiting to be sworn in, stood Richard Gresham himself. Surrey had no opportunity to object to certain individuals as jurors, as that right had been removed for treason cases in 1542.

The trial chamber was packed. Seated on the King's Bench were Chancellor Thomas Wriothesley in his very grand official robes, John Dudley, once the recipient of an angry letter from Surrey, Edward Seymour and William Paget. Surrey entered still accompanied by the Constable of the Tower and preceded by an official bearing the executioner's axe, its blade turned away from the prisoner. When the charges were read out it would have been the first time he knew in detail of what he was accused.[11] He pleaded not guilty to the charge of treason.

So there was Surrey, on his own, thinking on his feet and with no copy of the indictment before him to which he could refer. Defending himself for his life before judges and jury, some of whom hated him, he had no right to call witnesses of his own or to be represented by a lawyer. Branded a 'false and malicious traitor and public enemy', Surrey admitted he had used the Confessor's arms but vigorously denied treasonous intentions, as it was within his rights and told the court that when the heralds had seen his designs they had raised no objections. In a modern court of law the intricacies would need to be explained for the benefit of the jury; not so at this and other Tudor trials.

Apart from the breaches in heraldry, much of the other accumulated material from interviewing witnesses was read out, even though it had no bearing on the case. There is no surviving transcript but there were witnesses, including foreign ambassadors, in the public gallery. Surrey agreed he had said his father was the obvious choice to govern in the event of a minority and, in comparison with other potential candidates, genuinely believed it to be the case. Faced with the accusation he had suggested to his sister she become the king's mistress, he said that was not true. When informed she had spoken of it to Sir Gawain Carew, he was angry that he would be condemned on 'the word of a wretched woman'.[12]

Surrey defended himself vigorously all day, but would have realised the whole trial was a sham and he was as good as dead. The Bill of Indictment asserting the use of the arms was the prerogative of the king only, even though blatantly incorrect, had been found to be 'a true bill' before his case ever came to court, so when Surrey claimed before the jury that he had the right to use them, he was in fact condemning himself. According to Van der Delft, when at last he had had enough of the charade he snapped and laced into the Privy Councillors, all of whom were present, and 'addressed words to them that could not have been pleasant for them to hear'. Paget he declared to be a 'catchpole', a medieval derogatory name reminding him he was the son of a bailiff, 'the kingdom has never been well since the king put mean creatures like thee into the government'.

The trial had begun at nine in the morning and by late afternoon their assembled lordships were ready to bring it to a close. The jury was kept cold, hungry and uncomfortable to encourage a quick verdict – a nasty but legal tactic Surrey's father had not been against using in his time.[13] Those jurors who felt uneasy about returning a guilty verdict probably had a visit from Wriothesley or Paget to help them make up their minds. As early as five o'clock a guilty verdict was declared. The axe blade was turned towards Surrey who, demanding to know of what he was guilty, shouted out, 'Surely you will find no law that justifies you, but I know the King wants to get rid of the noble blood around him and to employ none but low people!'[14]

It was Wriothesley who pronounced the death sentence; it was to be the death of an untitled common man dragged through the streets on a hurdle to his death at Tyburn. Surrey hardly needed to pay attention as the Lord Chancellor described the process of hanging, drawing and quartering in all its horror. Many times he had witnessed others suffer the same end – he knew only too well what it entailed.

The Bill of Attainder, introduced into the House of Lords on 18 January, declared Norfolk and his son to be high traitors whose lands, chattels, titles and offices were forfeit. The next morning, 19 January, a Wednesday, the Lieutenant and Constable of the Tower walked with Surrey from his cell as far as the drawbridge. Overnight his sentence had been commuted to beheading, so instead of being dragged to Tyburn, two London sheriffs took him into their custody and walked with him to Tower Hill where, after the usual empty ritual of the executioner begging forgiveness and the accused admitting he was justly condemned, Henry Howard was killed with one blow of the axe.[15]

The reformer John Barlow, dean of Westbury, had in 1538 called Surrey 'the most foolish proud boy that is in England', the very characteristics that had now brought about his downfall. The arms of Edward the Confessor he had been within his rights to bear, but it was neither the time nor the place to have pursued that right. The Bill of Attainder became law on Thursday 27 January and his father, attainted and divested of the dukedom, title and all his worldly goods, and not having to face trial since he had already confessed, prepared himself for the same short walk to Tower Hill either the next day or in the very near future.

# Chapter 32

# 1547: A New Regime

On January 31 1547 Ambassador Odet de Selve wrote to Francis I, 'Have just heard that the Prince is proclaimed by the heralds King of England and Ireland and heir to all his late father's dominions; and that yesterday Norfolk [*sic*] was secretly beheaded in the Tower'.[1] He had been misinformed, for in the early hours of 28 January it was not Thomas Howard but Henry VIII whom the Grim Reaper visited, five years almost to the day since the House of Lords had found Katherine Howard guilty of treason. It is thought the former duke survived because the Council feared such a high-profile execution would not make for a good public image at the beginning of a new reign.

However, he remained incarcerated, largely in the great fortress's Beauchamp Tower, for the whole of the reign of Edward VI, but with increasing levels of comfort from early on, including garments made by a tailor named Bridges, a good supply of bedding, five paid servants and a very generous amount of spending money. Other concessions included permission to walk and ride in the Tower precincts, but always under supervision, a visit from his estranged wife, Elizabeth Stafford, which must have made interesting listening, and one from his daughter Mary in the winter of 1549. Surrey's son, another Thomas Howard, his grandfather's heir should his attainder ever be lifted, was allowed to visit in April 1551.[2]

Great recyclers that the Tudors were, just as Thomas Howard in his own heyday had hovered ready to pounce over the spoils of the condemned, so his accusers did well out of him, with Edward Seymour getting his clothes, fine chapel plate and jewels, including his garter insignia, and splitting his livestock and provisions with the Lady (Princess) Mary. Thomas Seymour was granted Chesworth House and its contents, although some of the luxury goods from there, such as carpets, beds and tapestries, were requisitioned for use in Edward VI's Nonsuch Palace near Cheam.[3] Norfolk House in Lambeth went to William Parr, Marquess of Northampton, the Dowager Queen Katherine Parr's younger brother.

King Henry VIII's will left clear instructions for the creation of a Regency Council of sixteen members for his 9-year-old son, all of whom would have an equal voice. Decisions were to be made by a majority vote with no one man holding a prominent position. It took only three days for his wishes to be overridden, with the Council unanimously electing the late Queen Jane's brother, Edward Seymour, Earl of Hertford, as 'Governor of the King's Person and Lord Protector of the Realm'.

In February, Paget and Anthony Denny drew up a book based on conversations they swore to have had with the ailing late monarch, and also on instructions they claim to have found in an odd additional clause in Henry's will concerning unfulfilled gifts and titles he had apparently intended to bestow before his death. Denny was one of the few men who had custody of the king's dry stamp, his facsimile signature which appears on the last page of the will indicating that Henry had been too weak to sign it properly.[4] Thanks to this controversial discovery of the 'unfulfilled gifts' clause, Protector Seymour became Duke of Somerset, a more appropriate status for a Protector, while his brother Thomas was made Baron Seymour of Sudeley. Wriothesley also benefited by gaining the title Earl of Southampton, while John Dudley became Earl of Warwick.

It was the start of the chain of traumatic events throughout the short reign of Edward VI that would witness power struggles, another war with Scotland, further religious reforms and in 1553 the young king making provision that should he die without heirs the throne would pass to Lady Jane Grey, a grandchild of Henry VIII's younger sister Mary and her husband Charles Brandon. She was also a daughter-in-law of John Dudley, who had in the intervening years ousted Somerset and taken the title Duke of Northumberland.

Edward VI was only 15 when he died in July 1553, possibly of tuberculosis, but had already concocted his 'devise', or plan, for the succession.[5] Sadly for Jane Grey it was fatally flawed, for although the Privy Council and other great men of the realm did sign Edward's document on 21 June, it did not automatically follow that the country at large would accept passing over Henry VIII's elder daughter Mary Tudor in favour of Jane Grey. Nor at the time of Edward VI's death had his 'devise' come before Parliament, which was on the agenda for September. While Jane's father-in-law, John Dudley, was out of London putting down rebellion and hoping to take Mary into custody, the Council made an about turn and pledged their allegiance to her. By 19 July, Jane Grey's reign was over after just nine days and Mary Tudor claimed the throne.[6]

On the evening of 3 August 1553, Queen Mary arrived in triumph at the Tower of London with a contingent of over 1000 retainers. Among prisoners kneeling before her on the grass were two old men, the younger of whom was 70-year-old Bishop Stephen Gardiner, who had resisted Seymour's rapid advance to Protestantism and had consequently been imprisoned in the Tower since June 1548. The other, now 80 years old, was Thomas Howard, erstwhile third Duke of Norfolk, by then halfway through his sixth year of imprisonment. Queen Mary helped them to their feet, announcing that they were her 'prisoners' now.

Howard's rehabilitation and restoration to some of his former offices was rapid. Kenninghall and Framlingham were restored to him, as were Norfolk House and Chesworth, and in September other property, some of which had been given to Edward Seymour and then at his demise in 1550 to John Dudley, was recovered, including his ducal coronet and garter regalia. As Earl Marshal he was responsible for arranging Queen Mary's coronation on 1 October and later in the month her first Parliament lifted the attainder and restored him as third Duke of Norfolk. With the attainder of the dead Surrey also reversed, his young son, restored in blood, would one day become fourth Duke of Norfolk.

Thomas Wyatt the Younger led a rebellion in January 1554 against the queen's plan to marry Charles V's son, Philip of Spain, a grandson of her mother's sister

Juana. Wyatt, son of Surrey's great friend, was one of the rowdy pack who had accompanied the earl on his vandalism episode ten years earlier. Norfolk, sent to quash the rebellion, at 81 and only recently released from six years of imprisonment, was a shadow of his former self and not the savvy general he once had been. His men turned on him, instead chanting for Wyatt and asking why they were fighting fellow Englishmen for the sake of Mary's Spanish fiancé, forcing Norfolk to make an ignominious retreat.

Thomas Howard, third Duke of Norfolk died on 25 August 1554 at Kenninghall, leaving the majority of his money, possessions and properties to his grandson and heir, who became fourth duke. To his daughter Mary, Duchess of Richmond and Somerset he left money for bringing up her late brother's children and for what he called her great expense when trying to secure her father's release. His long-suffering wife, Elizabeth Stafford, outlived him by only four years.

The Flodden duke had passed away thirty years earlier and his son's 1554 funeral, although less spectacular, was on similar lines, followed by a large feast and the giving of traditional aid to the poor. This Howard duke though would not be buried at Thetford as his father and grandfather had been. By now Thetford priory was redundant, the Howard coffins already moved to St Michael's at Framlingham, where he also would be laid to rest in a most elaborate tomb.

The Earl of Surrey's remains, which after his execution had been buried at the church of All Hallows close to the Tower, were moved to Framlingham in 1614, where he rests with his wife Frances de Vere in a magnificent tomb. Apart from its ornate richness and fashionable bright colours, one other feature distinguishes it from the rest – the coronet is not on his head, instead lying beside his right thigh, signifying the gruesome nature of his death.

# Epilogue

In the intervening three decades between the deaths of the second and third Dukes of Norfolk the Howard dynasty had provided two queens consort, both of whom met violent deaths, and survived the chaos and carnage of Henry VIII's reign, but only just. Their deadly entanglement with the Tudors, however, was not over yet.

Surrey's heir, the fourth duke, married two great heiresses, the first of whom, Mary Fitzalan, daughter of the Earl of Arundel, brought Arundel Castle in Sussex into Howard ownership but died aged only 16, eight weeks after the birth of her son Philip, while his second wife was the heiress of Lord Chancellor Thomas Audley. The fourth duke was executed for treason and his dukedom forfeited in June 1572 for plotting to depose his kinswoman Queen Elizabeth in favour of Mary, Queen of Scots whom he was hoping to marry. His son, Philip Howard, a Roman Catholic who refused to convert, died in the Tower in 1595 and the Norfolk dukedom was not restored to Thomas Howard, Earl of Arundel, Philip's great-grandson, until 1660.

In time, the ducal branch of the family made Arundel Castle their main home. Of the East Anglian properties only one wing of the great mansion at Kenninghall remains, and is now a private dwelling, while the ruins of Framlingham Castle are in the care of English Heritage. In 1842 it was decided to change the family name to Fitzalan-Howard as an acknowledgement of the fourth duke's marriage and is not associated with Elizabeth Fitzalan who married into the Mowbray family in 1382. The family motto is *Sola Virtus Invicta* (virtue alone is unconquered), while the shield, or escutcheon, bears the arms of Howard, Brotherton, Warenne and Fitzalan, but with no reference to their Mowbray ancestry.[1]

## Appendix

# What Became of Norfolk House?

For all its history there is precious little surviving detailed information about Norfolk House, the original property possibly came to the Howards via their Mowbray ancestors in 1483. Thomas Fitzalan, a son of the fourth Earl of Arundel, was married in Lambeth in 1405 and one of his heirs at his death in 1415 was his sister Elizabeth Fitzalan, mother of John Mowbray, future second Mowbray Duke of Norfolk,[1] however, the current Fitzalan Street in Lambeth was a late eighteenth-century creation, originally named Union Street. Excavations carried out in 1988 and 1990 indicated Norfolk House had been an impressive building, largely of early sixteenth-century date which could have replaced or improved and extended an earlier house and would correspond with the restoration of the dukedom in 1514.[2]

Eighteenth- and nineteenth-century writers Daniel Lysons (1792), Manning and Bray (1814), Thomas Allan (1826) and John Tanswell (1863) present almost identical accounts – namely that the house was lost by the third Howard Duke of Norfolk at his attainder and transferred to William Parr but regained by him in the first year of Queen Mary's reign.[3] According to Lysons in 1792, 'Where Norfolk Row now stands, in the smith's shop belonging to Betts's stocking manufactory, the back part of which is opposite to that row, there is an old chimney-piece formerly belonging to one of the rooms [of Norfolk House]'. According to Allen in 1826, 'at present none of the original buildings remain, the site of it being taken up with the extensive distillery of Messrs. Hodges and Son, and several houses in Paradise-row, including a malt-house'.

Sir Howard Roberts and Walter H. Godfrey, writing in 1951, present the best sequence of events. In 1524, as we already know, Norfolk House and freehold and copyhold (tenanted) lands in Lambeth went as part of her widow's settlement to Agnes Tilney for life, with whom, the authors inform us, Katherine Howard 'spent her neglected childhood', and Duchess Agnes lost it at her attainder in 1542. It was restored to her stepson, Thomas Howard the third Duke, who used it as his suburban residence until his own attainder in 1547, when his estates were seized and the house granted to William Parr, Marquess of Northampton, brother of Henry VIII's last wife, but it was restored to him in 1553. His grandson, son of the beheaded Henry Howard, became fourth duke and shortly afterwards sold the estate to a Richard Garthe and a John Dyster for £400, and from then on the estate was carved up into ever-smaller portions.

The property is described in the sale as 'a capital messuage [that is, the main house] "wherein the ancestors of the said duke have accustomed to lye"; two inns, formerly called the George and the Bell, the former being annexed to the mansion house on the west and the Bell, on the east; Bell Close, at the rear of the Bell, containing two acres, two perches; 23½ acres in "Cottmansfeld"; an acre of pasture in St George's Field; a close lying near the Bishop of Rochester's House [by then called Carlisle House] containing four acres; three acres of meadow near Prince's Meadows; and eight acres of marsh called "the Hopes"'.

Garthe and Dyster divided the property into three parts, which they then sold. The part which included Norfolk House itself and the Bell and Bell Close, was sold to John Glascocke and then to Margaret Parker, wife of Archbishop Parker, and, at her death in 1570, passed to her younger son, Matthew, who died in 1575 leaving the property to his brother John, who within a few years had divided it into three. The western portion, on which stood the main part of the original house, and where a large part of the Novotel and part of Palace View Apartments (formerly premises of the Royal Pharmaceutical Society) stand now, he sold in 1590 to Archbishop Whitgift, and Sir George Paule bought the house from Whitgift's son in 1608, living there until his death in 1635.

From the details of the 1590 sale some idea can be gained of the size of Norfolk House and the layout of the main buildings, although this was nearly half a century after the Dowager Duchess of Norfolk had lost it at her attainder. There was a large gateway from 'the King's highway' (now Lambeth Road) leading into a paved yard. On the west was the Duke's chapel which, by 1590, had been partitioned to make a hall, buttery and parlour and a number of small rooms; on the east were the kitchen offices with 'a greate chamber' on the first floor, a gallery, oratory and several closets and the hall opening on to the garden at the south. (Was this range the original great hall, adapted since Agnes's time?) The total width of the garden (remaining around the actual dwelling) was 125 feet, and it is a reasonable assumption that the street frontage of the house was approximately the same.[4]

The association of Norfolk House with Lambeth delftware began after further sales and exchanges had taken place, when in 1680 the potter, James Barston, set up business on part of the site of Norfolk House and began production of tin glazed earthenware; in time this site would become the Doulton factory in Lambeth.

According to the *Report on the Archaeological Excavations at 113–129 Lambeth Road S.E.1* sponsored by Vestey Estates Ltd.,[5] a nineteenth-century candle factory (shown on the Ordnance Survey Map of 1872) had contaminated the site in the south, so the archaeologists' efforts were concentrated on the north side. All that could be excavated was on Lambeth Road where glazed floor tiles indicated a building of high status, the major part of the remains excavated dating from the early sixteenth century.

Only a very small part of what was once here was found, and a good deal of artist William Wyatt's reconstruction had to be conjectural, based on details from surviving buildings of similar type and date. From this and the rest of the evidence, the present writer concludes that Norfolk House had many features in common with Gainsborough Old Hall in North Lincolnshire.

Of note at the Norfolk House excavation was the presence of a large number of vitrified bricks and various types of moulded brick which afforded some idea of the appearance of the northern, street front, wall. Vitrified (over-fired) bricks, then the height of fashion, were used in the grander Tudor buildings to form glossy black diaper patterns to break up the monotony of bright red brickwork. They too are to be found at Gainsborough. Linear development of Norfolk House along the street frontage was approximately 35 metres (105 feet) in length, which with the addition of a building, not included in the measurements on the plans, compares favourably with the measurements given by Roberts and Godfrey; this is not far off the dimensions of the north elevation of Gainsborough Old Hall.[6]

# Notes

## Introduction

1. The Lincolnshire Rising, the Pilgrimage of Grace and Francis Bigod's Rebellion took place between October 1536 and the following February.
2. Katherine Howard is first mentioned on 22 November 1539, see Gairdner, James *et al.*, *Letters and Papers of Henry VIII*, (HMSO, London, 1898); she married Henry on 28 July 1540 and was executed on 13 February 1542.
3. If Katherine had been born in 1521 it would make her 18 or 19 in July 1540 when she became queen.
4. The *Spanish Chronicle* was written some years after Queen Katherine's death and has many inaccuracies, see Hume, Martin, *Chronicle of King Henry VIII of England*, (George Bell and Sons, London, 1889).
5. Strickland, Agnes, *Lives of the Queens of England*, 12 vols., 1840–1848, (1867 Harper, New York).
6. See also Delorme, Mary, 'Facts, Not Opinions: Agnes Strickland' in *History Today* vol. 38, (London, 1988).
7. Ottwell Johnson, writing to his brother John Johnson, a merchant of the Staple at Calais, describing the execution of Queen Katherine Howard. See Ellis, Sir Henry, *Original Letters Illustrative of English History*, second edition vol. 2, (London, 1825); Letter CXLVII.

## Prologue

1. Barlings Abbey was a Premonstratensian house, a member of an order of canons regular founded by St Norbert at Prémontré near Laon, France, in 1120.

## Chapter 1: The Howards of East Anglia

1. PRO SP 1/227, fo.97. Cromwell had been attainted, that is condemned without trial, a tactic he had used against others, hence 'stricken with his own staff'.
2. The king's father, Henry VII, had carefully managed the 'new' nobility that emerged after the Battle of Bosworth.

3. Mowbray blood included that of the Plantagenets, Capets, Segraves, Bigods, Warennes, de Bohuns, Percys and Fitzalans.
4. See Roberts, Marilyn, *The Mowbray Legacy*, Chapter 4, (Queens-Haven Publications, Lincolnshire, 2012).
5. For example, a 1438 document refers to Margaret Mowbray as the widow of Robert Howard *armiger*, that is, an arms bearer, Warwickshire Record Office CR 1886/282.
6. Brenan, Gerald & Edward Phillips Statham, *The House of Howard*, (Hutchinson and Co, London, 1907) and also Robinson, John Martin, *The Dukes of Norfolk*, (Phillimore & Co Ltd, Chichester, 1995), claimed Robert Howard held important positions. Anne Crawford, Robert Howard's son's biographer (see note 8 below) could find no reference to these claims,
7. Charles V of France's closest male relative was Edward III of England, his sister Isabella's son, but the French rejected his claim to the throne and it passed to Charles's cousin, Philip, Count of Valois.
8. For full details of his life see Crawford, Anne, *Yorkist Lord*, (Continuum, London, 2010).
9. See 'Household Accounts of Sir John Howard (1462–1471)' in Turner, T.H. (ed.), *Manners and Household Expenses in England in the Thirteenth and Fifteenth Centuries,* (Roxburghe Club, 1841). This is Household Book 1 (H.B.I).
10. Crawford, Chapter 8, gives an account of projects, contacts, commissions, trading, bills, invoices, properties/tenants, purchases, building, finances, charity and even his love of chess and music; Chapter 9 details his business interests.
11. Calendar of Patent Rolls 1467–77, (HMSO, London, 1900), p.204.
12. 'Summons to a Parliament at Westminster on 26 November next', Calendar of Close Rolls, Edward IV vol. 2, 1468–1476, pp.167–178.
13. Crawford, p.185, note 35.

## Chapter 2: The Mowbray Inheritance

1. Roberts, Marilyn, *Lady Anne Mowbray: The High and Excellent Princess*, (Queens-Haven Publications, Lincolnshire, 2012), pp.6–7.
2. Ibid., pp.13–22
3. Black, W.H. (ed.), *Illustrations of Ancient State and Chivalry from manuscripts preserved in the Ashmolean Museum*, (Roxburgh Club, 1840). Also, Roberts, Marilyn, *Lady Anne Mowbray: The High and Excellent Princess,* pp.23–29.
4. For the original Act of Parliament of 1478 see *Rotuli Parliamentorum*, vol. 6, pp.169–70.
5. Speculation in later centuries that he had entered into some sort of compensation arrangement with Edward IV, as his cousin Berkeley had, has never been corroborated and evidence of any associated documentation to that effect is not known.
6. Roberts, Marilyn, *Lady Anne Mowbray: The High and Excellent Princess,* pp.34–57. Anne's coffin had been relocated to the convent of the Minoresses

near the Tower for the duration of the construction of the Henry VII chapel at Westminster Abbey and was never returned.
7. Warwick, Professor Roger, 'Anne Mowbray: skeletal remains of a medieval child', in *The London Archaeologist,* vol. 57, (London, 1986).
8. Lands still held by Anne Mowbray's mother, Elizabeth Talbot, fourth duchess, were less than might have been expected, as she had already made over extensive lands and properties to Edward IV before her daughter's marriage, as recorded in Arundel Castle A. C. MSS MD 1499.
9. Pronay, Nicholas; Cox, John (eds.), *The Crowland Chronicle Continuations: 1459–1486,* (Alan Sutton, London, 1986).
10. See Crawford p.187 fn. 26; H.B. II pp.378–9 and pp.383–4 for the hire of the boats.
11. For the Thomas Basin reference see Weir, Alison, *The Princes in the Tower*, (Pimlico, London, 1992), p.61.
12. Sutton, Anne and Livia Visser-Fuchs, *The Royal Funerals of the House of York at Windsor*, (Richard III society, 2005), p.37.
13. Much of the narrative of what happened in the three months between the death of Edward IV and the coronation of Gloucester as King Richard III is found in the observations of three contemporaries: the Italian Domenico Mancini, the *Crowland (Croyland) Chronicle* Second Continuator, and John Rous, the chantry priest of Guy's Cliffe in Warwickshire, with Polydore Vergil and Sir Thomas More writing some decades later. All the accounts present problems, however, and are littered with 'as men say', 'I have heard' and so on. The *Rous Roll*, English version BL Add MS 48976; Latin version, College of Arms, London; Wengemer G.B. and Curtright T., *The History of Richard III*, the Centre for Thomas More Studies.
https://thomasmorestudies.org/wp-content/uploads/2020/08/Richard.pdf.
14. Carson, Annette, *Richard of Gloucester as Lord Protector and High Constable of England*, (Imprimis Imprimatur, 2015).
15. For the hired boats see Crawford, p.108; also H.B. II p.402. Ann Wroe in *Perkin* examines the meeting pp.67–69 and says the archbishop and Sir Thomas Howard took the prince away by boat.
16. See Domenico Mancini's account in Armstrong, C.A.J. (ed.), *De Occupatione Regni Anglie per Riccardum, The Usurpation of Richard III*, (Sutton Publishing, Stroud, 1984).

# Chapter 3: The Duke of Norfolk

1. Castor, Helen, *Blood and Roses*, (Faber& Faber, London, 2004), p.290.
2. Payne Collier, J. (ed.), *Household Books of John Duke of Norfolk and Thomas Earl of Surrey 1481–1490*, (Roxburgh Club, London, 1844), H.B.II pp.xiii.
3. Tucker, Melvyn J., *The Life of Thomas Howard, Earl of Surrey and Second Duke of Norfolk 1443–1524*, (Mouton, The Hague, 1964), pp.38–45.

4. Crawford in *Yorkist Lord*, p.93; see also Crawford, Anne, 'John Howard, Duke of Norfolk: a possible murderer of the Princes' in *The Ricardian*, vol. V, 1981.
5. For coronation details see Sutton, Anne F. and Hammond, P. W., *The Coronation of Richard III: the Extant Documents*, (Alan Sutton, Gloucester, 1983).
6. In 1674 workmen at the Tower dug up a wooden box containing two small human skeletons from under a staircase.
7. His great-granddaughter, Katherine Howard, spent part of her early to mid-teens there in the care of her step-grandmother the Dowager Duchess Agnes in the 1530s.
8. Parliament (1483), '6. *An Act for the Attaynder of Margaret Countesse of Richmond*', (Rotuli Parliamentorum).
9. Titulus Regius; for details of the Act and how it was found in the Tower in the seventeenth century see Bryce, Tracy, *Titulus Regius: The title of the King*, Richard III Society of Canada. www.richardiii.ca/titulus-regius-the-title-of-the-king.
10. Details of the location from Battlefields Trust. www.battlefieldstrust.com.
11. Brenan & Statham, in *The House of Howard* claimed that when Norfolk's visor fell off Oxford refused to fight on because it would have been an uneven contest, 'It must be recollected that Oxford was over twenty years his adversary's junior. He was also under deep obligations to Norfolk for the manner in which he [when Sir John Howard] had treated his (Oxford's) widowed mother', Brenan p.55; no references given for sources.
12. For details of the discovery and identification of the remains of Richard III see University of Leicester: www.le.ac.uk/richard-iii.
13. Ashdown-Hill, John 'The Opening of the tombs of the dukes of Richmond and Norfolk Framlingham April 1841' in *The Ricardian* vol. 18 (2008).
14. Crawford, p.152.

## Chapter 4: Rehabilitation

1. Sir Gilbert Talbot of Grafton (1452–1517) a younger son of John Talbot Earl of Shrewsbury and brother of Anne Mowbray's mother, Elizabeth Talbot, and of the Eleanor Talbot said to have been pre-contracted to Edward IV.
2. For the meaning and implication of attainder see Lander, J. R., 'Attainder and Forfeiture, 1453 to 1509' in *The Historical Journal*, vol. 4, no. 2, 1961, pp.119–151.
3. Hutchinson, Robert, *House of Treason: The Rise and Fall of a Tudor Dynasty*, (Phoenix, London, 2009), p.9.
4. Weever *Rolls of Parliament*, vol. vi, p.478.
5. Leland, John, *Antiquarii De Rebus Britannicis Collectanea*, vol. 3, (Hearne, T., (ed.), Oxford, 1770) p.274.
6. Ellis, Sir Henry (ed.), 'Queen Margaret of Scotland to her father Henry VII' in *Original Letters Illustrative of English History* second edition, vol. 1 p.41, Letter XX, (Harding *et al.*, London, 1825).

7. The restitution of the remainder of Surrey's lands may be found in the Act of Restitution (copy) Arundel Castle Archives G2/9.
8. L&P vol. 1, no. 880, Wolsey to Fox, 30 September 1511.
9. https://maryrose.org/the-history-of-the-mary-rose/#1510.
10. Spont, Alfred, *Letters and Papers Relating to the War with France, 1512–13*, pp.97–8. Can be read in full at www.navyrecords.org.uk/letters-and-papers-relating-to-the-war-with-france-1512-1513/.
11. Ellis, *Original Letters Illustrative of English History Third Series* vol. 1, (Bentley, London, 1846), p.154, Letter LXII Thomas Howard to Wolsey immediately after taking over from his brother: 'Scribbled in great haste on the Mary Rose at Plymouth, at half past eleven on the night of 7 May'; see also L&P vol. 1, no. 1852.
12. Ellis, *Original Letters Illustrative of English History First Series* second edition vol. I (Bentley, London, 1825) Letter XXVII, p 76, James IV to Henry VIII, 24 May 1513.
13. Statutes of the Realm, vol. 3, Henry VIII, (Dawson, London, 1817).

# Chapter 5: Saviours of the Realm: Flodden

1. Goodwin, George, *Fatal Rivalry, Flodden 1513*, (Weidenfeld and Nicholson, London, 2014), p.176, citing *Grafton Chronicle*, (Johnson *et al.*, London, 1809), p.271.
2. Surrey's second letter to James IV 'Written in the field in Woolerhaughe, 7 September, 5 o'clock in the afternoon'. It was signed by himself and eighteen of his commanders. He requested that James send a messenger with a signed agreement to meet him on the actual Milfield Plain. Ellis, Sir Henry, Second edition vol. 1, Letter XXXI, p.85.
3. Thanks to Clive Hallam-Baker of the *Remembering Flodden Project* for his thoughts on the state of the terrain and Surrey's mobility problems. See also L.A.B. Scotland's excellent short film *Remembering Flodden Project* https://www.bbc.co.uk/programmes/p01gnx1g.
4. Hutchinson, Robert, *House of Treason: The Rise and Fall of a Tudor Dynasty*, (Phoenix, London, 2009), p.29, citing *Hall's Chronicle*, (Johnson *et al.*, London, 1809), p.561.
5. Lindsay, Robert, *The Chronicles of Scotland*, (Blackwood and Sons, Edinburgh and London, 1899), p.277. (*Pitscottie Chronicles* frequently referred to as *The Pitscottie Chronicles*.)
6. Surrey's 400-man artillery corps was led by Nicholas Appleyard and included twenty-two guns, eighteen 2-pounder falcons and four 4-pounder serpentines. Lighter and more manoeuvrable than the heavy Scottish siege guns, they were more suited to the conditions and location.
7. Accounts of the battle can be found in L&P vol. 1, no. 2236 and no. 2246 4; the Earl of Surrey made forty knights on the battlefield, including his son Lord Edmund Howard and Nicholas Appleyard, L&P vol. 1, no. 2246 4 ii.

8. Ellis, *Original Letters* second edition, vol. 1, 1825 pp.88–9, Letter XXXII, Katherine of Aragon to Henry VIII regarding Lord Admiral Thomas Howard's letter to her.
9. See *The Sad Tale of King James IV's Body*, Dr Tony Pollard, BBC News Scotland; www.bbc.co.uk/news/uk-scotland-23993363.
10. Ridgard, John (ed.), *Medieval Framlingham*, Suffolk Record Society 27 (Boydell Press, Dover New Hampshire, 1985), p.6, 153, inventory of 1524; plate gilt, 'ii grett pottis with the scottishe kingis armys on the hed of theym, 300 ounces'.
11. Details of the dukedom and a description of the ceremony can be found in BL Egerton Ms 985 fol. 59.
12. For Letters Patent and granting the Augmentation to the Howard arms see Arundel Castle Archives G1/83.
13. Ellis, *Original Letters* second edition vol.1, 1825, pp.115–117, Letter XXXIX, Mary Queen of France to King Henry the Eighth.
14. Grafton, Richard, *Chronicle or History of England 1189–1558*, 2 vols. (Johnson *et al.*, London, 1809), p.293.
15. L&P vol. 2, no. 3259, Nicolo Sagudino writing on 19 May 1517. He was secretary to Alvise Foscari, the Venetian Ambassador to England.
16. L&P vol. 3, part I, p.cxxxiv; Hall, *Chronicle* p.624.
17. For details of his funeral and life see Martin, Thomas, *History of Thetford*, (J. Nichols, London, 1779), Appendix VIII.
18. Thomas Hawley was created Carlisle Herald in 1514, Norroy King of Arms in 1534 and Clarenceux King of Arms in 1536; he died in 1557.
19. Following its closure in 1540 (it was one of the last priories to be dissolved), the third Howard duke had the family remains removed to the Church of St Michael the Archangel, Framlingham.

## Chapter 6: A Great Matter

1. In its latter days the western parts of original and ancient Roman Empire had collapsed in the fifth century AD; Eastern territories centred on Constantinople were later referred to as the Byzantine Empire.
2. Starkey, David, *Six Wives*, (Vintage, London, 2004), p.290.
3. George Wyatt is quoted by George Cavendish in his *The Life of Cardinal Wolsey*, (Weller-singer, Samuel, Chiswick, 1825).
4. Leviticus 20:21.
5. Twenty-four years later Elizabeth, who had led a miserable life, related her story in a letter to Thomas Cromwell, see Wood, Mary Anne Everett, *Letters of Royal and Illustrious Ladies of Great Britain* vol. II, (Henry Colburn, London, 1846), Letter CXLVIII, p.360 ff.
6. A small part remains and is now a private house: Thurley, Simon, *Royal Palaces of Tudor England*, (Yale University Press, London, 1993), p.41–43.
7. Wood, p.223–225 Letter XC.

8. PRO SP 60/1 fo. 114. Dr William Butts c.1485–1545, personal physician to Henry VIII.
9. L&P vol. 4 Introduction p.ccclxxii for the sweating sickness description; Dr Butts also treated Anne Boleyn during this outbreak. For Duchess Agnes's 1528 letter to Wolsey see this book, Chapter 12.
10. L&P vol. 4, no. 5778, 16 July – the original, on two skins of vellum, is very badly mutilated.
11. L&P vol. 4, no. 5994, 7 October 1529; Clement VII, Giulio di Giuliano de' Medici, in office 1523–1534.
12. BL Add. MS 19398, f.44.
13. Eustace Chapuys to the Emperor Charles V: Spain vol. 4, part 1, no. 228, 9 December 1529, de Gayangos, Pascual (ed.), (HMSO, London, 1879).
14. Chapuys to the Emperor Charles V, CSP Spain vol. 4, part 1, no. 232, 13 December.
15. Chapuys to Charles V, CSP Spain, vol. 4, part 1, no. 257, 6 February 1530.
16. *Collectanea satis copiosa,* BL Shelfmark: Cotton Ms. Cleopatra E vi, fols.37v-38. This document can be viewed on the British Library website, and has Henry VIII's comments written all over it.
17. Admiral Lord Nelson was buried in the crypt of St Paul's Cathedral, 9 January 1806. The black marble sarcophagus on the top of his tomb was made by Benedetto da Rovezzano (1474–1552) for Cardinal Wolsey; Nelson is not buried in the sarcophagus itself. Henry VIII had plans for it himself as part of a lavish tomb, but they came to nothing.

## Chapter 7: Times of Change

1. Katherine was sent to live at The More, a fine palace in Hertfordshire, late in 1531. Between May 1532 and her final move to Kimbolton Castle in 1534 she had also been held at Hatfield Palace, Elsyng Palace, Ampthill Castle and Buckden Towers.
2. L&P vol. 5, no. 238, 14 May, Chapuys to Charles V, 'At the desire of the same lady [Anne Boleyn] the Duchess of Norfolk has been sent home, because she spoke too freely, and declared herself more than they liked for the Queen'.
3. Griffith, Ralph, Rhys ap Thomas and his Family: *A Study in the Wars of the Roses and Early Tudor Politics*, (University of Wales Press, Cardiff, 1993), pp.106, 110–11.
4. Burgh, Borow or Borough, pronounced 'borough'; one of his daughters-in-law was the young Katherine Parr.
5. L&P vol. 6, no. 584, 2 June. For details of the journey to the Tower, the coronation, people present and the cost of the proceedings see L&P vol. 6, entries beginning no. 556, 29 May to no 585, 2 June.
6. L&P vol. 6, no. 1111, 10 September.
7. Richard Rex 'Royal Supremacy (1531–1535)' in *Henry VIII Man and Monarch*, British Library Exhibition Catalogue, Susan Doran and David Starkey (eds.), (BL, London, 2009), pp.127–129.

8. L&P vol. 8, no. 1, 1 January 1535.
9. The Act of Supremacy 1534: TNA C 65/143, m.5, no. 8.
10. See Roberts, Marilyn, *The Mowbray Legacy* Appendix G. The remains of the Axholme Charterhouse may be seen on Google Maps, Postcode DN9 1AD, Melwood Hill.
11. L&P vol. 8, no. 666, 5 May 1536.

## Chapter 8: Choler and Agony

1. L&P vol. 9, no. 1036, Chapuys to Charles V, 30 December.
2. L&P vol. 10, no. 282, Chapuys to Charles V, 10 February 1536.
3. Ives, Eric, *The Life and Death of Anne Boleyn*, (Blackwell, Oxford, 2005), p.334–335.
4. L&P vol. 10, no 782, Chapuys to Charles V, 2 May.
5. See the Middlesex Jury's Indictment complete with fictitious dates and graphic details, L&P vol. 10, no. 876, 15 May.
6. Commission to Thomas Howard Duke of Norfolk as Lord Steward of England to assemble a jury of peers to try Anne and George Boleyn: TNA KB 8/9, membrane 17.
7. L&P vol. 10, no. 282, Eustace Chapuys to Antoine Perrenot, a leading diplomat for the Hapsburgs and later a cardinal, 10 February 1536. This is the first recorded reference to Jane Seymour.
8. L&P vol. 11, no. 48; Lord Thomas and those who knew him interrogated.
9. Daubeney was involved in a bitter and protracted dispute with the Lisles over lands; see St Clare Byrne, Muriel (ed.), *The Lisle Letters*, (Secker & Warburg, London, 1983), in particular pp.337–343.
10. L&P vol. 11, no. 108, Lord Husee to Lord Lisle, 18 July 1536. Henry had entertained thoughts of Fitzroy succeeding him.
11. L&P vol. 11, no. 221, 3 August 1536, Chapuys to Antoine Perrenot. See also L&P vol. 11, no. 228, Castelnau, Bishop of Tarbes to Cardinal Du Bellay, 4 August.
12. L&P vol. 11, no. 233, 5 August 1536, Norfolk to Cromwell.

## Chapter 9: The Northern Rebellions

1. *Valor Ecclesiasticus*, 1535; TNA E344/22 f2.
2. For the pattern of monastic suppression at the Dissolution, its effect on the religious orders, its relationship to the outbreak of rebellion, and the long term social and economic impact of the exchange of such massive wealth see Peyton, Nick, 'The Dissolution of the English Monasteries: A Quantitative Investigation', in *LSE Economic History Working Papers*, no. 316, (London, December 2020).

3. L&P vol. 11, no. 458, 16 September.
4. Recording of the events of the rebellion begins in L&P vol. 11, no. 531, 3 October, and continues intermittently for the next twelve months.
5. L&P vol. 11, no. 533, 3 October.
6. L&P vol. 12, part 1, no. 6, 1 January 1537, *The manner of the taking of Robert Aske in Lincolnshire, and the use of the same Robert unto his passage from York.*
7. Sawcliffe medieval village and moated site, Roxby cum Risby. 1017554 | Historic England. https://historicengland.org.uk/listing/the-list/list-entry/1017554.
8. L&P vol. 11: for the list of those required to provide men see no. 580, 7 October. For Lord William Howard's letter to Cromwell see no. 636, 10 October.
9. CSP Spain vol. 5, part 2, no. 104, 7 October.
10. L&P vol. 11, no. 642.
11. L&P vol. 11, no. 780 (2) 'Answer to the petitions of the traitors and rebels in Lincolnshire'.
12. L&P vol. 11, no. 780, 19 October.
13. L&P vol. 12, part 1, nos. 97 and 98, 16 January 1537.
14. L&P vol. 12, part 1, no. 478 Norfolk to Cromwell 21 February 1537.
15. L&P vol. 12, part 1, no. 479 Henry VIII to the Duke of Norfolk, 22 February.
16. Hutchinson, p.119; TNA SP 1/116/ 108.
17. Ridley, Jasper, *Henry VIII,* (Penguin Books, London, 1984).
18. L&P vol. 12, part 1, no. 734, 26 March 1537.
19. Bindoff, *History of Parliament*, Ref Volumes 1509–1558, (Secker & Warburg, London, 1982).
20. L&P vol. 11, no. 805, 20 October.
21. L&P vol. 12, part 2, no. 229, Norfolk to Cromwell, 8 July.

## Chapter 10: A birth, a Death and a Betrothal

1. Hutchinson, Robert, *House of Treason: The Rise and Fall of a Tudor Dynasty*, (Phoenix, London, 2009), chapter 5, p.121, note 74.
2. The other party is not known, although there has been speculation, but no proof, it might have been Jane Seymour's brother, Edward.
3. Porter, Linda, *Katherine the Queen,* (Macmillan, London, 2010), pp.123–124 describes the preparations.
4. The Council of the North as set up by Henry VIII in 1536 was the updating and permanently locating of a body that had been in existence since the time of Edward IV, See Reid, Rachel R., *The King's Council in the North*, (Longmans, Green and Co., London, 1921), pp.41, 59, 243.
5. L&P vol. 12, part 2, no. 971.
6. L&P vol. 12, part 2, no. 1004.
7. L&P vol. 12, part 2, no. 1285, ambassador Castillon to Francis I, 30 December.

8. Hans Holbein the Younger: *Christina of Denmark, Duchess of Milan*, National Gallery, London; Inventory number NG2475; location Room 12.
9. L&P vol. 10, no. 669 Thomas Warley writing to Lady Lisle, 14 April 1536. The church is now the Garden Museum.
10. Hans Holbein the Younger: *Thomas Howard, Duke of Norfolk*, 1539, oil on panel, 80.1 x 61.4 cm. Royal Collection RCIN 404439.
11. www.rct.uk/collection.
12. Ibid.
13. The document for the surrender of Thetford Priory: TNA E 322/240.
14. The Six Articles Act, 1539, see Gee, Henry and William John Hardy, *Documents Illustrative of English Church History Compiled from Original Sources*, (Macmillan, London, 1896), pp.303—319. See in full at Project Canterbury: The Six Articles Act, 1539. (http//anglicanhistory.org).
15. Hans Holbein the Younger: *Anne of Cleves*, 1539, Musée du Louvre, Paris, Richelieu Wing, Room 19.

# Chapter 11: Lord Edmund Howard

1. He enrolled on 3 February 1511; on the old calendar it would have been recorded as 1510.
2. For the Jousting Rules see BL Shelfmark: Harley Charter 83 H 1.
3. *Hall's Chronicle*, p.519.
4. For the grant see L&P vol. 1, part 2, no. 3325.
5. Ellis *Original Letters Series III* vol. 1, (London, 1846), Letter LXIV pp.160–163.
6. His appointment is recorded in L&P vol. 5, no. 220, grant 14; April 1531.
7. L&P vol. 5, no. 1042, Lord Edmund Howard to Cromwell, 21 May 1532.
8. After Edmund's death Margaret Mundy married a Henry Manox; whether this is the same Manox who had behaved inappropriately with her stepdaughter Katherine is unclear.
9. L&P vol. 7, no. 1179, 21 September.
10. L&P vol. 8, no. 1103, 24 July 1535.
11. L&P vol. 5, no. 1757, Miscellaneous 1532.
12. L&P vol. 12, part 2, no. 466.
13. The title of Lord Deputy of Calais was in use from 1507; the current incumbent Arthur Plantagenet, Viscount Lisle, was an illegitimate son of Edward IV and therefore an uncle of Henry VIII.
14. *Lisle letters* selected by Muriel St Clare Byrne, Chapter 3, letter 49 pp.68–69; facsimile copy plate 7 p.70. Although the messenger is instructed to deliver the letter 'post haste for thy lyffe', the tenor is surely humorous.
15. The chief mourner was Elizabeth Boleyn's half-sister Katherine (Rhys) Daubeney.
16. L&P vol. 13, part 1, no. 464, 9 March 1538.

17. L&P vol. 13, part 1, no. 465, 9 March 1538.
18. L&P vol. 13, part 1, no. 659 Edmund Howard to Lord Lisle 2 April 1538.
19. L&P vol. 13, part 1, no. 800, Lord Edmund Howard to Lord Lisle, 18 April 1538.
20. L&P vol. 14, part 1, no. 172, London, 31 January 1539.
21. L&P vol. 14, part 1, no. 906 (17); the exact date is not known, but was before 29 April when he is mentioned as 'Lord Edm. Howard, knight, deceased'.

## Chapter 12: Our Wife Agnes

1. For the full text of the will of Thomas Howard second Duke of Norfolk see *Testamenta vetusta:* (Nicolas, Nicholas Harris, London, 1826), vol. 2, pp.602–604.
2. Weever, John, *Ancient Funerall Monuments*, (Thomas Harper, London, 1631) p.835.
3. Inventory of the late duke's goods, 1524: plate gilt 'ii grett pottis with the Scottishe kingis armys on the hed of theym, 300 ounces'. Ridgard, John, (ed.), *Medieval Framlingham*, Suffolk Record Society vol. 27 (1985), p.6; 1st Edition (Boydell Press, 14 November 1985).
4. For the troubles of William Ashby see Chapter 23 and L&P vol. 17, no. 28, 16 January 1542.
5. The dispensation was granted Pope Alexander VI.
6. For earlier Tilneys in some detail see *History of Parliament*, Lincolnshire, Boydell and Brewer. Later generations may be found in *Tilney Families*, Bristow, Cyril, (Tonbridge, 1988).
7. Glenne, Michael, *Henry VIII's Fifth Wife: the Story of Catherine Howard*, Chapter 3 'The Grandmother', (Robert M. McBride, New York, 1948). (The Publisher died in 1970; all efforts have been made to trace any copyright holders.)
8. Green, R., *History, Topography, and Antiquities of Framlingham and Saxsted*, (London, 1834), p.66; the will of John Howard's widow Margaret Chedworth made in May 1490 confirms she was still calling herself Duchess of Norfolk.
9. BL Harl. MS 6148, fols. 44–44v.
10. L&P vol. 4, no. 4710: 8 September 1528. The full text can be found in Green, Mary Anne Everett (ed.), *Letters of Royal and Illustrious Ladies of Great Britain* vol. 2, 1846. pp.26–30.

## Chapter 13: Chesworth and Lambeth

1. See 'Horsham: Manors and other estates' in *A History of the County of Sussex*: vol. 6, part 2: Bramber Rape (North-Western Part) including Horsham (1986), pp.156–166.

2. 'The King ... took to wife Katharine, daughter to the late Lord Edmund Howard, thinking now in his [old] age to have obtained a jewel for womanhood.' The Council writing to William Paget (on diplomatic service in France) on the arrest of Katherine, L&P vol. 16, no. 1334, 12 November 1541.
3. The site of Norfolk House post code for Google maps is SE1 7LS. The Google satellite and street views put Norfolk House into context with Lambeth Palace opposite and the Palace of Westminster across the river.
4. Roberts, Sir Howard and Walter H., Godfrey, (eds.) *Survey of London, Volume 23: Lambeth: South Bank and Vauxhall,* (LCC, London, 1951), pp.137–140, 'Norfolk House and Old Paradise Street'.
5. *Report on the archaeological excavations at 113–129 Lambeth Road S.E.1, sponsored by Vestey Estates Ltd.,* Department of Greater London Archaeology. Museum of London. See Appendix for excavation site record reference numbers and details of the findings.
6. Roberts and Godfrey, *Survey of London.*
7. *Palatium Archiepiscopi Cantuariensis propae Londinum vulgo Lambeth House* (Lambeth House: Palace of the Archbishop of Canterbury, London) Wenceslaus Holler 1647, detail. Courtesy Metropolitan Museum of Art Harris Brisbane Dick Fund, 1917. Public Domain.
8. For further details, see Appendix, *What Became of Norfolk House?*
9. Brenan and Statham, p.269.
10. See also Chapter 26.The image from the long-disappeared tomb was recorded by Henry Lilly, Rouge Dragon in *The Genealogie of the Princelie Familie of the Howards,* which is now in the Archives of The Duke of Norfolk at Arundel Castle. Also NPG Lithographs by William Henry Kearney NPG D38987.
11. Brenan & Statham pp.268/9.
12. Starkey, David, *Six Wives.*
13. In recent years some researchers concluded there were fewer boarders in the duchess's household than previously thought.
14. Strickland, Agnes in *The Queens of England,* (Harper, New York, 1867), Strickland sees the old lady almost as 'weak-minded', whereas David Starkey says she had a 'sharp forensic brain', Starkey, *Six Wives.*
15. Glenne, Michael, *Henry VIII's Fifth Wife: the Story of Catherine Howard,* Chapter 3 'The Grandmother'. Glenne appears to have relied heavily on the Victorian and Edwardian writers and his own lively imagination for his information.
16. Fraser, Antonia, *The Six Wives of Henry VIII,* (Weidenfeld & Nicholson, 1992), p.198. The Duke of Buckingham had over 200 household staff – the more you had the greater the status symbol; added to these would be a large number of outdoor staff.
17. The letter of 10 October 'Written at my lady's house at Cheseworth' [Chesworth] appears to be one of the last mentions of the Horsham mansion in extant public documents: L&P vol. 11, no. 636, 10 October 1536. There is another mention in private correspondence of the third duke in the 1540s, and in arrangements for it to be transferred to Thomas Seymour in 1547.

18. When she received her first salary as a maid of honour to Anne of Cleves, Katherine reimbursed fellow Norfolk House resident Francis Dereham for money he had paid out to secure material and various trinkets for her.
19. For the list of beds and of gifts to Katherine see L&P vol. 15, no. 686, 18 May, Accounts of The King's Wardrobe.
20. For 'son compagnon de lit' see L&P vol. 16, no. 1359, 19 November 1541, Chapuys to Charles V.
21. Brenan and Statham, p.270; this was not correct: the infamous 'Culpeper letter' shows she could both read and write.
22. Katherine Parr, whose first two marriages had been arranged, had hoped to marry as her third husband Jane Seymour's brother, Thomas, but Henry intervened and chose her as his own sixth bride. After his death she married Seymour and was given custody of Princess Elizabeth, who lived with them.
23. L&P vol. 12, part 2, no. 35, 5 June 1537.

## Chapter 14: The Maidens' Chamber

1. Wilkinson, Josephine, *Katherine Howard: the Tragic Story of Henry VIII's Fifth Queen*, (John Murray, London, 2016) and Denny, Joanna, *Katherine Howard: A Tudor Conspiracy*. Joanna Denny saw her as having been sexually aware at a very young age and a victim of what would today be regarded as child abuse.
2. For details and the tragic outcome of Katherine Howard's involvement with Henry Manox, Francis Dereham and a third lover see Chapters 15–26.
3. Manox testified later he had started working there 'five years past', meaning 1536.
4. Brenan & Statham, *The House of Howard*.
5. Herbert, Henry William, *Memoirs of Henry VIII of England, with the fortunes, fates and characters of his six wives*, (New York, 1855), p.418.
6. Ibid., p.419.
7. Smith, Lacey Baldwin, *A Tudor Tragedy*, p.55.
8. Years later their son Edward was the second husband of Agnes ap Rhys, the daughter of Rhys ap Gruffyd and Duchess Agnes's daughter Katherine Howard.
9. Herbert, Henry William, p.419.
10. See Josephine Wilkinson, p.viii, Family tree.
11. For the duties of a gentleman usher and other household employees see Jones, Paul van Brunt, *The Household of a Tudor Nobleman*, (Torch Press, Cedar Rapids, 1918).
12. L& P vol. 16, no. 1400.
13. L& P vol. 16, no. 1469, 22 December 1541.
14. The whole of the testimonies, including the question of the pre-contract, will be examined on a daily basis in Chapters 20–25.

15. Burnett, Gilbert (Bishop of Salisbury), *The History of the Reformation of the Church of England*, (G. Appleton, New York, 1843) vol. IV, pp.504–505: the Confession of Katherine Howard. (The original printing R. Chiswell, London, 1681.)
16. Warnicke, Retha, *Wicked Women of Tudor England*, (Palgrave Macmillan, London, 2012).

## Chapter 15: Mistress Katherine Leaves Home

1. The church of St Mary-at-Lambeth, dating from the fourteenth century, was largely rebuilt in the nineteenth, although much of the tower is original. Unfortunately, the Victorians showed little regard for commemorating its Howard burials in the chapel constructed by the second Duke of Norfolk in 1522, two years before his death. The recording of a now lost very fine memorial brass in St Mary's church would suggest his remains were reinterred in Lambeth.
2. Robinson, Rev. Hastings, *Original letters Relative to the English Reformation*, (Parker Society, Cambridge, 1847), pp.201–202. The Reformers Richard Hilles and Henry Bullinger corresponded about the Londoners being aware of Henry's visits to Norfolk House and Bishop Gardiner's palace in June 1540.
3. L&P vol. 14, part 2, no. 572, 22 November 1539. The 'mother of the maidens' (the maids of honour) is a Mrs Stoner while the maidens themselves are listed as: Katharine Howard, ? Sturton, Dorothy Braye, Anne Basset, Katharine Cary and Mary Norres. Howard, Carey and Norres (Norris) all had connections to the Duke of Norfolk.
4. L&P vol. 16, no. 12, Marillac to Anne de Montmorency, Constable of France.
5. The Katherine Howard Holbein miniature Royal Collection RCIN 422293; the (possible) Elizabeth Seymour portrait is in the Toledo Museum of Art, Ohio Object number 1926.57; the seventeen-year-old in the style of Holbein in The Metropolitan Museum, New York; Katherine mannequin courtesy of Pauline Loven, costume@crowseye.co.uk
6. Strickland, Agnes, *Queens of England*, 1867, p.303.
7. According to Brenan and Statham, p.269.
8. Ibid.
9. Herbert, Henry William, *Memoirs of Henry VIII of England, with the fortunes, fates and characters of his six wives*, (New York, 1855), p.427.
10. L&P vol. 16, no. 1409; also no. 1416.
11. L&P vol. 14, part 2, no. 469.

## Chapter 16: 1540: Two More Wives

1. L&P vol. 15, no. 22, 5 January 1540.
2. L&P vol. 14, part 2, no. 718, 22 December 1539, When Anne Basset wrote to her mother, Lady Lisle, that the king is aware she is taking great care of Anne

of Cleves, it was from York Place (Whitehall Palace): presumably Katherine Howard and the other maids were there with her.
3. L&P vol. 15, no. 22, writing 5 January 1540.
4. Ibid.
5. According to *Hall's Chronicle*, the speaker, if he ever existed, is unnamed.
6. Francis I (1517–1545) was the Duke of Lorraine from 1544–1545, who married Christina of Denmark in 1541 and died at the age of 27. Christina, who had borne him three children in three years, did not remarry and lived to be 68.
7. Brenan and Statham, p.278–9
8. Ibid., p.277.
9. L&P vol. 15, no. 613 (12), grants in April 1540, the goods of the murderers.
10. L&P vol. 15, no. 686, 18 May, the quilts; Accounts of The King's Wardrobe.
11. Attributed to Henry Howard, Earl of Surrey speaking after the execution of Thomas Cromwell.

# Chapter 17: No Other Wish but His

1. L&P vol. 16, no. 12: Marillac, 3 September 1540. His comment on the current fashion is often misinterpreted and does not imply that neither Jane Seymour nor Anne of Cleves had ever followed this French style. Marillac was writing in French so Katherine's motto could have been in English, but no examples survive, as everything associated with her was destroyed after her death.
2. Strickland, *Lives of the Queens III*; for the coin see Starkey, *Six Wives* p.810.
3. 'The King ... took to wife Katherine, daughter to the late lord Edmund Howard, thinking (now in his old) age to have obtained a jewel for womanhood.' L&P vol. 16, no. 1334, 12 November 1541.
4. L&P vol. 16, no. 314. Apart from her interest as regent of the Netherlands for her brother the Emperor Charles V, the Dowager Queen of Hungary would have taken an interest in the proceedings as she had kindly given Anne of Cleves safe conduct through the Netherlands and provided an escort for her as far as Calais.
5. Spain vol. 6, part 1, no. 149, Chapuys to the Queen of Hungary, 8 January.
6. Ibid.
7. Ibid.
8. Ibid.
9. L&P vol. 15, no. 850, (12 Dr Chamber; 13 Dr Butts; 14 the ladies Rutland, Rochford and Edgcombe, who had concluded the marriage was not consummated).
10. 'They ... are going to send as ambassador the above Lord William – a good young gentleman, but not suitable for such business.' Chapuys to the Queen of Hungary, CSP Spain, vol. 6, part 1, no. 149, 8 January.
11. L&P vol. 16, no. 589.

12. L&P vol. 16, no. 662, Chapuys to Charles V, 27 March 1541. Wyatt had once been an admirer of Anne Boleyn: perhaps it was some perverse revenge on the king's part that he was pardoned 'on condition that not only should he confess his guilt but also take back his wife from whom he had been separated upwards of fifteen years, on pain of death if he be untrue to her henceforth'.
13. Herbert, Henry William, *Memoirs of Henry VIII of England, with the fortunes, fates and characters of his six wives*, (New York, 1855), p.425.
14. L&P vol. 16, no. 1489, 12 April.
15. L&P vol. 16, no. 864, 26 May.
16. L&P vol. 16, no. 868, Marillac to Francis 1.

## Chapter 18: Faces from the Past

1. Brenan and Statham, p.280
2. L&P vol. 15, no. 875, from Joan Bulmer in York to Katherine Howard, 12 July 1540.
3. L&P vol. 16, no. 1321, 5 November 1541, 'young Bulmer's wife, who was her bedfellow and also entertained by Deram'. It is stated plainly that 'Kath. Tylney, [is] now chamberer with the Queen'.
4. Burnet, Gilbert, *The History of the Reformation of the Church of England*, vol. VI, doc LXXII.
5. The chronology is difficult. David Loades in *Catherine Howard: The adulterous wife of Henry VIII*, (Amberley, Stroud, 2012), p.113 sees the downcast Dereham wanting to leave Lambeth behind in late 1539 and finally going in January 1540. If this was so and if it was already apparent that Henry was interested in Katherine, then his attraction to her could have begun before he had yet seen Anne of Cleves.
6. Loades, p.115 sees Agnes sounding out Queen Katherine, who tells her to bring him with her next time she comes to court.
7. SP 1/168 f. 85.
8. Derby is recorded in L&P vol. 16, no. 268 at a meeting of the Privy Council at Windsor on 26 November 1540 'Thos. Derby, the Queen's secretary, put up a complaint against Sir Edw. Willoughby, and it was decreed to send for Willoughby'. Huttoft is recorded as a potential Secretary to Anne of Cleves and then was in Katherine's service, L&P vol. 15, no. 21, 5 January 1540.
9. Brenan and Statham, p.299.
10. Ryrie, Alec, 'Lassells [Lascelles], John (d. 1546), courtier and religious activist' in *Oxford Dictionary of National Biography*, (2008).
11. Lascelles was arraigned for heresy on 12 July 1546. Offered the chance to recant, he refused and was burned at the stake at Smithfield four days later, at the same time as the martyr Anne Askew.

## Chapter 19: The Northern Progress

1. L&P vol. 16, no. 941, Mariallac to Francis I, 30 June.
2. See Thornton, Tim, 'Henry VIII's Progress Through Yorkshire in 1541 and its Implications for Northern Identities', in *Northern History*, vol. 46, no. 2, September 2009.
3. L&P vol. 16, no. 1088, Henry VIII's visit to Lincoln.
4. L&P vol. 16, no. 1391 (Grant 18) November 1541; 'Page *alias* Clerk, of Kedby, in Lyndesey, Linc., [the Trent side village of Keadby in the northern part of Lincolnshire] spinster. Pardon (at the request of Queen Katherine) for all felonies committed by her.
5. L&P vol. 16, no. 1088, Henry VIII's visit to Lincoln, 'On the morrow, Wednesday, the King rode to the castle and viewed it and the city'.
6. Ibid.
7. Some authors have put the Hatfield events at Hatfield, the town in Hertfordshire, but it was definitely the Yorkshire village about eight miles north-east of Doncaster.
8. L&P vol. 16, no. 1339, 13 November.
9. The residence, which was retained by the Crown and allocated to the Council of the North, became the official residence of the President of the Council in 1561.
10. L&P vol. 16, no. 1183, Marillac to Francis I, 16 September.
11. Minns, E. H., 'Documents relating to the dissolution of the monastery of Thornton Curtis in the county of Lincoln left by the Rev Charles Parkyn to Pembroke College, Cambridge' in *Proceedings of the Cambridge Antiquarian Society*, 10, (Cambridge, 1898), pp.482–95.
12. L&P vol. 16, no. 1253, Marillac to Francis I, 12 October.
13. L&P vol. 16, no. 1287; also L&P vol. 16, no. 1339, fn. 11 puts the date at about 25 October.
14. Josephine Wilkinson, p.151, sees Alice as having gone into the service of Lord William and meeting Anthony Restwold there.
15. L&P vol. 16, no. 1339.

## Chapter 20: A Time of Reckoning

1. L&P vol.16, no. 1320, 5 November.
2. For the possibility Manox had married soon after Dereham replaced him in Katherine's affections see www.queens-haven.co.uk.
3. 'My lord Prince' was Henry's son Prince Edward.
4. TNA SP1/167/138 5 November 1541 deposition of Henry Manox; also L&P vol. 16, no. 1321.
5. TNA SP1/167/157 Dereham's deposition in the Tower, 5 November.

6. L&P vol. 16, no. 1334, included in the letter from the Council to Paget in France.
7. Marillac wrote to Francis I about Norfolk being recalled, L&P vol. 16, no. 1332, 11 November.
8. Ibid.
9. Chapuys, CSP Spain vol. 6, part 1, no. 201; also Marillac to Francis I, L&P vol. 16, no. 1332.
10. Agnes Strickland, *Queens of England.*
11. L&P vol. 16, no. 1325 Cranmer to Henry VIII.
12. Ibid.
13. L&P vol. 16, no. 1317, 4 November. Cotes, a tailor working for the duchess, had no significant information and appears not to have been questioned again.
14. Burnett, Gilbert, *The History of the Reformation of the Church of England*, (G. Appleton, New York, 1843) vol. IV, Book 3, Records, number LXXI pp.504–505: the Confession of Katherine Howard. (A collection of sources used in the original printing for R. Chiswell, London, 1681.)
15. Ibid.
16. L&P vol. 16, no. 1325, Cranmer to Henry VIII. But as he closed his account of the interview to Henry, Cranmer made it clear to the king that Katherine claimed to have been forced into sex with Dereham, TNA SP1/167, f. 121.
17. L&P vol. 16, no. 1331, 11 November. Katherine's Uncle Norfolk was one of the signatories.
18. Ibid.
19. The Chapuys version of events, L&P vol. 16, no. 1328, writing 10 November.
20. L&P vol. 16, no. 1342 Marillac to Francis I, written 14 November.

## Chapter 21: Master Thomas Culpeper

1. From Culpeper's own deposition in November 1541, L&P vol. 16, no. 1339.
2. L&P vol. 16, no. 1366.
3. '... at her uncle's, Sir John Culpepper, at Holingbourne, in the nursery, as the play-fellow of his little heir, Thomas Culpeper, with whom her name was afterwards to be painfully connected in the page of history.'
4. Burnet, Gilbert, *The History of the Reformation of the Church of England*, vol. IV, doc LXXII.
5. Henry had said he was a big man in need of a big wife, L&P vol. 12, part 2, no. 1285, Ambassador Castillon to Francis I, 30 December 1537.
6. L&P vol. 16, no. 589, Marillac to Francis I, 3 March 1541.
7. Ibid.
8. This came out at their cross-examinations in November 1541.
9. L&P vol. 16, no. 1359, 19 November; CSP Spain 6, part 1, no. 207.
10. TNA SP1/167, f.131.
11. L&P vol. 16, no. 1337.

12. TNA SP1 /167, f.131.
13. Garbett, Henrietta 'The Old Palace of Lincoln' in Rait, R. S. (ed.), *English Episcopal Palaces – Province of Canterbury*, (New York, 1911), pp.186–88.
14. TNA SP 1/167/155 Margaret Benet, and SP 1/167/162 Joan Bulmer.
15. From Culpeper's own deposition in November 1541, L&P vol. 16, no. 1339.
16. SP1/167, f.131; also L&P vol. 16, no. 1337, 13 November.
17. SP1/167, f.159.
18. L&P vol. 16, no. 1130.
19. SP 1/167, f.133.
20. L&P vol. 15, no. 850 (14).
21. SP1/167, f. 133.
22. L&P vol. 16, no. 1338, Margaret Morton's confession to Sir Anthony Browne, 13 November 1541.

## Chapter 22: As Long as Life Endures

1. L&P vol. 16, no. 1314, 3 November 1541 '... to enlarge the King's chace of Hatfield, Yorks., in which his game of red deer is well replenished, the manor of Armethorpe, Yorks., parcel of the late monastery of Roche, and the manor of Crowyll [Crowle], Linc., parcel of Selby Priory, shall be joined to it from Christmas next coming'.
2. L&P vol. 16, no. 1333, Sir Ralph Sadler to Cranmer and Others, 12 November. Summaries of evidence given so far can be found in L&P 1336–1343, 13 November.
3. L&P vol. 16, no. 1339, Culpeper testified that Lady Rochford had provoked him to love the queen.
4. L&P vol. 16, no. 1337.
5. L&P vol. 16, no. 1338, 13 November; the place was Lyddington in Rutland, where they stayed from the end of July to 1 August.
6. L&P vol. 16, no. 1401, Chapuys to Charles V, writing on 3 December.
7. L&P vol. 16, no. 1340, Lady Rochford; this was just the beginning: Jane had extensive valuables at her home at Blickling in Norfolk, including a spectacular carved and draped bed worth a fortune.
8. L&P vol. 16, no. 1343.
9. Now held by TNA, Ref: SP1/167 folio 14; also published in L&P vol. 16, no. 1134: date unknown, but placed in L&P at 31 August 1541 (the editors later considered that it should have been placed in early August).
10. Warnicke, Retha M., *Wicked Women of Tudor England: Queens, Aristocrats, Commoners (Queenship and Power)*, (Palgrave Macmillan, London, 2012), and *ODNB* 'Katherine Howard' 2004.
11. TNA catalogue ref SP 1/167, f. 131. A photograph of the Culpeper Letter may be found at Six Wives in the Archives: Howard's end – The National Archives blog. https://blog.nationalarchives.gov.uk/six-wives-archives-

howards-end/#note-31198-4. Josephine Wilkinson in *Katherine Howard: the tragic story of Henry VIII's fifth queen* sees Katherine as cultivating Culpeper because he was in a position to advise her of the king's attitude toward her at any one time, p.125.
12. He classed as being 'a gentleman', the 'persuasion' used against Culpeper would not be as vigorous as that meted out to Dereham, in theory at least.
13. L&P vol. 16, no. 1333, Sir Ralph Sadler to Cranmer and others, written on November 12.
14. L&P vol. 16, no. 1389.
15. L&P vol. 16, no. 1342, Marillac to Francis I, 14 November.
16. L&P vol. 16, no. 1348.
17. L&P vol. 16, no. 1353, The Privy Council, 16 November.
18. L&P vol. 16, no. 1359, 19 November.
19. L&P vol. 16, no. 1366, Marillac to Francis I, 22 November.
20. L&P vol. 16, no. 1385, 30 November.

## Chapter 23: The Fate of Dereham and Culpeper

1. L&P vol. 16, no. 1394, The Privy Council to Wriothesley, 1 December.
2. Rumour had it that the men themselves carried out the torture on Anne Askew which is not certain, but they were believed to have been present.
3. L&P vol. 16, no. 1395, 1 December. Trial of Culpeper and Dereham for Treason: indictment found at Doncaster, 24 November.
4. Ibid.
5. Many thanks to Shaun Clark, formerly of Gainsborough Old Hall, who searched in vain for traces of a lost external entrance to the tower bedroom stairs.
6. L&P vol. 16, no. 1395, 1 December.
7. L&P vol. 16, no. 1396, Francis I. to Marillac, 1 December.
8. L&P vol. 16, no. 1426, 7 December. Marillac to Francis I; the duke had retreated to his mansion at Kenninghall in Norfolk.
9. L&P vol. 16, no. 1398 and 1400.
10. L&P vol. 16, no. 1408. They had also spent some time on Pewson, the servant whom the duchess sent to Hampton Court ostensibly to buy wood, but in reality to find out what was happening about Dereham.
11. Ibid.
12. L&P vol. 16, no. 1409; also 1416.
13. Young Rhys was the elder son of the late Rhys ap Gruffydd and Agnes's daughter, now Katherine Bridgewater.
14. L&P vol. 16, no. 1411, 5 December; also no 1414, 6 December.
15. L&P vol. 16, no. 1414.
16. Agnes Strickland (without references) says his teeth were forced out and he was subjected to the 'Duke of Exeter's daughter' (the rack), which is repeated by Antonia Fraser, *Six Wives of Henry VIII* p 348, referencing Strickland.

17. L&P vol. 16, no. 1416 (2).
18. L&P vol. 16, no. 1422.
19. Ibid.
20. L&P vol. 16, no. 1414.
21. L&P vol. 16, no. 1423.
22. L&P vol. 16, no. 1425.
23. L&P vol. 16, no. 1426.

## Chapter 24: The Sorrow of the Women

1. L&P vol. 16, no. 1430, letter from the Council with the King to the Council in London, 8 December.
2. L&P vol. 16, no. 1433, 9, and no. 1437, 10 December.
3. L&P vol. 16, no. 1433, 9 December.
4. Ibid.
5. L&P vol. 16, no. 1432, 9 December, The Privy Council.
6. L&P vol. 16, no. 1437 10 December, the Council with the King to the Council in London.
7. L&P vol. 16, no. 1438, Westminster, Saturday 10 December, about 8 o'clock in the morning.
8. L&P vol. 16, no. 1440.
9. A mark was not an actual coin, but a term used in accounting for a worth of 100 (pre-decimal) pence, or 13 shillings and fourpence, that is two-thirds of £1; thus, for example, goods estimated at 600 marks would be worth £400 in 1540. The Bank of England Inflation Calculator estimates that goods and services costing £400 in 1540 give an equivalent of £305,000 in November 2023.
10. L&P vol. 16, no. 1445. David Starkey compares the £1000 a year allowance made by Henry VII to the young Katherine of Aragon as being equivalent to the annual income of a substantial baron: *Six Wives* p.81.
11. L&P vol. 16, no. 1444, 12 December.
12. L&P vol. 16, no. 1447, 13 December.
13. L&P vol. 16, no. 1453.
14. L&P vol. 16, no. 1454.
15. L&P vol. 16, no. 1461, Tilney questioned 19 December.
16. Ibid.; and Lacey Baldwin Smith, p.62.
17. L& P vol. 16, no. 1469, 22 December.
18. Ibid.
19. L&P vol. 16, no. 1467; letter of 21 December relating events of the twentieth. The Bank of England Inflation Calculator gives an equivalent of £3,303,000 in November 2023.
20. L&P vol. 16, no. 1471.
21. L&P vol. 16, no. 1472.

## Chapter 25: That Vicious Life Before

1. L&P vol. 17, no. 2, 1 January 1542.
2. Ibid.; this, obviously pertaining to the case of Lady Rochford, received the Royal Assent on the 11 February.
3. L&P vol. 17, no. 28 II, Acts printed in the Statutes at Large, but not entered on the Parliament Roll (C. 21), 16 January 1542.
4. L&P vol. 17, no. 34, Marillac to Francis I, 17 January.
5. L&P vol. 16, no. 1328, Chapuys to the Queen of Hungary, 10 November; CSP Spain vol. 6, part 1, no. 204.
6. See Burnet, *History of the Reformation*; if Bishop of *Westminster* is correct this would have been Thomas Thirlby, the only person ever to hold the position (1540–1550).
7. L&P vol. 17, no. 63, Chapuys to Charles V, CSP Spain vol. 6 part 1, no. 228, 29 January.
8. L&P vol. 17, no. 92, Chapuys to Charles V, CSP Spain vol. 6, part 1, no. 230, 9 February.
9. Ibid.
10. Lady Jane Grey was the granddaughter of Suffolk and Henry VIII's sister, Mary Tudor. Her position as a grandchild of Henry VII led to her claiming the throne in 1553 for which she was executed on 12 February 1554.
11. L&P vol. 17, no. 100 Marillac to Francis I, 13 February.
12. www.bankofengland.co.uk/monetary-policy/inflation/inflation-calculator.
13. Hume, Martin A. Sharp, *Chronicle of King Henry VIII of England Being a Contemporary Record of Some of the Principal Events of the Reigns of Henry VIII and Edward VI, Written in Spanish by an Unknown Hand*, (George Bell and Sons, London, 1889).
14. The account of Katherine Howard's last words written on February 15, 1542, by the merchant Ottwell Johnson in a letter to his brother John can be found in Ellis, Sir Henry (ed.), *Original Letters, Illustrative of English History*, 1825: Volume II to 1586; letter CXLVII.
15. Bell, Doyne C., *Notices of the Historical Persons buried in the Church of St Peter ad Vincula*, (John Murray, London,1877).

## Chapter 26: All Has Changed

1. See L&P vol. 17 – Grants in May, no. 25: Agnes Duchess of Norfolk, late of Lambeth, Surrey, widow. General pardon for treasons committed before 14 Feb. 33 Hen. VIII. Westm., 5 May. Pat. 34 Hen. VIII.
2. The King's Jewels and Plate: Large folio volume of numbered leaves, dated at the beginning 24 April 34 Hen. VIII., and signed by the king on the first page, containing an inventory of the king's money, jewels, plate, tapestry, and other goods in charge of Anthony Denny, keeper of the Palace of Westminster. With

numerous marginal notes recording the subsequent disposal of the various items, it includes a long descriptive list of pictures, maps, musical instruments, weapons, clocks etc.
The Whitehall Inventory 1542: TNA PRO E315/160 and PRO E101/472/2, and at the British Library, BL Lansdowne Rolls 14 & 15. See Hayward, Maria A., *The 1542 Inventory of Whitehall: the palace and its keeper*, vols. 1 & 2, (Illuminata Publishers for The Society of Antiquaries, London, 2004).

3. 'Agnes duchess of Norfolk late of Lambeth, Surr., widow. Grant, for life, of the manors or lordships of Stoke alias Stoke Hall, Suff., of Reigate, Surr., of Sheringham, Welles, Wiveton, Warram, Stafford Barningham and Hecham, Norf., and of lands in Colchester, Essex, with all appurtenances in Stoke, Neylond, Polstede, Boxworth and Higham, Suff., and the other places aforenamed, except the rectory and advowson of Hicham; which premises the said Duchess lately held for life, with remainder to Thomas duke of Norfolk and his heirs, and forfeited by her late attainder; rent free, with profits from Michaelmas last. Greenwich, 18 May 34 Hen. VIII. Del. Westm., 20 May. (58.) 'Confirmation to Thos. duke of Norfolk of the mansion in South Lambeth [Norfolk House] and lands there which lady Agnes Duchess of Norfolk lately held, in exchange for the site, &c., of the late priory of Clerkenwell; and also of his copyhold of the messuage called the Bell and other lands in Lambeth of the abp. of Canterbury.' L&P vol. 18, part 1: 1543.
4. Agnes's will: TNA Prob 11/30, Records of the Prerogative Court of Canterbury: Pynnyng.
5. Nichols, John Bowyer, *Illustrations of the Literary History of the Eighteenth Century consisting of authentic memoirs and original letters of eminent persons* vol. VI, (J.B. Nichols, London, 1779), Letter 51 p.385–387, from J.C. Brooke to R. Gough.
6. *The Genealogie of the Princelie Familie of the Howards exactly deduced in a right line from 970 to 1638*, by Henry Lilly, Rouge Dragon. Now in the Archives of The Duke of Norfolk at Arundel Castle, it was done for Thomas Howard, Earl of Arundel and Surrey (the 'Collector' Earl) in 1638, a great-great grandson of the third Duke of Norfolk.
7. I am indebted to Sara Rodger, Assistant Librarian to the Duke of Norfolk, for showing me this glorious book and its wonderful contents, which, in their remarkable condition and freshness, look as though they were compiled only yesterday.

# Chapter 27: Those Katherine Left Behind

1. The author is conducting further research into the life of Henry Manox and the possibility of his marriage to Edmund Howard's widow.
2. See Henry VIII's Tomb – College of St George. https://www.stgeorges-windsor.org/image_of_the_month/henry-viiis-tomb/.

## Chapter 28: Scotland and France

1. L&P vol. 17, no. 996 to the Council, and L&P vol. 17, no. 997 to Wriothesley and Gardiner.
2. The current reincarnations of these streets may be seen at Google maps satellite and streetview, Postcode EC2V7. Guildhall, not far away, would be of tremendous significance to Surrey in the not-too-distant future.
3. For Surrey's poetry and the rampage through London see Childs, Jessie, 'The Fury of Reckless Youth' in *Henry VIII's Last Victim*, Chapter 11, (St Martin's Press, New York, 2006).

## Chapter 29: Lieutenant General of the King on Sea and Land

1. Nothing remains of the house today; a few details may be found at Norfolk Heritage Explorer NHER Number 359, Site of St Leonard's Priory, Norwich.
2. Simon Thurley describes the house and contents in 'Palace for a Nouveau Riche King' in *History Today* 41, 1991, p.14. (Surrey House, which was never completed, was sacked during Kett's rebellion of 1549 and fell into ruin.)
3. TNA SP 1/209/128.
4. TNA SP 1/210/30.
5. CSP Venice vol. 5, no. 373.
6. Childs, p.245; Oxburgh Hall Bedingfeld MS, Paget to Surrey, 17 January 1546.
7. Beer, Barrett L., 'A Critique of the Protectorate: An Unpublished Letter of Sir William Paget to the Duke of Somerset' in *Huntington Library Quarterly*, vol. 34, no. 3, 1971, pp.277–283.
8. CSP Spain vol. 8, no. 370, Francis Van der Delft to Charles V, 24 December 1546. Van der Delft had replaced Chapuys in 1543.
9. L&P vol. 21, part 2, no. 287, 19 October.

## Chapter 30: The 'poure prisoner'

1. L&P vol. 16, no. 1447, The Privy Council, 13 December 1541.
2. CSP Spain vol. 8, no. 364, Van der Delft to Charles V, 14 December.
3. BL Cotton MS Titus B I, fol. 101v.
4. Sir John Gate, or Gates, was married to Denny's sister Mary and was also related to Carew.
5. Childs, p.274; TNA LR 2/115/18.
6. L&P vol. 21, part 2, no. 548, John Gate, Sir Richard Southwell and Wymond Carew to Henry VIII, Report on events at Kenninghall, 14 December.

7. The inventories for the Norfolk assets can be found in TNA LR 2/117; documents recording the dispersal of the contents of Kenninghall are LR 2/115 and 116.
8. CSP Spain vol. 8, no. 370. Van der Delft to the Emperor, 24 December.
9. Kaulek, Jean. *Correspondence Politique* de *MM de Castillon et de Marillac*, (Felix Algan, Paris, 1885,) p.261.
10. Lord Herbert of Cherbury, *Life and Raigne of King Henry the Eighth*, (Thomas Whittaker, London, 1649), pp.563–4
11. Ibid., pp.566–7.
12. CSP Spain vol. 8, no. 370. Van der Delft to the Emperor, 24 December.

## Chapter 31: A question of heraldry

1. For the use of the 'difference' see Fox-Davies, Arthur Charles, *A Complete Guide to Heraldry*, (T. C. & E. C. Jack, London, 1909), Chapter 31.
2. The Second Succession Act, 1536 (28 Hen.8 c. 18).
3. TNA PRO SP 1/223, fo.34.
4. See also Moore, Peter R., 'The Heraldic Charge Against the Earl of Surrey' in *English Historical Review,* Volume CXVI, 2001 (OUP, Oxford, 2001), pp.557–583.
5. Attributed arms of Saint and King Edward the Confessor were used by Richard II who revered him and is depicted with him and John the Baptist on the Wilton Diptych now in the National Gallery, NG 4451. www.npg.org.uk.
6. Baga de Secretis Pouch XIV. M. 9. TNA.
7. Baga de Secretis Pouch XIV M. 8, dated 11 January, TNA.
8. Lord Herbert of Cherbury, pp.567–9.
9. Ibid.
10. For the coat see TNA PRO E101/60/22.fo.1. An account rendered by Sir Walter Stonore, lieutenant of the Tower, 'Money to be received for the late Earl of Surrey's board, &c., viz., board from 8 Dec. to 19 Jan. 38 Hen. VIII, 24l., attendants, coal, &c.' Also included was 'a coat of "right sattyn" against his arraignment' and an allowance for coal, wall hangings and plate. (Accts. Exch. K.R.60/22.)
11. Childs, p.304.
12. CSP Spain vol. 9, Van der Delft to Charles V, 23 January 1547.
13. Childs, p.307.
14. Ibid., p.308.
15. BL Cotton MS Titus B I, fols. 136–7. Anthony Anthony, an official of the Tower, described the execution as happening exactly as expected, see Childs, p.311, whereas the *Spanish Chronicle* (which had over-embellished the last moments of Surrey's cousin Katherine Howard and was not written by an actual witness) states that 'Surrey spoke a great deal [until] they would not let him talk anymore', *Spanish Chronicle* p.148.

## Chapter 32: 1547: A New Regime

1. L&P vol. 21, part 2, no. 761, Odet de Selve to Francis I, 31 January 1547.
2. Hutchinson pp.202–3.
3. Surrey History Centre Ref no. LM/1090/2, 'Inventory of furnishings in the manor house of Chesworth, Horsham, Sussex, and in its outbuildings'. One entry is annotated as having been delivered to the Lord Admiral [Thomas, Lord Seymour of Sudeley, Lord Admiral 1547–1549, to whom the manor was granted following the forfeiture of Thomas Howard, Duke of Norfolk in 1547; see LM/COR/2/2-3 for letters of 3–5 April 1547 relating to the preparation of this inventory.
Thomas Seymour's enjoyment of the property was short lived: LM/1090/1 records the sequestration of his goods and chattels on 20 January 1549, two months before his execution. Images of these documents can be seen online at www.surreyarchives.co.uk.
4. The King's will: TNA E 23/4, fol. 16v. David Starkey describes this awarding of titles as typical of 'the shameless back-scratching of the alliance', Starkey, *The Reign of Henry VIII*, (Franklin Watts, London, 1986), p.142. Jessie Childs calls the will the most controversial document of Henry's reign, p.63 note 5, while G. R. Elton calls the changes to the king's will 'convenient', Elton, G. R., *Reform and Reformation*, (Hodder Arnold, Totnes, 1989), p.332. For those authorised in August 1546 to use 'the drie' stamp and how it should be used until 10 May 1547, see L&P vol. 21, part 1, no. 1537 (34), Hampton Court, 31 August 1546.
5. For an excellent photograph of this document online see www.innertemplelibrary.org.uk/collections/manuscript-collection/edward-vis-devise-for-the-succession.
6. Thirteen if including the days between Edward VI's death and Jane's proclamation. Some months earlier Mary had been restored to the status of princess, although her place in the succession remained ambiguous.

## Epilogue

1. The shield differs from that of the Tudor Howards in that the Howard arms are now in the first quarter and Brotherton in the second, while the tail of the lion in the fourth quarter curves outwards, indicating Fitzalan, whereas that of the Mowbray lion curved inwards.

## Appendix: What Became of Norfolk House?

1. Berkeley Castle Muniments BCM/D/4: The Arundel Inheritance.
2. See also Norfolk House – Sites and Monuments excavations: Norfolk House, 113–125 Lambeth Road, SE1. 1988 excavation: Site record NOR88, Greater

London SMR no. 091297; 1990 excavation: Site record NOR90, Greater London SMR no. 091324-7.
3. Lysons, Daniel 'Lambeth', in *The Environs of London: volume 1: County of Surrey,* (Cadell and Davies, London, 1792); Manning, Rev. Owen and William Bray, Esq, *History and Antiquities of the County of Surrey,* vol. 3, (John Nichols, London, 1814); Allen, Thomas in '*A History of Lambeth and the archiepiscopal palace'*, (J. Nichols, London, 1826); Tanswell, John, *The Histories and Antiquities of Lambeth,* (F. Picton, London, 1863). Some of these authors state the house was sold by the third duke, but it was his grandson and successor who sold it.
4. Roberts, Sir Howard and Walter H. Godfrey, (eds.) 'Norfolk House and Old Paradise Street' in *Survey of London, Volume 23: Lambeth: South Bank and Vauxhall,* (LCC, 1951), pp.137–140.
5. Webber, Michael D., 'The Norfolk House Excavations 1973 and 1990' in *The Pharmaceutical Journal,* December 1991.
6. Lindley, Phillip G. (ed.), *Gainsborough Old Hall,* (Society of Lincolnshire History and Archaeology, Lincoln, 1991). In particular P. G. Lindley, 'Structure, Sequence and Status: the Archaeological History of Gainsborough Old Hall to c.1600'; N. Field, 'Excavation of the West Range'; M.V. Clark, 'The West range: Survey and Analysis'; M.W. Thompson, 'The Architectural Context of Gainsborough Old Hall'.

# Bibliography

## Abbreviations

BL: British Library
CSP Spain: Calendar of State Papers Spain
CSP Venice: Calendar of State Papers Relating To English Affairs in the Archives of Venice
CUP: Cambridge University Press
HMSO: His/Her Majesty's Stationery Office
L&P: Letters and Papers Foreign and Domestic of Henry VIII
NPG: National Portrait Gallery
OUP: Oxford University Press
RCIN: Royal Collection Identification Number
PRO: documents held by the Public Record Office prior to its merging with the Historical Manuscripts Commission to form The National Archives.
TNA: The National Archives

## Primary Sources

Arundel Castle Archives
The British Library
The National Archives

Beer, Barrett L., 'A Critique of the Protectorate: An Unpublished Letter of Sir William Paget to the Duke of Somerset' in *Huntington Library Quarterly*, vol. 34, no. 3, (University of Pennsylvania, 1971).
Black, W.H. (ed.), *Illustrations of Ancient State and Chivalry from manuscripts preserved in the Ashmolean Museum*, (Roxburghe Club, Oxford, 1840).
Brewer, Gairdner and Brodie, *Letters and Papers of Henry VIII*, vols. 1–21 (HMSO, London, 1898–1932).
Burnett, Gilbert (Bishop of Salisbury), *The History of the Reformation of the Church of England*, (G. Appleton, New York, 1843) vol. IV. (The original printing R. Chiswell, London, 1681.)
CSP Spain vols. 4–6, Pasqual de Gayangos (ed.) 1879–1895, (HMSO, London, 1895).

*Bibliography*

CSP Venice: Calendar of State Papers Relating to English Affairs in the Archives of Venice, vol. 5, Rawdon Brown (ed.), (HMSO, London, 1873).
Cavendish, George, *The Life of Cardinal Wolsey*, (Weller-Singer, Samuel, Chiswick, 1825).
Cherbury, Lord Herbert of, *Life and Raigne of King Henry the Eighth*, (Thomas Whittaker, London, 1649).
Collier, John Payne (ed.), *Household Books of John, Duke of Norfolk and Thomas, Earl of Surrey, 1481–1490*, (Roxburghe Club, 1844). This is Household Book II (H.B.II).
Ellis, Sir Henry, *Original Letters Illustrative of English History First Series*, second edition, vol. 1, (Harding et al, London, 1825).
Ellis, Sir Henry, *Original Letters Illustrative of English History First Series*, second edition, vol. 2, (Harding *et al.*, London, 1825).
Ellis, Sir Henry, *Original Letters Illustrative of English History Third Series*, vol. 1, (Bentley, London, 1846).
Ellis, Sir Henry, Polydore Vergil, c.1470–1555, (Camden society, London, 1844).
Grafton, Richard, *Chronicle or History of England 1189–1558*, 2 vols., (J. Johnson, London, 1809).
Green, Mary Anne Everett (née Wood), *Letters of Royal and Illustrious Ladies of Great Britain* vol. 2, (Henry Colburn, London, 1846).
Hall, Edward, *Hall's Chronicle*, Sir Henry Ellis (ed.), (Johnson *et al.*, London, 1809).
Hume, Martin A. Sharp, *Chronicle of King Henry VIII of England Being a Contemporary Record of Some of the Principal Events of the Reigns of Henry VIII and Edward VI, Written in Spanish by an Unknown Hand*, (George Bell and Sons, London, 1889). Translated from Spanish and published with notes by historian, Martin Hume, who appears to have accepted it as fact.
Kaulek, Jean, *Correspondence Politique de MM de Castillon et de Marillac*, (Felix Algan, Paris, 1885).
Lilly, Henry, *The Genealogie of the Princelie Familie of the Howards*, (which is now in the Archives of The Duke of Norfolk at Arundel Castle).
Lindsay, Robert, *The Chronicles of Scotland*, (Blackwood and Sons, Edinburgh and London, 1899). (The Pitscottie Chronicles).
Nicolas, Nicholas Harris, *Testamenta vetusta: being illustrations from wills, of manners, customs, &c. as well as of the descents and possessions of many distinguished families. From the reign of Henry the Second to the accession of Queen Elizabeth*, (London, Eyre and Spottiswoode, 1826).
Nichols, John Bowyer, *Illustrations of the Literary History of the Eighteenth Century consisting of authentic memoirs and original letters of eminent persons*, vol. VI, (J. B. Nichols, London, 1779).
Pronay, Nicholas and Cox, John (eds.), *The Crowland Chronicle Continuations: 1459–1486*, (Alan Sutton, London, 1986).
Riley, H. T. (ed.), *Ingulph's Chronicle of Croyland Abbey*, (London, 1854).
Robinson, Rev. Hastings, *Original letters Relative to the English Reformation*, (Parker Society, Cambridge, 1847).

*Rotuli Parliamentorum*, (London, 1771).
St Clare Byrne, Muriel (ed.), *The Lisle Letters*, (Secker & Warburg, London, 1983).
Spont, Alfred (ed.), *Letters and Papers Relating to the War with France, 1512–13*, (The Navy records Society, 1897).
Coates, Tim (ed.), *Letters of Henry VIII, 1526–29*, (The Stationery Office, London, 2001).
Surrey History Centre, Papers of the, 1547: LM/COR/2/2; LM/COR/2/2; LM/1090/2; LM/COR/2/2-3; LM/1090/1. Images of these documents referring to the surrender of Chesworth House can be seen online at www.surreyarchives.co.uk.
Turner, T. H. (ed.), 'Household Accounts of Sir John Howard (1462–1471)' in *Manners and Household Expenses in England in the Thirteenth and Fifteenth Centuries*, (Roxburghe Club, 1841). This is Household Book I (H.B.I).
Weever, John, *Ancient Funerall Monuments*, (Thomas Harper, London, 1631).
Wriothesley, Charles, *Chronicles of England, 1485–1559*, (Camden Society, London, 1875).

## Secondary Sources

Allen, Thomas, *A History of Lambeth and the Archiepiscopal Palace*, (J. Nichols, London, 1826).
Amin, Nathen, *The House of Beaufort, The Bastard Line That Captured the Crown*, (Amberley, Stroud, 2017).
Armstrong. C. A. J., *Domenico Mancini: De Occupatione Regni Anglie per Riccardum Tercium*, (The Occupation of the Throne of England by Richard III), (Sutton Publishing, Stroud, 1984).
Ashdown-Hill, John, 'The Opening of the Tombs of the dukes of Richmond and Norfolk, Framlingham April 1841', in *The Ricardian* vol. 18 (2008).
Baggs, A. P. *et al.*, *A History of the County of Sussex*: vol. 6, part 2, (Victoria County History, London, 1986).
Baldwin Smith, Lacey, *A Tudor Tragedy*, (Jonathan Cape, London, 1961).
Bateson, M., 'Aske's Examination' in *English Historical Review* 5, (1890).
Bell, Doyne C., *Notices of the Historical Persons Buried in the Church of St Peter ad Vincula in the Tower of London*, (John Murray, London, 1877).
Bindoff, S. T. (ed.), *The House of Commons 1509–1558*, (Secker & Warburg, London, 1982).
Bollond, Charlotte and Cooper, Tarnya, *The Real Tudors: Kings and Queens Rediscovered*, (National Portrait Gallery, London, 2014).
Brenan, Gerald and Statham, Edward Phillips, *The House of Howard*, (Hutchinson and Co, London, 1907).
Castor, Helen, *Blood and Roses*, (Faber & Faber, London, 2004).
Childs, Jessie, *Henry VIII's Last Victim*, (St Martin's Press, New York, 2006).
Crawford, Anne, *Yorkist Lord*, (Continuum, London, 2010).
Crawford, Anne, 'John Howard, Duke of Norfolk: a possible murderer of the Princes' in *The Ricardian, vol.* V, 1981.

## Bibliography

Delorme, Mary, 'Facts, Not Opinions: Agnes Strickland' in *History Today* vol. 38, (London, 1988).

Denny, Joanna, *Katherine Howard: A Tudor Conspiracy*, (Portrait, London, 2005).

Department of Greater London Archaeology, *Report on the archaeological excavations at 113–129 Lambeth Road S.E.1, sponsored by Vestey Estates Ltd.*, (Museum of London).

Dicks, John, *The History and Legacy of Old Castles and Abbeys*, (J. Dicks, London, 1850).

Elton, G. R., *Reform and Reformation*, (Hodder Arnold, Totnes, 1989).

Everett, Michael, *The Rise of Thomas Cromwell*, (Yale University Press, London, 2015).

Fox, Julia, *Jane Boleyn: The Infamous Lady Rochford*, (Weidenfeld and Nicholson, London, 2007).

Fox-Davies, Arthur Charles, *A Complete Guide to Heraldry*, (T. C. & E. C. Jack, London, 1909).

Foyle, Jonathan, *Lincoln Cathedral: The Biography of a Great Building*, (Scala Arts and Heritage, London, 2015).

Fraser, Antonia, *The Six Wives of Henry VIII*, (Phoenix, London, 1992).

Garbett, Henrietta 'The Old Palace of Lincoln' in Rait, R. S. (ed.), *English Episcopal Palaces – Province of Canterbury*, (New York, 1911).

Gee, Henry and Hardy, William John, *Documents Illustrative of English Church History Compiled from Original Sources*, (Macmillan, London, 1896).

Glenne, Michael, *Henry VIII's Fifth Wife: the Story of Catherine Howard*, (Robert M. McBride, New York, 1948). (The Publisher died in 1970; all efforts have been made to trace any copyright holders.)

Goodwin, George, *Fatal Rivalry, Flodden 1513*, (Weidenfeld and Nicholson, London, 2014).

Green, R., *History, Topography, and Antiquities of Framlingham and Saxsted*, (London, 1834).

Griffith, Ralph, *Rhys ap Thomas and his Family: A Study in the Wars of the Roses and Early Tudor Politics*, (University of Wales Press, Cardiff, 1993).

Grummitt, D., *The Calais Garrison: War and Military Service in England, 1436–1588*, (Boydell Press, Woodbridge, 2008).

Gunn, S. J., *Charles Brandon, Duke of Suffolk, c.1484–1545*, (Basil Blackwell, Oxford, 1988).

Hallam-Baker, Clive, *The Battle of Flodden Why and How*, (The Remembering Flodden Project, 2013).

Harris, Barbara, 'Marriage Sixteenth century Style: Elizabeth Stafford and the Third Duke of Norfolk' in *Journal of Social History*, vol. 15, (OUP, 1981).

Harris, Barbara, *Aristocratic Women 1450–1550, Marriage and Family, Property and Careers*, (OUP, 2002).

Hayward, Maria A., *The 1542 Inventory of Whitehall: the palace and its keeper*, vols. 1 & 2, (Illuminata Publishers for The Society of Antiquaries of London, London, 2004).

Head, David M., *The Ebbs and Flows of Fortune: the Life of Thomas Howard, Third Duke of Norfolk*, (University of Georgia Press, 1995).

Head, David M., 'Beying ledde and seduced by the Dyvil: the attainder of Lord Thomas Howard', in *Sixteenth Century Journal* vol. 13 (1982) pp.3–16.

Herbert, Henry William, *Memoirs of Henry VIII of England, with the fortunes, fates and characters of his six wives*, (Miller et al., New York, 1855).

Hoyle, R. W., and Ramsdale, J. B., 'The Northern Progress of 1541', in *Northern History*, XLI: 2, (2004).

Hoyle, R. W., *The Pilgrimage of Grace and the Politics of the 1530s*, (OUP, Oxford, 2001).

Hunter, Joseph, 'An Account of King Henry the Eighth's Progress in Lincolnshire' in *The Archaeological Journal*, (Archaeological Institute of Great Britain and Ireland, London, 1848).

Hutchinson, Robert, *House of Treason: The Rise and Fall of a Tudor Dynasty*, (Phoenix, London, 2009).

Ives, Eric, *Lady Jane Grey: A Tudor Mystery*, (Wiley-Blackwell, Chichester, 2009).

Ives, Eric, *The Life and Death of Anne Boleyn*, (Wiley-Blackwell, Chichester, 2005).

Jones, Paul van Brunt, *The Household of a Tudor Nobleman*, (Torch Press, Cedar Rapids, 1918).

Jones, Michael K. and Underwood, Malcolm G., *The King's Mother: Lady Margaret Beaufort*, (CUP, Cambridge, 1992).

Kendall, Paul M., *Richard the Third*, (W.W. Norton and Company Inc., New York, 1956).

Lander, J. R., 'Attainder and Forfeiture, 1453 to 1509', *The Historical Journal*, vol. 4, no. 2, (1961).

Leland, John, *Antiquarii De Rebus Britannicis Collectanea*, vol. 3, (Hearne, T., (ed.), Oxford, 1770).

Lindley, Phillip G., (ed.), *Gainsborough Old Hall*, (Society of Lincolnshire History and Archaeology, Lincoln, 1991).

Loades, David, *Catherine Howard: The adulterous wife of Henry VIII*, (Amberley, Stroud, 2012).

Lodge, Edmund, *Portraits of Illustrious Personages of Great Britain*, (Harding et al., London, 1823).

Lysons, Daniel, 'Lambeth' in *The Environs of London: vol. 1: County of Surrey*, (Cadell and Davies, London, 1792).

McFarlane, K. B., *The Nobility of Later Medieval England*, (Clarendon Press, Oxford, 1973).

Mackay, Lauren, *Inside the Tudor Court,* (Amberley, Stroud, 2014).

MacNalty, Arthur S., *Henry VIII: A Difficult Patient*, (Christopher Johnson, Norwich, 1952).

Manning, Rev. Owen and William Bray Esq., *History and Antiquities of the County of Surrey*, vol. 3, (John Nichols, London 1814).

Martin, Thomas, *History of Thetford*, (J. Nichols, London, 1779).

Miller, Helen, *Henry VIII and the English Nobility*, (Blackwell, Oxford, 1896).

Minns, E.H., 'Documents relating to the dissolution of the monastery of Thornton Curtis in the county of Lincoln left by the Rev Charles Parkyn to Pembroke

College, Cambridge' in *Proceedings of the Cambridge Antiquarian Society*, 10, (Cambridge, 1898).

Moore, Peter R., 'The Heraldic Charge Against the Earl of Surrey' in *English Historical Review*, Volume CXVI, (OUP, Oxford, 2001).

Norwich, John Julius, *Four Princes, and the Obsessions that Formed Modern Europe*, (John Murray, London, 2016).

Penn, Thomas, *Winter King, The Dawn of Tudor England*, (Penguin, London, 2011).

Peyton, Nick, 'The Dissolution of the English Monasteries: A Quantitative Investigation', in *LSE Economic History Working Papers No: 316,* (London, 2020).

Pollard, A. J., *Richard III and the Princes in the Tower*, (Alan Sutton, Stroud, 1991).

Pollard, A. J., *Warwick the Kingmaker, Politics, Power and Fame*, (Continuum, London, 2007).

Pollard, Dr Tony, *The Sad Tale of King James IV's Body*, BBC News Scotland. www.bbc.co.uk/news/uk-scotland-23993363.

Porter, Linda, *Katherine the Queen*, (Macmillan, London, 2010).

Prescott, Andrew, *English Historical Documents*, (British Library, London, 1988).

Reid, Rachel R., *The King's Council in the North*, (Longmans, Green and Co., London, 1921).

Rex, Richard, 'Royal Supremacy (1531–1535)' in *Henry VIII Man and Monarch*, British Library Exhibition Catalogue, Susan Doran and David Starkey (eds.), (British Library, London, 2009).

Ridgard, John (ed.), *Medieval Framlingham*, Suffolk Record Society 27 (Boydell Press, Dover, New Hampshire, 1985).

Ridley, Jasper, *Henry VIII*, (Penguin Books, London, 1984).

Roberts, Sir Howard and Godfrey, Walter H. (eds.), 'Norfolk House and Old Paradise Street' in *Survey of London, vol. 23: Lambeth: South Bank and Vauxhall*, (LCC, 1951).

Roberts, Marilyn, *The Mowbray Legacy*, (Queens-Haven Publications, Lincolnshire, 2012).

Roberts, Marilyn, *Lady Anne Mowbray: The High and Excellent Princess*, (Queens-Haven Publications, Lincolnshire, 2013).

Robinson, John Martin, *The Dukes of Norfolk*, (Phillimore & Co Ltd, Chichester, 1995).

Ross, Charles, *Edward IV*, (Eyre Methuen Ltd., London, 1974).

Rowse, A.L., *Bosworth Field and The Wars of The Roses*, (Wordsworth Editions, Ware, 1999).

Ryrie, Alec, 'Lassells [Lascelles], John (d.1546), courtier and religious activist', in *Oxford Dictionary of National Biography*, (2008).

Russell, Gareth, *Young and Damned and Fair*, (William Collins, London, 2017).

Sansom C. J., 'The Wakefield Conspiracy of 1541 and Henry VIII's Progress to the North Reconsidered', in *Northen History: a review of the history of the North of England* vol. 45 (No. 2, 2008).

Santiuste, David, *Edward IV and the Wars of the Roses*, (Pen & Sword Books, Barnsley, 2017).

Scarisbrick, J. J., *Henry VIII*, (Yale, 2011).
Sessions, William, *Henry Howard, the Poet Earl of Surrey: A Life*, (OUP, Oxford, 1999).
Strickland, Agnes, *Lives of the Queens of England*, 12 vols. 1840–1848, (Harper, New York, 1867).
Sutton, Anne and Visser-Fuchs, Livia, *The Royal Funerals of the House of York at Windsor*, (Richard III society, 2005),
Sutton, Anne and |Hammond, P. W., *The Coronation of Richard III: the Extant Documents,* (Alan Sutton, Gloucester, 1983).
Starkey, David, *Henry, Virtuous Prince*, (Harper Press, London, 2008).
Starkey, David, *Six Wives*, (Vintage, London, 2004).
Starkey, David, *The Reign of Henry VIII*, (Franklin Watts, London, 1986).
Terry, Francis (ed.), *A Guide to the History, Archaeology and Current Proposals for the Church of St-Mary-at-Lambeth*, (Vauxhall Society and Tradescant Trust, London, 1980).
Thornton, Tim, 'Henry VIII's Progress Through Yorkshire in 1541 and its Implications for Northern Identities' in *Northern History*, vol. 46, no. 2, (September 2009).
Thurley, Simon, 'Palace for a Nouveau Riche King' in *History Today* 41, (1991).
Thurley, Simon, *Royal Palaces of Tudor England*, (Yale University Press, London, 1993).
Tremlett, Giles, *Katherine of Aragon, Henry's Spanish Queen*, (Faber & Faber, London, 2010).
Tucker, Melvyn J., *The Life of Thomas Howard, Earl of Surrey and Second Duke of Norfolk 1443–1524*, (Mouton, The Hague, 1964).
Virgoe, R., 'The recovery of the Howards in East Anglia,1485-1529' in Ives, Knecht and Scarisbrick. J. J. (eds.), *Wealth and Power in Tudor England*, (1978).
Walford, Edward, *Old and New London* Vol. VI, (Cassell *et al.*, London, 1899).
Warnicke, Retha M., *The Marrying of Anne of Cleves: Royal Protocol in early modern England*, (CUP, Cambridge, 2000).
Warnicke, Retha M., *Wicked Women of Tudor England: Queens, Aristocrats, Commoners*, (Palgrave Macmillan, London, 2012).
Warwick, Professor Roger 'Anne Mowbray: skeletal remains of a medieval child' in *The London Archaeologist* vol. 57, (London, 1986).
Webber, Michael D., 'The Norfolk House Excavations 1973 and 1990' in *The Pharmaceutical Journal*, December 1991.
Weir, Alison, *The Princes in the Tower*, (Pimlico, London, 1992).
Wilkinson, Josephine, *Katherine Howard: the Tragic Story of Henry VIII's Fifth Queen*, (John Murray, London, 2016).
Wilson, Derek, *In the Lion's Court: Power, Ambition and Sudden Death in the Reign of Henry VIII*, (Pimlico, London, 2002).
Wroe, Ann, *Perkin: a Story of Deception*, (Vintage Books, London, 2003).

# Index

Ackworth, Joan, see Bulmer, Joan
Acts of Succession 1534 and 1536, 37, 41, 163
Act of Suppression 1536, 44, 50
Act of Supremacy 1534, 37, 44
Agnes, (née Tilney), Duchess of Norfolk, see Howard, Agnes
Anjou, Margaret of, Queen Consort of England, 4
Aragon, Katherine of, Queen Consort of England, 17, 18, 19, 28, 29, 34, 35, 39, 56, 64, 93, 117, 143, 195n
Arthur, Prince of Wales, 16, 30, 35
Arundel Castle, 149, 171
Arundel, Miss Millicent, 154
Ashby, William, 63, 109, 132–134, 152
Aske, Robert, 46–50
Askew, Anne, 129, 190n
Attainder, 41, 88, 135, 136, 141, 142, 145, 148, 167, 169
Audley, Thomas, 34, 36, 51, 92, 100, 107, 110, 129, 133, 143, 144, 171

Barker, Christopher, 163, 164
Barlings Abbey, Lincolnshire, xvi, 26, 50, 175n
Barlow, John, 167
Basset, Anne, 86, 113, 144, 188n
Battles:
    Barnet, 4
    Bosworth, xvi, 13–16
    Flodden, 20–25, 56, 163
    Tewkesbury, 4, 8, 12,
    Towton, 3
    Solway Moss, 153
    Spurs, The, 20

Baynton, Sir Edward, 76, 112, 113
Baynton, Lady Isabel (née Leigh), 76, 93, 104, 113
Beaufort family, 12
Beaufort, Lady Margaret, 11–12, 18
Benet, Margaret, 119, 133, 142, 151
Berkeley, Lord William, 'the Waster', x, 6, 176n
Bigod, Sir Francis, 48, 50
Blount, Elizabeth, 'Bessie', 29
Boleyn, Anne, Queen Consort of England, x, xi, xii, 5, 17, 27, 31, 32, 33, 35–36, 37, 39–42, 58, 71, 72, 100, 126, 127, 137, 143, 147, 182n, 190n
Boleyn, Elizabeth, (née Howard), Countess of Wiltshire, x, xi, 5, 17, 29, 31, 32, 40, 53, 60, 80, 149
Boleyn, George, Viscount Rochford, x, 32, 38, 40, 41, 104, 120
Boleyn, Jane, Viscountess Rochford, 104, 116, 118–124, 140–141, 144–148
Boleyn, Mary (Carey), x, 25, 29, 80
Boleyn, Thomas, Earl of Wiltshire, x, 29, 32
Boulogne, 154–157
Brandon, Charles, Duke of Suffolk, 56, 105, 118, 145, 155, 169
Bray, Dorothy, 119, 188n
Brereton, Sir William, 40
Bridgewater, Katherine, see Howard, Katherine, Countess of Bridgewater
Brotherton, Thomas of, Earl of Norfolk, xi, 2, 163, 165, 171, 200n

Browne, Sir Anthony, 107, 122, 124, 134, 144
Buckingham, Edward Stafford, 3rd Duke of, 13, 25–26, 30, 186n
Buckingham, Henry Stafford, 2nd Duke of, 8, 9, 11, 12–13
Bullinger, Henry, 80, 188n
Bulmer, Joan (née Ackworth), 76, 77, 78, 84, 97, 108, 119, 128, 136, 142, 151
Burgh, Lord Thomas, 35, 45, 103, 164
Butler, Eleanor (née Talbot), 9
Butts, Dr William, 30, 181n, 189n

Caistor, Lincolnshire, 45, 46, 49
Calais, 3, 4, 13, 35, 46, 58–61
Campeggio, Lorenzo, 30, 31
Carthusians, 37–38, 130, 159
Chapuys, Eustace, 31, 32, 37, 39, 42, 46, 72, 85, 91, 92, 93, 95, 110, 114, 127, 143, 144, 145, 152
Charles V, Holy Roman Emperor, 28, 32, 52, 53, 55, 152
Chedworth, Margaret, Duchess of Norfolk, x, 64, 185n
Chesworth House, Horsham, 2, 34, 63, 67, 70, 71, 74, 99, 133, 137, 168, 169, 186n
Christina of Denmark, Duchess of Milan, 56, 87, 189n
Clarence, George, Duke of, 16, 93
Clarence, Lionel, Duke of, xi
Clement VII, Pope, 31, 36, 181n
Cleves, Anne of, Queen Consort of England, xi, xii, xiii, 55, 61, 81, 82–88, 91–92, 95, 120
Cleves, John, Duke of, xi
Cleves, William, Duke of, 55
College of Arms, 165
Cranmer, Thomas, 35, 45, 55, 65, 77, 87, 100, 105–6, 107, 109–114, 126, 144
Cromwell, Thomas, xiii, 1, 33, 36, 37, 40, 44, 45, 52, 55, 61, 83, 88, 146
Culpeper, Joyce, x, 57, 115

Culpeper letter, the, xv, 124–125, 147, 187n, 193n
Culpeper, Thomas, 72, 78, 115–121, 122–128, 129–131, 134, 135, 136, 141, 145, 146, 151

Damport, Robert, 78, 109, 131, 132, 133, 134, 139, 142, 152
Daubeney, Henry, Earl of Bridgewater, 41–42
Daubeney, Katherine (née Howard) Countess of Bridgewater *see* Howard, Lady Katherine
Denny, Sir Anthony, 161, 168, 169, 196n
Dereham, Francis, 76–79, 84, 97–99, 103, 104, 105, 107–112, 115, 119, 121, 122, 127, 128–136, 138, 141, 145, 151, 187n
Devereux, Walter, Lord Ferrers, 32
Doncaster, 48, 127, 129
Douglas, Archibald, Earl of Angus, 24
Douglas, Lady Margaret, 24, 41, 83, 113, 126
Dowager Duchess of Norfolk, the, *see* Howard, Agnes
Dudley, Edmund, 157
Dudley, John, later Duke of Northumberland, 156, 157, 162, 165, 166, 169

Edward the Confessor, 163–164, 165, 166, 167
Edward III, xi, 2, 3, 25, 164, 176n
Edward IV, 3, 4, 6–10, 26, 37, 93, 94
Edward V, 8, 9–10, 15, 103
Edward VI, 106, 151, 157, 168, 169
Elizabeth of York, Queen Consort, xi, 13, 16, 17
Elizabeth, Princess, later Queen Elizabeth I, 36, 41, 42, 73, 95, 111, 145, 151, 171
Epworth, North Lincolnshire, 2, 37, 130
Evil May Day Riots 1517, 25

# Index

Ferdinand of Aragon, xi, 28
Fisher, John, Bishop, 37, 38
Fitzalan, Elizabeth, Duchess of
    Norfolk, x, 2, 172
Fitzalan, Mary, Duchess of Norfolk, 171
Fitzroy, Henry, Duke of Richmond and
    Somerset, 29, 32, 33, 34, 36, 38,
    41, 42, 43
Fitzwilliam, William, Earl of
    Southampton, 94, 107, 109, 122,
    131, 132, 138, 145, 161
Framlingham, Suffolk, 3, 6, 15, 24, 26,
    54, 61, 150, 169, 170, 171
Francis I of France, 28, 34, 36, 130,
    137, 152

Gage, Sir John, 132, 164, 166, 167
Gainsborough Old Hall, Lincolnshire,
    35, 45, 69, 103, 120, 150, 173–174
Garden Museum, formerly St Mary's
    Church, Lambeth, 80, 151
Gardiner, Stephen, Bishop, 88, 100,
    153, 157, 169
Gate, John, 161
*Genealogie of the Princelie Familie of
    the Howards,* Henry Lilly,
    149–150, 186n, 197n
Greenwich Palace, 7, 36, 39, 85, 86,
    93, 117, 130, 139, 140
Gresham, Sir Richard, 154, 166
Grey, Lady Jane, 111, 145, 169, 196n
Grey, Sir Richard, 103
Guildhall, London, 9, 129, 130, 166, 198n

Hall, Mary, *see* Lascelles, Mary
Hampton Court, 28, 51, 52, 91, 93,
    106, 109, 110, 113, 114, 116, 123,
    126, 130, 134, 194n
Hastings, William, 1st Baron Hastings,
    8, 10
Hatfield, Yorks, 105, 120, 122,
    124, 191n
Hawley, Thomas, Rouge Croix
    Pursuivant, 21, 26, 180n
Heneage, Sir Thomas, 110

Henry V, 2, 11
Henry VI, 3, 4, 11–12
Henry VII, 12, 13, 14
Henry VIII, xi–xvi, 1, 17–20, 24–27,
    28–33, 34–38, 39–43, 44–49,
    51–55, 56, 59, 65, 67–68, 72, 74,
    80–83, 85–89, 90–95, 97–99,
    101–106, 109–114, 115–121,
    126–127, 129, 130, 134, 135–137,
    139, 143, 144, 148, 153, 154,
    155–157, 162, 163, 168–169
Hilles, Richard, 80, 188n
Holbein, Hans, the Younger, 53, 54, 55,
    81, 82, 86
Holland, Bess, 30, 155, 161
Holy Roman Empire, 28
Houghton, John, 37
Howard Chapel, Lambeth,
    *see* St Mary's Church, Lambeth
HOWARD FAMILY x-xvi, 1–5, 171
Howard, current family motto, 171
Howard, Agnes (née Tilney), Dowager
    Duchess of Norfolk, x, xiv–xvi,
    16–17, 23, 30, 32–36, 41, 46, 52,
    53, 60, 62–66, 67–73, 74–78,
    80–84, 86–88, 97–100, 108, 109,
    110, 115, 117, 127–128, 129–134,
    135–140, 142, 146, 148, 149–50,
    152, 160, 161, 172, 197n
    Husband's outstanding bequests to
        and her immense wealth, 62–63,
        136–137, 139, 146
    Katherine Howard causing
        problems for, xiii, 52, 74–75,
        77–78
    Arrest and interrogation, 129,
        131–133, 135–136
    Attainder and life imprisonment,
        137, 142, 146
    Release from the Tower, 148
    Death and tomb design, 148–150
Howard, Anne, sister-in-law to
    Katherine Howard, 133, 136, 142
Howard, Charles, brother of Katherine
    Howard, 91, 114, 126

Howard, Charles, 2nd Baron
  Effingham, 151
Howard, Lady Douglas, 151
Howard, Lord Edmund, father of
  Katherine Howard, x, xi, xiv, 5, 17,
  22–23, 25, 34, 35, 56–61, 81, 129,
  158, 179n
Howard, Sir Edward, x, 18, 19
Howard Elizabeth, Countess of
  Oxford, 2, 4, 14
Howard, Elizabeth, Countess of
  Wiltshire see Boleyn, Elizabeth
Howard, Elizabeth, Duchess of
  Norfolk see Stafford, Elizabeth
Howard, Frances, (née de Vere),
  Countess of Surrey, 34, 41,
  161, 170
Howard, Lord Henry, Earl of Surrey x,
  1, 26, 33, 34, 41, 47, 51, 69, 89, 93,
  147, 153–154, 155–158, 159–162,
  163–167, 168, 169, 170, 171, 172
Howard, Sir John, x, 2
Howard, John, 1st Howard Duke of
  Norfolk, 3, 4, 5, 6–7, 10, 11, 12, 13,
  14, 15, 26
Howard, Lady Katherine (Rhys,
  Daubeney), Countess of
  Bridgewater, x, xiv, 32–33, 41–42,
  64, 78, 93, 99–100, 133–134,
  136–137, 138, 140, 142, 145, 146,
  151, 160
Howard, Katherine, Queen Consort of
  England and Ireland, x–xvi, 1, 5,
  17, 27, 34, 36, 52, 57, 58, 60, 61,
  63, 67–73, 74–79, 80–84, 85–89,
  90–95, 97–106, 107–114, 115–121,
  122–128, 129–134, 137–140,
  141–147, 148, 153, 159, 168,
  187n, 188n
  Appearance xiv 81–82
  Upbringing 67–73
  Manox and Dereham 74–79
  Comes to notice of Henry VIII
    80–84
  Becomes queen 85–89

Unfulfilled life as consort to Henry
  VIII 90–95
The return of Dereham 97–100
The Northern Progress 101–106
Her past revealed 107–110
Interrogation and confession
  110–114
Meetings with Culpeper revealed
  115–121
Beginning of house arrest 122–128
Former associates questioned
  further 129–134
The Bill of Attainder 141–144
Taken to the Tower; her execution
  145–147
Howard, Margaret (née Gamage), Lady
  William Howard, 139, 142, 148
Howard, Margaret (née Mundy), Lady
  Edmund Howard, 59, 152, 184n
Howard, Lady Margaret (née Mowbray),
  see Mowbray, Lady Margaret
Howard, Mary, Duchess of Richmond
  and Somerset, x, 34, 36, 41, 42,
  113, 155, 161, 166, 168, 170
Howard Nicholas, x, 4
Howard, Philip, 171
Howard, (Sir?) Robert, x, 2
Howard, Thomas, Earl of Surrey, later
  2nd Duke of Norfolk, xi, xii, xvi,
  4, 5, 10, 11, 16–17, 18, 19, 20–27,
  62–63, 64,
Howard, Lord Thomas, Earl of Surrey,
  later 3rd Duke of Norfolk, x, xii,
  xvi, 5, 17, 19, 20, 22, 23, 25–26,
  27, 29–30, 31–33, 34–38, 39–43,
  44–46, 47–50, 51, 52, 53–55, 62,
  64, 73, 76, 81–83, 84, 88, 91,
  92, 100, 101, 102, 109–110, 113,
  118, 120, 122, 126–128, 129, 131,
  134, 137, 141, 142, 144, 146,
  147, 148, 151, 153–154, 155, 156,
  157, 158, 159–162, 164, 165, 167,
  168–170, 172
  His fear of Henry VIII xii, 42–43,
    46–47, 51, 81, 131, 137

And the Northern Rebellions
1536–1537, 46–50
Appearance 53–54
Imprisonment and attainder
159–160, 165, 168
Released by Queen Mary 169
Death and funeral, 170
Howard, Thomas, Earl of Arundel and Surrey, 149
Howard, Lord Thomas, son of Duchess Agnes, x, 41, 52, 64, 83, 126
Howard, William, 1
Howard, Lord William, x, 23, 46, 52, 58, 64, 71, 78, 91, 93, 99, 105, 107, 108, 132–139, 142, 146, 148, 151, 152
Hull, Yorks, 50, 104, 121, 125
Hundred Years' War, the, 3
Hungary, Mary Queen of, 91, 95, 114, 143
Hussey, Thomas, 156

Islay Herald, 21

James IV of Scotland, 16, 19, 20–24
James V of Scotland, 24, 34, 102, 104, 153
John of Gaunt, Duke of Lancaster, xi, 2, 12
Johnson, Ottwell, 147
Julius II, Pope, 30, 31

Katherine Howard, Queen Consort of England and Ireland, see Howard, Katherine
Kendall, Thomas, 45, 49
Kenninghall, Norfolk, 17, 30, 42, 113, 137, 155, 161, 169, 170
Knyvett, Edmund, 2
Knyvett, Thomas, 56

Lambeth, Surrey, xiii, 24, 53, 60, 61, 62, 63, 67–73, 76, 80, 82, 83, 87, 92, 93, 99, 106, 107, 109, 111, 129, 131, 132, 133, 136, 137, 138, 139, 146, 148, 149, 150, 151, 162, 168,
172–173; *see also* Norfolk House, Lambeth and St Mary's Church, Lambeth
Lambeth Palace, 67, 68, 109, 186n
Lascelles, Mary (later Hall), 75, 76, 78, 84, 99, 105, 106, 107, 108, 133, 135
Lascelles, John, 99–100, 107, 129, 190
Lawrence, Robert, 37
Leigh, Isabel, *see* Baynton, Lady Isabel
Leigh, Ralph 57
Lincolnshire xvi, 2, 35, 37, 44–50, 63, 69, 129
Lincolnshire Rising, the, 1536, 45–50
Lincoln city, 101–103, 105, 118–119, 128, 130
Lincoln Bishop's Palace, 103, 115, 118, 119
Lincoln Castle, 50, 102–103, 130, 191n
Lincoln Cathedral, 102–103, 118
Lorraine, Francis, Duke of, 87
Louis XII of France, 24
Louth, Lincolnshire, 45, 47, 50
Low Melwood Priory, Lincolnshire, 37, 130, 182n

Mackerel, Matthew, xvi, 26, 27, 50
Manox, Henry, 52, 53, 74–76, 77, 78, 79, 99, 107, 108, 112, 130, 132, 133, 139, 152, 184n
Marillac, Charles de, 72, 85–86, 90, 93, 95, 101, 104, 105, 110, 114, 115, 116, 120, 126, 127, 128, 130, 131, 134, 141, 142, 145–146, 152, 189n
Mary of Guise, 52, 105
Mary, Queen of Scots, 52, 153, 171
*Mary Rose*, 18, 19, 155
Mary Tudor, dowager Queen Consort of France, 24, 28, 65, 145, 169
Mary Tudor, Queen Mary I, 28, 32, 37, 41, 57, 64, 65, 83, 91, 95, 101, 113, 151, 169
Misprision of treason, 99, 133, 135, 142, 160

Moigne, Sir Thomas, 46, 47, 49, 102
Moleyns, Catherine, x, 4
More, Sir Thomas, 24, 31, 34, 37, 38
Morton, John, 12
Mouat, Prof. Francis, 147
MOWBRAY FAMILY, x, xiii, 2, 3, 4, 5, 44, 150
Mowbray, Lady Anne, x, 6–7, 9, 10, 64
Mowbray Lady Isabel, x, 7
Mowbray John, 2nd Duke of Norfolk, x, 2
Mowbray John, 3rd Duke of Norfolk, x
Mowbray John, 4th Duke of Norfolk, x, 4, 5, 6
Mowbray, Katherine (née Neville), Duchess of Norfolk, x, 6, 7, 11, 12, 65
Mowbray, Lady Margaret, mother of John Howard, Duke of Norfolk, x, 2, 7
Mowbray, Lord Thomas ex, 1405, x, 2
Mowbray Thomas, 1st Mowbray Duke of Norfolk, x, 2, 11, 37, 163–164
Mundy, John, 25, 59
Mundy, Margaret, *see* Howard, Margaret

Neville, Anne, Queen Consort of England, 8
Neville, Cecily, Duchess of York, 6, 8, 11
Neville Katherine, *see* Mowbray, Katherine, Duchess of Norfolk
Norfolk, dukes of, *see* Howard and Mowbray families
Norfolk House, Lambeth, xiii, xv, 24, 53, 60, 61, 63, 67–72, 76–79, 80, 84, 86–87, 97–98, 108, 109, 111, 115, 117, 119, 123, 127, 131, 133, 134, 136, 137, 138–139, 148, 150, 161, 162, 168, 169, 172–174, 186n
Norris, Sir Henry, 40, 81, 115, 119
Northern Progress, the, 1541, 99, 101–106, 111, 118–121, 122

Oath of Succession, 37
Oath of Supremacy, 37, 44
Oatlands Palace, 1, 90, 130, 134, 136
Oxford, John de Vere, 13th Earl of, 4, 13, 14, 178n

Page, Helen, *alias* Clarke, 102
Paget, Sir William, 90, 105, 156–157, 158, 160, 166, 168
Parr, Katherine, Queen Consort of England and Ireland, xi, 35, 73, 103, 119, 154, 164, 168
Parr, Thomas, 119
Parr, William, 168
Pewson, Andrew, 109, 194n
Philip of Spain, 169
Pilgrimage of Grace, the, 1536, 45, 47, 49, 94, 159
Plantagenet, Arthur, Lord Lisle, 60, 94, 113, 142, 144, 184n
Plantagenet, Edward, Earl of Warwick, 16, 93
Plantagenet, Joan, 2
Plantagenet, Margaret, *see* Pole, Margaret, Countess of Salisbury
Plantagenet, Richard, Duke of York, 3, 8, 9
Pole, Sir Geoffrey, 94
Pole, Henry, Lord Montagu, 94
Pole, Margaret, Countess of Salisbury, 90, 93, 94, 95, 96, 126, 132, 136
Pole, Reginald, Cardinal, 93, 94, 95
Pollard, Richard, 131, 132, 136, 137
Pontefract Castle, Yorks, 103, 111, 121, 123, 130, 134
Prince Richard, Duke of York, x, 6, 8, 9–10, 12
Princes in the Tower *see* Edward V and Prince Richard, Duke of York

Reformation Parliament of 1529–1536, 34, 36
Restwold, Alice, *see* Wilkes, Alice
Reynolds, Richard, 38
Rhys ap Gruffydd, 32, 34

Rhys ap Thomas, 32
Rice (Rhys), Agnes, 137, 151
Rice (Rhys), Griffith, 'young Rhys', 132, 137, 151
Rice (Rhys), Thomas, 137, 151
Rich, Sir Richard, 45, 129, 131, 132, 133
Richard III, 8–9, 10, 12, 13, 14, 15
Richard, Duke of York, *see* Plantagenet, Richard
Rochford, Lady *see* Boleyn, Jane
Rochford, George, *see* Boleyn, George
Russell, Lord John, 105, 107, 122, 124

St Mary's Church, Lambeth, 53, 68, 77, 80, 108, 131, 132, 148, 149, 150, 188n; *see also* Garden Museum, Lambeth
St Peter ad Vincula, Tower of London, 41, 146, 147
Sadler, Sir Ralph, 123, 126, 131, 134, 136, 139
Sagudino, Nicolo, 25, 180n
Sawcliffe village, Lincolnshire, 46, 130, 183n
Scutt, John, 94, 95
Segrave, Elizabeth, 2
Selve, Odet de 168
Seymour, Edward, Earl of Hertford, later Duke of Somerset, 41, 100, 156–157, 160, 162, 165, 166, 168, 169
Seymour, Jane, Queen Consort of England, xi, 41, 51–52, 81, 148
Seymour, Sir John, xi, 41
Seymour, Thomas, Baron Seymour of Sudeley, 154, 168, 169, 187n, 200n
Shookborough, John, 59
Simnel, Lambert, 16–17
Smeaton, Mark, 39–40
Southwell, Sir Richard, 159, 161
*Spanish Chronicle, The*, xiii, 74, 146, 199n
Stafford, Elizabeth, Duchess of Norfolk, x, 30, 42, 64, 149, 168, 170, 181n
Stafford, Edward *see* Buckingham, Edward

Stafford, Henry, *see* Buckingham, Henry
Starkey, David, 28, 186n, 200n
Surrey, earls of, *see* Howard
Swynford, Katherine, xi, 12, 103
Syon House, formerly Syon Abbey, 7, 28, 41, 113, 126, 144, 145

Talbot, Elizabeth, Duchess of Norfolk, x, 7, 64
Tendring, Alice, x, 1, 3, 15
Tendring Hall, Stoke by Nayland, Suffolk, 3, 7, 15
Teshe, Thomas, 73
Thetford Priory, Norfolk, xvi, 15, 25–26, 30, 42, 52, 54, 63, 148, 150, 170
Thornton Abbey, Lincolnshire, 105
TILNEY FAMILY, 63, 76
Tilney, Agnes, Duchess of Norfolk, *see* Howard, Agnes,
Tilney, Edmund, 152
Tilney, Elizabeth, Countess of Surrey, x, xi, 5, 16, 29, 56, 64
Tilney (Tylney) Katherine, 70, 72, 77, 93, 97, 108, 118, 119, 121, 122, 123, 128, 133, 138, 142, 151
Tilney (Tylney) Malyn, 108, 133, 138, 142, 152
Tilney, Sir Philip, 108, 138
Tonge, Thomas, York Herald, 21
Tudor, Edmund, Earl of Richmond, 12
Tudor, Henry *see* Henry VII
Tudor, Jasper, Earl of Pembroke, 11, 12
Tudor Margaret, Queen Consort of Scotland, 16–17, 21, 24, 41, 105
Tudor, Owen, 11
Treasons Act 1534, 39, 38, 39, 99
Treaty of Perpetual Peace 1502, 16, 19, 20, 23
Tyburn, 38, 50, 130, 136, 167

Van der Delft, Francis, 157, 160, 161, 162, 166
Valois, Catherine of, Queen Consort of England, 11
Valois, House of 3, 176n

*Valor ecclesiasticus*, 44
Voltaire, 28

Wakefield, Yorks, 95, 102
Waldegrave, Edward, 84, 108, 133, 151
Wallop, Sir John, 93
Wars of the Roses, 3
Webster, Augustine, 37–38, 130
Weston, Sir Francis, 40
Wharton, Sir Thomas, 153
Whitehall Palace, *see* York Place, 86
Wilkes, Alice, 72, 77, 78, 105, 107, 132, 133, 136, 138, 142, 151
Wilton, Lord Grey of, 155, 157
Wolsey, Thomas, Cardinal, 18, 19, 24, 25, 28, 29, 31, 33, 57–58, 63, 65–66, 181n

Woodville, Anthony, 8, 103
Woodville, Elizabeth, Queen Consort of England, 8, 9, 13
Wyatt, George, 28
Wyatt, Thomas, the elder, 92, 144, 153, 190n
Wyatt, Thomas, the younger, 153, 169, 170

York Place, renamed Whitehall Palace, 31, 66, 67, 86, 188n
York, Anne of, Countess of Surrey, 29, 64
York, city of, 64, 73, 101, 102, 104, 121, 125
York, King's Manor, 104, 120, 121
York, Richard Duke of, *see* Plantagenet, Richard